Sandy Blythe had a promising Australian Rules Football career ahead of him when a car accident left him a paraplegic. Refocusing his athletic abilities, he turned to wheelchair basketball, and sixteen years later, he co-captained the Australian men's wheelchair basketball team to a historic gold medal at the Atlanta Paralympics. Off court, Sandy runs a disability management company that advises companies on how to make their premises accessible, in compliance with relevant legislation. He is also a polished motivational and humorous speaker.

Blythe Spirit

Blythe Spirit

SANDY BLYTHE

Pan Macmillan Australia

First published 2000 in Macmillan by Pan Macmillan Australia Pty Limited
St Martins Tower, 31 Market Street, Sydney

Copyright © Sandy Blythe 2000

All rights reserved. No part of this book may be reproduced or transmitted
in any form or by any means, electronic or mechanical, including photocopying,
recording or by any information storage and retrieval system, without prior
permission in writing from the publisher.

National Library of Australia
cataloguing-in-publication data:

Blythe, Sandy.
Blythe Spirit.

ISBN 0 7329 1027 7

1. Blythe, Sandy. 2. Paralympics (10th: 1996: Atlanta, Ga.).
3. Basketball players – Australia – Biography.
4. Paraplegics – Australia – Biography.
5. Wheelchair basketball. I. Title.

796.3238092

Typeset in 11/14pt Garamond by Midland Typesetters
Printed in Australia by McPherson's Printing Group

*To the Brownlow Medal parents, Al and Rosie,
who win the award year after year
in all number of ways.*

ACKNOWLEDGEMENTS

The writing of this book is due to so many people. Should you not be listed in print, you know who you are and what you have done.

To Cathy, for her constant support through the dark days, and friendship through the lighter ones. And for her writing the 'letter from a friend', which adds a truly different perspective to this book.

To Laurie Prosser for his foreword, and for his undying support during my days at Ballarat.

To the students of Ballarat University who supported me throughout and railed against discriminatory issues I faced upon my return to study after my car accident.

To the people of Derrinallum and district who supported me, the farm and my mum and dad, Al and Rosie, through the years.

To everyone who came and spent time at the Austin Hospital day after day, week after week.

To every member of the Australian Wheelchair Basketball Team, both past and present, who share ownership of the team's achievements and current world status.

To the Australian Paralympic Committee, which provides constant financial support and organisation for Paralympic athletes, assisting them simply to be the best that they can be.

To Wheelchair Sports Victoria who supported my development in the early days.

To Rob Woodhouse and the staff at Elite Sports Properties. Rob, from our initial chat over a coffee, your vision, enthusiasm, belief and support have created a number of opportunities for me. Thanks, Big Fella.

To Peter Forrester for the initial support and 'push' to put pen to paper, and your belief that there was a story to tell.

To the staff of Pan Macmillan, particularly Vanessa Mickan and Tom Gilliatt, for their support and enthusiasm and constant availability to a virgin author.

To Paula for her word processing and input, and for cajoling and encouraging me, always in a positive way, helping me to get to the finish line.

To Andrew Sanderson, my partner at Morris–Walker, who gave me space and time to put this story together.

When all else is lost, the future remains.

Laurie Prosser

CONTENTS

Acknowledgements		ix
Foreword		xv
Introduction		xvii
Chapter 1	Full Circle	1
Chapter 2	Me BC (Before Crash)	5
Chapter 3	The Accident: Green Grass and Broken Glass	19
Chapter 4	Horror on the Hill (Wards Seven and Eight)	37
Chapter 5	Rehabilitation	57
Chapter 6	Back to Ballarat	81
Chapter 7	Plane to Perth	117
Chapter 8	Back to the Austin	139
Chapter 9	The Big Wide World	169
Chapter 10	Back to Basketball	173
Chapter 11	The Gold Medal Journey	189
Chapter 12	Gold and Home	223
Chapter 13	New Horizons	229
Chapter 14	Towards 2000	241
Epilogue		247

FOREWORD

Sandy Blythe's is a wonderful story of human endeavour, stubborn spirit, and abundant humour. It will touch the hearts of many, and it offers us a chance to reflect on our lives, and find inspiration for the future.

My life changed forever one day when, as a Senior Lecturer in Physical Education at the University of Ballarat, I watched Sandy undertake a practical examination for Olympic gymnastics. This young man had entered university with a promising AFL career ahead of him. But at the age of nineteen his future changed suddenly when he was involved in a devastating car accident that left him a paraplegic. Sandy fought back, rebuilt his life, and showed us all that a person can achieve their goals no matter what.

'Seeing is believing,' I thought as I watched him mastering

the Roman rings and parallel bars. Until that moment, I had believed it was virtually impossible to perform such physically demanding routines while trailing uncooperative legs. But I was wrong. As a student with a disability, Sandy had the option to take a written exam instead of a practical, but he chose the practical examination. That sums up Sandy: choosing the path with the greatest reward, regardless of the obstacles.

I can only imagine how hard it must have been for him, as a teenager, to face the end of his dream to play AFL, but it was not long before Sandy switched his focus to a new dream. One that would bring him the honour of representing his country in the international arena. I was elated—but not surprised—in 1996 when Sandy co-captained the Australian men's wheelchair basketball team to a gold medal at the Atlanta Paralympics.

Sandy's tenacity, patience, adaptability and good humour have stood him in good stead on the long road from hospital bed to Paralympic stadium. He'll probably laugh at me for saying this, but when I think of Sandy I am constantly reminded of the words of the great British wartime leader, Sir Winston Churchill, in an address to his people in their darkest hour: 'never, never, never give up'!

May Sandy's journey from tragedy to triumph provide you with the inspiraton, hope and laughter Sandy has brought to my own life.

Laurie Prosser

INTRODUCTION

I feel that my life has been unique. Having grown up in relative ease to have a clear and simple life plan, I survived a brutal and bloody car accident to face many barriers and crossroads, and to overcome countless challenges. I have seen life from very different perspectives.

My reason for writing this book is to share the journey of this different life, to provide a little inspiration and hope to people with similar realities, and to create an awareness of what it is like to have your world turned upside down, and what it takes to turn it back. Because there but for the grace of God go us all. This is my story.

FULL CIRCLE

Tears, exhaustion, passion, exhilaration, finality.

The buzzer sounded minutes ago, signifying the culmination of a dream. The Australian wheelchair basketball team have done the impossible, winning the gold medal at the 1996 Atlanta Paralympic Games in front of 10,500 spectators. And for me, it feels like the culmination of a very long journey.

The quest for fulfilment of a sporting dream began many years ago for me, and back then I had certainly not considered wheelchair basketball as the vehicle for my success. But sometimes in life you have to take what you can get, or at least be flexible with your goals. I could never have imagined that being hugged by eleven sweaty, elated men in wheelchairs could feel so good, but then I suppose their dreams had been diverted from their initial paths too.

I find myself thinking about how I should react, rather than just reacting. David and Troy leap onto the ring and cut the sacred basketball net from our hoop; the media film this; players cry; people who dislike each other intensely, hug; and I just sit there. I had sometimes wondered what it would be like to climb the highest mountain. I think I'm just finding out: absolute exhaustion, numbness, disbelief and relief. Thank God it's over.

We are ushered off court and down into the bowels of the stadium so the presentation ceremony can be organised. A mass of well-wishers continue to present themselves, many of whom I don't know, and yet they call me by name. The British team, now vanquished, is nearby. A shell-shocked, shattered aura surrounds them, reminding me of the fine line between success and failure. The American team is overheard bitching that they have finished third despite having lost only one game. We don't care. Winners are grinners.

When the Australian team was issued with uniforms, we were given a special tracksuit to be worn during medal presentation ceremonies. Ever the optimist, I hadn't truly cared about its terrible design, as it had not been at the forefront of my mind that I would actually have to wear it. There is no point getting excited about crossing a bridge before you get to it, and as we had gone into the Games ranked sixth, the bridge had looked particularly wide. The Australian Paralympic Committee had also included in every athlete's uniform pack a small card with the words to 'Advance Australia Fair' on it.

I felt that it would be somewhat superfluous to my needs and had not even packed it; and now they are going to hear me sing.

The music starts and the Americans, bronze medal winners, enter the show court at the Omni Stadium, followed by the sad, sad Brits. Then it's our moment. Richard Oliver, the former Australian captain at his fifth and final Paralympics, leads the team out, sporting the basketball net around his neck. Richard, a hard, grizzly character and one of the architects of the development of wheelchair basketball, is aglow. He is not alone, and has eleven glowing team mates for company, me included. As we enter the stadium, the crowd stands and applauds. The underdogs from downunder have nailed it. The first senior gold medal ever for Australian basketball, benchmarking the development of our game, in front of a loyal home crowd at an American Paralympics.

The Americans receive their bronze medals, then the British team their silver. It's our time. Orfeo Ceccenato, the big Italian man is first to receive his medal, and so it goes down the line until it's my turn. The gold medal is hung around my neck and I'm presented with a posy of flowers. What do you say at a moment like this? All the players link arms as Australia's anthem rings out around the stadium. We break into song and it becomes immediately apparent that, when it comes to singing, we make bloody good basketballers. But then, I'd never planned to sing 'Advance Australia Fair' in Atlanta.

ME BC

(BEFORE CRASH)

I was raised in the shadow of Mount Elephant, near Derrinallum in the Western Plains. Many people have heard of the mountain, which looks like a sleeping elephant, but fewer know of the small town called Derrinallum and its population of approximately three hundred. I grew up on 'Barbary', a 250-hectare sheep, cattle and cropping farm close to Derrinallum.

My dad, Al, was a career farmer, and has been involved in the land all his life. He was schooled at Geelong Grammar, where he became renowned for his passion for sport. One of my earliest memories is of shop keepers (particularly in shoe shops) asking me if I was going to be as tough a footballer as him. After leaving school, Al had a distinguished football career with Camperdown in the Hampden League, where he gained the reputation of running only in straight lines. He obviously had the belief that the shortest way to the football was from A to B, a route which did not involve skirting the packs. This at times led him to being not exactly adored by the opposition fans. He delighted in telling me of the time that, on leaving the field at half time, he was hit by an elderly lady with an umbrella. After this show of aggression—and a points win to the umbrella holder—he had his jaw broken in the second half of the match. To this day he can still clunk it on demand as a party trick. He is tough.

In my eyes, Al was the consummate professional farmer, who worked hard from sunrise to sunset, and it was in this guise that I got to know him best. Whether he ploughed paddocks on the tractor, or sheared sheep in the shearing shed, I was often beside him and he always seemed to be in control. This, however, as it is with all people, was an illusion. Once, after shearing, the family had grouped to dip all the sheep for lice. Dipping involved herding sheep through a chemical bath, which in our case was a circular pit of about two metres in depth. Each sheep had to be totally submerged to ensure their heads were deliced as well as their bodies. Near the end of the day, when the dip had become full of the remnants of numerous sheep, and their excrement was floating on the surface, Al went to submerge a sheep by leaning on the back of its head with an implement similar to a broomstick. Tired and perhaps not concentrating, he slipped, and into the dip he went. And all this while I wasn't even watching. As soon as I heard the splash, I realised that I had missed something special. As seriously as only a naïve little boy could be, I asked him to repeat his plunge so I could watch. Ignoring me, he hauled himself out of the dip using words that I was only to learn later in life. And there was to be no replay.

Rosie, my mum, was raised on a farm at Leslie Manor and was educated at Toorak Ladies College. After marrying Al she became the number one farm assistant, Al's best team mate. It didn't matter whether it was driving trucks, bailing hay or cooking up a storm for a hungry herd of shearers, Rosie was 'odd job'. However it should be noted that her female charms were useful in many and varied ways. As I grew older, she would recount how quickly she used to get through the weighbridge at the Berrybank Silo, where the ageing and somewhat deviate weighbridge attendant would invite her back for a drink. There was no way the other farmers could compete with Al's secret weapon. She still denies taking up the attendant's offer, but may, I suspect, have fluttered the odd eyelash.

My only brother, Tony (Bud) is three years older than I am, and was always keen to show me the way. That the way may well have been the wrong one was of little concern to him. Our relationship verged on violent and for many years the only reason that it was only verging was the three-year age difference. Just as I was reaching my prime fighting size, we were involved in a discussion (all-in brawl) when Al intervened. As I turned back to watch the television, Bud belted me from behind and then bolted. I didn't see him for the remainder of the evening. In the morning, Rosie confronted me, saying: 'I don't suppose you'll care that your brother has a broken hand from hitting you on the head'. I answered no and laughed.

Once, when he was sixteen or seventeen, Bud was driving the Land Rover, towing me in a non-operative small Massey Ferguson tractor. In his favourite position—one of power and control over his little brother—he accelerated the Land Rover to fifty kilometres an hour, with me trying to hang on to the lurching, skidding Fergie, pleading with him to slow down. He didn't, but somehow we came away unharmed. Bud now admits that, at the time, he did not quite grasp the potential consequences of setting a land-speed record for a small grey Ferguson tractor.

Thankfully things improved over time between us. This may be in part due to increased common sense and perhaps even battle fatigue as we got older. Bud still whinges of the cold affecting the plate in the knuckle on his small finger!

Fred, a red kelpie, and Ding, a border-collie–pointer cross (unusual and definitely unplanned!) were the other constants in all our lives. Throughout his entire life Fred had aspirations to talk, and was often not that far away from it. Having been recruited from the Maryborough saleyards, he was on permanent loan from one of our shearers. He was a first-class sheepdog, but his personality and intelligence outshone these skills. Al and Fred were constant work companions, and Al would often recount Fred's exploits. When checking lambing ewes with Al from the back of the Land Rover, Fred would spot a sheep having trouble completing a birth. With a despairing yelp (interpreted by Al as 'you bloody idiot, look what you've missed!') Fred would jump off the moving Land Rover at his own initiative and catch the poor unfortunate sheep. But age wearied Fred, and in his latter years he seemed to think it was time for retirement and superannuation. At shearing time, Al would wake Fred, and take him to the sheepyards bright and early to organise the sheep for the first run. Come time for the second run, Al would realise that Fred had gone AWOL, only to find him back at the house, reclined under a tree with a look of 'I'm too old for that'.

Ding was lucky in life in that he had one at all. He had no sheepdog skills of any note (although in later years he developed some mimicking skills from observation of Fred and others), and escaped the farmer's traditional rationalism about extra mouths to feed only because he was Bud's pet. Determined to prove that cats were in fact tree dwellers, Ding constantly sent them skyward in rapid retreat of his advances, ensuring that all the stray cats had enhanced cardiovascular fitness. Or he practised his statue-like 'pointing'. That he may have been pointing at a car, or a tree, or a piece of machinery was apparently of no consequence to our frustrated hunter.

Of course Fred and Ding sometimes teamed up, their favourite activity being unaccompanied rabbiting. With the long, leggy Ding built for speed, and Fred, the squat kelpie, for cunning, they made a useful team. The plan was for Fred to wait by the burrow whilst Ding chased the rabbits back to their home. Ding would arrive home breathless and somewhat guilt stricken.

Many minutes later, the older Fred would trudge in, struggling to keep himself upright, with the poor unfortunate rabbit deceased and wet, clasped between his teeth. Looking at Al, he seemed to say, 'Look, boss: proof!'

Being a kid on a farm is so different from growing up in a city. From an early age I had to find my own amusements. Usually I would go rabbit trapping or kick the football alone— or, for a special treat, with Dad. Sometimes we'd play cricket on the rolled backyard pitch. But of course, there were always the farm jobs. As I got older these increased from feeding the dogs to crutching sheep, carting hay and driving tractors. One of the biggest highlights of living on a farm was being able to ride a motorbike from an early age.

A motorbike served the dual purpose of amusement and functionality when checking paddocks, mustering sheep and getting around the farm. First for the Yamaha 100cc and later for the 175cc, I developed a small racetrack on the side of a hill near the house. This track was used so often that grass never grew. Bud and I had many a time trial, along with the obligatory crashes, though amazingly with no injuries. One particularly wet and slippery day, Bud and I convinced Al to have a go around the track. Coming into a right-angle corner on his second lap, he used too much front brake and dropped the motorbike into the mud. His amusement level was particularly low, our mirth level particularly high, and his racing career over. He never went around the track again. Accidents on the motorbike were not always on the racetrack. One day when I was thirteen I was mustering sheep with Rosie, who was driving the Land Rover. As we moved the sheep towards a gate, we suddenly became aware that another gate had inadvertently been left open. In my urgency to get to the gate before the sheep, I powered through the first gate, leaning into the corner (as you do) and hit a loose rock on the ground. This saw me being launched off the bike, which somersaulted and landed in a crashing heap immediately next to me. At this stage it should be noted that the bike was only six months old. Rosie rushed over in the Land Rover with her first query being 'Is the bike OK?' At this point I was still lying dazed on the ground. The bike had handled the spectacular dismount quite well, its only injuries being a broken indicator and footstand, and a split petrol tank. My injuries basically involved my pride due to Rosie's apparent lack of concern. (She still denies this story.)

With the motorbike a means of transport around the farm, and rabbit skins easy pocket money, I invested in my own ferrets at the age of twelve. One of them soon went to heaven, assisted on her way by one of the farm dogs. Only Willy remained, a white, sturdy, robust, half-back flanker type of a ferret. Many an hour was spent waiting for Willy to return after placing him down a rabbit burrow and listening to him inflicting his brutality on a poor unsuspecting rabbit. After his victory by knockout, I suspect he dined on the losing rabbit, only to then fall prey to the peril of a full stomach: sleep. A long time later, he would trudge wearily from deep within the earth with an apologetic look plastered upon his ferrety face. Or so I told myself. Another chance would be given, and another sleep would be taken. And so it was with much sadness that one fine day I took Willy to a burrow on top of a stony hill and let him go and seek his bounty, only for me to walk away. If you love something, set it free.

Every year, one of the greatest fears for farmers is fire, fanned by hot summer winds, and often uncontrollable due to the vagaries of burning tumbleweed. On a particularly hot day early in February one year, a large grass fire was burning out of control and threatening Barbary. Thankfully for us, the wind changed, removing the danger to our farm, but increasing it to others. Al, Bud and myself went to the aid of our neighbours on the Acco truck along with a large tank of water, pump and hoses. At one stage we felt we were doing a great job stopping the fire in heavy smoke by the side of a road, but when the smoke cleared we realised that the fire had already gone through. Later that same day in an area of stony country a farmer's house seemed certain to burn. The fire fighters on the nearby road could see there was no access to the fire sweeping towards it. When everyone had all but given up, Al had someone cut the fence and drove his truck straight up and over a rocky barrier, shredding the tyres. Others followed and the house was saved. It was one of my earliest lessons about leadership, passion and commitment.

To get to school I travelled four kilometres with Al or Rosie to the bus stop; picking up the children of two of our neighbours on the way. The bus then proceeded to Derrinallum, which was a further fourteen kilometres away. In the evening, one of the neighbours would pick us up where the bus dropped us off, and if it was raining all we could do was hope that they were not late.

Derrinallum Primary School was a typical small country school, with a focus on sport. Academically my efforts were inconsistent, meaning I ranged from good to horrible. High school was a huge change. It was much bigger, having more than two hundred students. Again my academic performance varied, usually improving just prior to or immediately after report time, depending on how big a serve I got from my teachers or Al and Rosie. During these years my love of sport flourished. Each year I won all the sprint and jumping events at the school and inter-school athletic carnivals. My major failing at school, however, was my lack of ability in any craft classes, including woodwork. No matter what it was that I was meant to make, some unfortunate aberration would occur. When given a thick piece of wood and asked to make a bowl by chiselling out a portion, the chisel always seemed to go through the bottom of the would-be bowl. And it got worse for bigger projects. But so long as the sports master was the woodwork teacher, and I continued to perform in the athletic arena, my marks never strayed far from a B grade. This was perhaps my first lesson in how far sport could take me.

As I progressed through the levels of school, the great question of what to do with my life became more and more important. To me, there always seemed a pretty clear answer, and it all revolved around my love of sport. I decided to complete a physical education teaching degree, while chasing the dream of AFL football as far as I could. On the completion of my football career I would return home to Barbary and take over the farm from Al and Rosie, since Bud appeared to be taking a different tack in life.

It became more important that I excel at school to accumulate the required marks to get into a tertiary course. At the beginning of Year Eleven, Al and Rosie made the commitment to send me to Geelong Grammar, which Bud had recently left. My start at the school had been delayed due to a lack of dollars, and so upon my arrival I found that I was the only new boy in Manifold House. Most of the other students had been boarding for many years and were not overly keen to help the sole new boy assimilate. Besides, I was missing the motorbike and the freedom of the farm. It seemed to me a classic case of being able to take the boy out of the country but not the country out of the boy. So I went home for a weekend and didn't go back.

Consequently, in Year Twelve I was back at Derrinallum High School, beginning what was then the Higher School Certificate (HSC) with a total of eleven other students, and being directed by the Year Coordinator, Barbara Tulloch. I took five subjects: Legal Studies, Biology, Accounting, English, and Politics. I was finally diligent about my studies. The practice examiners' comments were not on whether or not I would pass but what mark I would get. So it was with some trepidation but also a little confidence that I met the postman on the day the results were released. They read: Legal Studies 64%, Biology 54%, Accounting 49%, English 46%, and Politics 43%. I had failed conclusively.

All my plans were now thrown into confusion. Should I do

my HSC again, despite a ten per cent examiners' penalty for repeating? Or should I go to the Ballarat School of Mines (SMB) for a Tertiary Orientation Program (TOP), a different course which could still gain me entry to a physical education degree? The HSC at Derrinallum seemed the easier path, with an amusing added incentive to return to the school. The principal, John Gilmore, was fond of me: he used to call me Thumper, and I had even dated his daughter for a time. He was keen to turn a blind eye to my academic indifference, in exchange for my returning to straighten out one of the school bullies and cleaning up his schoolyard, so to speak. He may have let the contract to another student, since I never went back. After much discussion it was decided that I would board in Ballarat for a year and complete a Physical Education TOP at the SMB, and hopefully attain sufficient marks to gain entry to Ballarat College of Advanced Education (which has since become the University of Ballarat).

Now that I had got older, as with all country boys, my thoughts had turned to transport, namely procuring my own. In the country the importance of having one's own transport is magnified since there is no public transport out on the farm. My desire to have the money to buy a car immediately on (or, even better, before) turning eighteen was great. Al and Rosie had always talked of self responsibility, and from a young age I had planned to make and save sufficient money for a good car to drive when I became eligible to hold a licence. For a number of years I had been saving money from carting hay on neighbouring farms, working in the shearing shed, odd jobs and even pocket money. Dad gave me a one-hectare paddock adjacent to the house, which I could crop and take any profits from in the year before I turned eighteen. The crop was a boomer and the profit was good. So shopping I went.

Camperdown, near Warrnambool and thirty kilometres from Barbary, was the nearest town with a number of car yards. And whilst the selection was not great I was lucky enough to find a car which appealed: a 1973 Celica with mag wheels, auburn exterior and sexy black interior. As is often the case, a little old lady had been the fastidious previous owner. For $3,000, and a good deal of negotiating, it became my pride and joy. But I had to be patient. I bought the car in November, four months before my eighteenth birthday, and so the car in all its glory was parked under cover in a hay shed.

There is no doubt that obtaining a driver's licence is rarely as difficult in the country as it is in the city, not least because of the difference in traffic. My test was on a particularly fine day in Lismore (an adjacent town to Derrinallum, and the nearest town with a police station). Lismore was of a similar size to Derrinallum, and during ten minutes of driving I only had to give way once. And this was to a fat golden Labrador asleep in the middle of the road. I don't really know if it is a fail if you run over a dog, but it soon woke up and staggered off the road, allowing me to proceed to the police station and accept the much-coveted piece of paper, my licence.

Boarding in Ballarat was an eye-opening experience. The first place I stayed in was occupied mostly by elderly people and alcoholics, along with only three students. When one of the boarders died, and remained undiscovered for two days, I decided it was time to seek new lodgings.

As the year unfolded, I settled well in Ballarat, becoming increasingly independent and eventually finding a home away from home, a girlfriend called Cathy, who was to play a major role in my life. I also found a degree of independence. This included not having to report in to parents by a pre-arranged time or be seen to be studying or be careful of alcohol. But, as with so many people, an early lesson of overindulgence stood me in good stead for future caution. It's happened to most of us. My learning experience involved Cathy, the lack of money which is a student's lot, and a particularly large flagon of Kaiser Stuhl Riesling. One evening midway through the year of the TOP course, I was with Cathy at her mother's unit, which they

Me BC (Before Crash)

shared. I suggested that we go out for a drink, but Cathy, being particularly studious, said that she had to stay in and watch a program on television for school. I volunteered to go to the bottle shop, but when I got there I looked in my wallet to find a particularly lonely five-dollar note. With my resources limited, but my enthusiasm undeterred, I selected the flagon and hurried back to the unit with my prize. I poured Cathy a drink, but she curled her nose and said, 'I'm not drinking that'. With two glasses now poured, and me feeling a little manic, I dubbed one glass 'this' and the other one 'that' and proceeded to consume stupendous amounts of the Riesling. Suffice to say, I remember saying hello to the two goldfish in their small bowl at some stage of the evening. (One was found floating the next morning, with, we suspect, alcoholic poisoning. And I understood how the fish felt.) I was put to bed on the divan by, and with, Cathy. Sometime later in the evening, I realised I was fast becoming unwell. In a desperate scrambling attempt to source the toilet I leapt out of bed and promptly ran into the wall, like Fred Flinstone, missing the door by some four feet, and leaving a Riesling and spaghetti deposit on the wall. This marvellous event occurred adjacent to Cathy's mother's bedroom. Turfed into the shower by Cathy, only to repeat the performance later on, I had a long night. Come the morn I was offered eggs on toast or corn flakes by Cathy, which had the (deliberate) effect of making me dry retch. Stupidly I made the effort to go to SMB, where I sat through English, with the teacher discussing Galileo and me desperately trying not to throw up on her. At recess I staggered outside and promptly dived head first into a bush. As I was being sick, a gardener with a wicked sense of humour asked me, 'What's the birdlife like in there?' That was enough. I surrendered and went home to my hostel and put myself to bed, only to be disturbed by a knock at the door. It was Rosie of all people, on the only time she visited me in Ballarat for the year. I told her I had a severe case of gastro, but I'm not sure she bought it. The country boy was growing up.

I worked solidly enough through the year to gain entry to a teaching degree in physical education. And with my plans back on track I went off to spend a summer at home, working at odd jobs around the farm until it became time to begin my tertiary study. My first year of university in Ballarat was relatively uneventful. I had accommodation at Beaufort House, a large student hostel which housed seventy-odd students, providing a bed and meals, and also an immediate built-in social life. Contact hours at the university amounted to twenty-four hours a week, which included theory lectures and a range of practical sport classes. At the end of the year I was to have a two-week observation placement in a school, Portland High, my first step towards becoming a real teacher.

But study was only a part of the real plan. From as early as I can remember my dream had been to play AFL football, but of course sometimes our dreams are not 'owned' by the people near and dear to us! A big moment in any aspiring footballer's life is the day when their parents proudly present them with their first pair of football boots. And on my day it became clear to me that Rosie did not share my dream with any of my intensity. With a great flourish, she handed me the box containing the 'boots'. Flinging the lid aside, my look of expectation and unmeasured euphoria instantaneously changed to one of horror and anger, in all the established traditions of a five-year-old having a career-best tantrum. Rosie, with all good intentions but with a limited football pedigree, had purchased a pair of Ron Barassi insignia boots, consisting totally of hard moulded plastic, including the uppers. Not the material that dreams are made of! To add final insult to injury, there was also a token plastic football lurking in the background. With a crisis meeting called between Al (the ex-footballer), me (the angry hopeful footballer), and Rosie (the shopper from hell and a member of the anti-football council), a revisit to Camperdown shopping centre was agreed upon. With the appropriate tools now in hand and on foot, my dream began.

I remember that from my first informal games at Derrinallum State School, my drive was constant to become the best footballer I could be. My real football career began in a humble fashion with five years in the Derrinallum U16 team during which I developed in size, football skills and nous. In my last year, whilst still eligible for the junior team, I also had the odd game in the seniors.

Every weekend for a number of weeks, trials were held for selection in the Victorian Teal Cup side, the best U17 team in the state. Two teams would play, and at the end of each match a composite team would be picked. So if you didn't perform on the day, you didn't play the following week and your chance of making the team was gone. Sometime during the selection process, a carnival was held in Shepparton in which four country teams from Victoria played off; from these four, one team would be selected to play our city counterparts. With perfect timing, in the first match of the carnival I played to all my abilities and beyond—so much so that the selectors approached me about not playing for the rest of the carnival for fear of injury. I had made an impact and had secured a position in the country team after only the first match. After the Victorian country versus city match, I was selected in the Victorian team. This team was a showcase of the best junior football talent in the state, and for every team member it was their greatest opportunity of their young lives to impress the AFL recruiting officers. The big league was getting closer.

In addition to the Teal Cup matches, I played with the Derrinallum Football Club senior team during my HSC and TOP years, as well as my first year at the University of Ballarat. The team won premierships in the latter two years, with me fortunate to win the Best and Fairest Award for Derrinallum in one of them.

Derrinallum was a good grounding for my football. We played in a hard, tough, physical league. In the second semi final in 1980, I was virtually knocked out by an opposition tough man, whose defence at the subsequent tribunal hearing was that I had inadvertently fallen over and hit my head on his boot. He received a four-week suspension. His case hadn't been helped by my advocate telling how I had been examined for a suspected broken jaw after the 'collision'. With no broken bones, and having recovered my senses for the team's grand final, I was in the wrong spot again. Late in the first quarter I was crouching over the ball, only to look up and see the opposition coach, a vicious hefty ruckman, charging towards me with his elbow cocked. I had no time to evade this incoming goliath and his elbow slammed into my ribs, taking all my wind with it. When the end of the game came, some three quarters later, we had won, but as the siren sounded I found myself swaying in the centre of the ground, lacking air, as the hordes of spectators converged. Al ran on, grabbed his spent son and led me off to lie on a table, and then to the doctor who informed me that I had suffered two broken ribs in the first quarter. But you must pay the price to attain your dreams, and mine were getting a little closer all the time.

Between the SMB and my first year at university, I had been invited to train with the St Kilda country squad. I was hoping that, after completing one year at Ballarat, I could transfer courses and move to Melbourne. The coordinator of the country squad was Laurie Prosser, one of the physical education lecturers at the college, a driven, passionate and idealistic man. As my first year at Ballarat drew to an end, I began to investigate the Rusden physical education course, which would allow me to give the big league a go. Unbelievably, I was told that no academic credits would be given for my time in Ballarat, and that I would have to repeat first year again. Rusden was no longer an option, so I got in touch with Geelong football club. They called back, but it was a few days too late.

THE ACCIDENT: GREEN GRASS AND BROKEN GLASS

November 23, 1981 was a superb day. The sun had risen early at Barbary, and I was pretty excited because I'd finished the academic year at Ballarat College. In addition to having summer holidays and jobs to plan for, I had also passed all the units in the first year of my physical education degree, so things were looking good.

Bud was at home and, with our relationship on the improve, it was with a tinge of regret that at 10 a.m. I headed back to Ballarat. It was a year to the day since I had been booked for speeding at 11 a.m. on my way back to Ballarat from Melbourne. For some reason the date had stuck in my mind, and in the preceding week it had occurred to me not to be on the road that morning. But with a night out and celebrations planned, I had forgotten my inner voice.

After driving the Celica for about forty minutes, I found

myself stuck behind a car which was moving along at about seventy-five kilometres an hour on a road with few passing opportunities. The car had a 'Phys Eds Stay On Top' sticker fixed to its silver bumper bar. I wondered who the driver was; I knew which cars most of the physical education students drove. This was a Falcon that certainly didn't have much go about it.

So through the twists and turns of Smythesdale and Scaresdale we drove, passing the old mine and gold fields. As we approached Ballarat we caught up with an even slower-moving car following a truck. This line of traffic continued like this for some time; despite a number of opportunities, neither car in front of me attempted to pass the truck.

When we got to approximately a mile outside Ballarat, the final passing opportunity arose. No one attempted to pass. After waiting a few moments I realised that, unless I passed at that precise moment, the opportunity would be lost and I would continue to chug into Ballarat. So I tried to. I indicated, pulled out, and accelerated, with the sun beating down, at 10.47 a.m. As I came alongside Phys Eds Stay On Top, the driver suddenly pulled out in an attempt to pass, which left us three abreast—the car immediately behind the truck, Phys Eds Stay On Top to their right, and me lurching to the right-hand verge of the road. Phys Eds Stay On Top didn't brake, didn't accelerate, and basically froze, doing nothing to avert the impending accident. I had to make an instant choice: either to run into his car, or take the Celica off the road and into long dry grass, thus avoiding a collision. I chose the latter. This was something I would live to think about for a very long time.

I drove the car off the road to the right, into unkempt grass about 1.2 metres high, and tried to brake. The Celica was still under my control, as although hastily made, it had been a conscious decision to leave the road. Changing gears in an effort to slow the car, whilst also attempting to brake from a road-exit speed of around eighty kilometres an hour, the major issue was

The Accident: Green Grass and Broken Glass

that I was driving blind. The Celica had a low seating position and I couldn't see anything through the long grass. On I hurtled. Then it happened. As I came over a small rise, there directly in front of the car was a dry creek bed. I had no options, I was about to stop. Just before I hit, the words 'Oh shit!' came from my mouth, and I locked my legs out straight onto the floor of the car in a desperate attempt to brace against the inevitable impact. My pride and joy, the Celica, slammed into the opposite creek bank.

The first part of the car to hit the creek bank was the front right-hand side, which meant the initial impact came up through my feet. The right-hand front wheel burst the floor open, sending all the force up through my straight legs and impacting on the bend in my body, the lower region of my spinal cord. After the car hit, it slid gently back down and rolled onto its side in the dry creek. I remember the sight of green grass, the sounds of tinkling glass and the blaring of the horn; and then I had a little sleep.

After a minute or so I came to, with the car back on its wheels, glass from my driver's side window all over me. The Phys Eds Stay On Top driver had been panic-stricken when my car left the road, and had stopped on the verge and run down to help. He had single-handedly pushed the Celica back onto its wheels. Whilst this was a great effort of strength, it probably did not do my spinal cord a lot of good. I said simply, 'Get an ambulance'. My diction was not so good because my teeth had gone through my chin; it wasn't a good look.

I realised well before the arrival of the ambulance that I had an incredible constant burning and sharp sensation of pain in my back, and that my feet weren't working properly. I could move my legs, but they suddenly seemed to be somewhat uncoordinated and clumsy. This felt like the only thing that was stopping me from getting out of the car and remonstrating with Phys Eds Stay On Top. I wanted to sit in the car and wait quietly for the ambulance, but even this was a forlorn wish. A crowd of concerned onlookers had quickly gathered, and a couple of these people were worried that I would lose consciousness. Whenever I went quiet people started asking inane questions. With a mouthful of loose teeth and intense pain in my back, I was not really interested in things like the state of the nation. The other real annoyance was the flies. The big, buzzy, annoying blowflies that Australia is renowned for were on the job. With blood all over my face, I was an easy target and my continued efforts to keep them at bay soon lagged.

I was able to look down, straight through the split car floor, to the ground and grass directly beneath the foot pedals. This was eerie, and left no doubt as to the severity of the impact. Simply put, I had gone from sixty-odd kilometres an hour to a dead stop in about ten centimetres.

A policeman arrived marginally before the ambulance. He did not appear to give a damn about my injuries or my pain levels; all that he was interested in was filling in his forms.

The ambulance finally arrived after what seemed an interminable time, but in reality was probably only fifteen minutes or so. The two ambulance officers traipsed down through the long grass to the Celica, which was now resting back from the creek, and asked the predictable question: 'How are you feeling?' 'Not well,' I replied. Or sounds to that effect, because I'm sure my reply was not particularly clear!

After basic questions as to what hurt and a general assessment of my injuries, I was eventually lifted out of the car, leaving my white car seat cover stained with the blood from my chin. Amazingly, both car doors were in perfect working order, despite the front of the car having been shattered by the engine. My removal was achieved slowly, but without a problem. I was placed onto an ambulance trolley immediately beside the car, and my back was carefully straightened. From there the ambulance officers and some volunteers had the task of carrying me back up to the roadway, and negotiating the bloody grass. This took a minute or two, with every bump slashing a burning scythe through my back. It was as I was lifted into the back of the ambulance that I first aired my fears that I had broken my back. It did not take a genius to work out I was in real trouble.

The ambulance officers were personable and caring, assuring me that I was OK, but any questions I asked were met with responses that were calming and noncommittal. I was told that I was going to Ballarat Base Hospital and that I'd probably not hurt my back as badly as I thought. The ambulance drove at twenty kilometres an hour for the five kilometres to the hospital, so as to minimise the bumps and consequent jarring of my back. And boy, it takes a long time to get anywhere when you're driving at that speed. We finally arrived at casualty with the ambulance backing up to the automatic entry doors, and the flies still annoying my blood-covered face.

I was unloaded from the ambulance, wheeled through the hospital corridors into a large examination room, and lifted onto an X-ray table. This was not pleasant. A broken back on a white, shiny, uncushioned X-ray table is not a delight at all, especially for what was to become an hour-and-a-half. Quickly, staff surrounded me. Someone asked if they could cut my T-shirt off and someone else asked if they could take my shorts off. I wondered why they hadn't taken my shoes off. I was pretty proud of my shoes. They were the latest Boston Adidas, bright yellow with orange stripes, and when I was wearing them I thought I was pretty cool. I lifted my head and I saw that they already had taken them off. I just hadn't noticed, as I couldn't feel my feet anymore.

Shocked and scared, I put my head back onto the narrow pillow, only to be confronted with the first nasogastric tube I had ever seen in my life. I didn't know that it would be far from my last. The doctor started pushing the tube up through my nose and down my throat. The sensation in the back of my throat made me gag. In an instant of frustration, a sense of violation and anger, I spontaneously pushed away the two attending doctors and the nursing staff, grabbed the tube and pulled it inch by inch back out of my throat and nose, and threw it across the room. It struck the examination-room wall on the full. The response from the coordinating doctor was 'Oh, it's a bit big, is it?' I gave him a somewhat grumpy reply, 'Yeah, it is.' So with that he picked up a smaller tube and began to insert it into my nose. In it went, a little better than the first effort. Then came the dreaded X-ray, which I thought would reveal all.

I asked the lead doctor if he thought I had broken my back, and whether I would be a paraplegic. He said he thought not. He was wrong, but to this day I respect him because he was one of the very few people prepared to put his hand up and say it as they thought it was—or, in lay terminology, to run straight at the ball.

X-rays were done in the same examination room, which at least meant that I did not have to be rolled around on the hard table. Pictures were taken from all angles, of my upper spine and of my lumbar spine from directly above, and to the left and right. I felt a little like a model, they took so many shots. And so, after another seemingly endless wait, the doctor came back, leaned close to my face and said simply: 'You have damaged your spinal cord; it's very serious. You are going to be transferred to the Spinal Injuries Unit at the Austin Hospital in Melbourne'.

I was shattered, and scared beyond comprehension. And yet the overwhelming sensation was that there were still so many unanswered questions. I had the feeling that the Spinal Injuries Unit would be the only place to find these answers. I had, however, grasped that things were particularly grim. The future that had looked so bright at the beginning of what was still that sunny day had taken a turn for the worse.

Preparations were made for me to be transferred to the waiting ambulance, which would transport me to the Austin Hospital. Before I left the examination room, I was offered drugs to deaden the pain, which emanated from my back, and seemed to take over my whole body.

Pain. I think it is perhaps one of the most difficult of human

The Accident: Green Grass and Broken Glass

sensations to describe. It can be physical or emotional, but most of all it is personal. It is so hard to share because it is one of the most intrinsic, internal feelings that human beings can have. And I had it in abundance. Yet something inside me resisted all offers of painkillers. I wanted to be able to show the specialists at the Austin Hospital my injuries, and my abilities. In other words, I wanted to do my personal best, and give myself the best chance, though I still did not know what that chance was.

I was moved from the examination room, through the stark antiseptic corridors, to the ambulance, which was waiting for me in the emergency bay. I was accompanied by a number of nursing staff, and the coordinating doctor. On the way, I was wheeled through the next-of-kin waiting area, and it was there that I saw Al and Rosie.

The police had notified them that their son had had an accident but was OK, and had requested that they come up to Ballarat. They immediately travelled the eighty kilometres from Barbary, believing that I was being X-rayed for, at worst, a broken arm or leg.

As my parents saw me, the attending doctor confronted them brusquely: 'Your son has a spinal injury; it is very serious and he is being transferred to the Austin Hospital.' For them, one can only imagine the shock. One moment they were thinking of perhaps an overnight stay in the Ballarat Hospital, and now this. It was as though they had been physically struck. Al and Rosie approached me with fear in their eyes. They found themselves back in the role of empathising parents, rather than the friends and guiding companions they had been to me during my adolescent years.

As I was loaded into the ambulance, I remember thinking that, even though it was still a beautiful summer's day and only a couple of hours had passed since the accident, it was going to be the longest day of my life.

I was joined in the ambulance by a nurse who was stunning. Slim and brunette, in her early twenties. Being a red-blooded nineteen-year-old, I lifted my head off the pillow to get a better look. I quickly dropped my head back, saying to myself, 'It's not worth it, Blythe. You're bloody crook.' At that moment, I realised more than ever how serious my minor accident was.

Generally Ballarat to Melbourne is approximately an hour-and-a-half's drive. Ballarat to Melbourne in my ambulance, which drove in the same way and at a similar speed to the one which carried me from the crash site, took about three hours, making it a long, long trip. A number of times on the trip, the nurse offered me drugs to relieve the pain, the intensity of which I am at a loss to explain. I refused and refused again.

The crew of my ambulance did not know exactly where to go and they had to make two attempts to deliver me to the right area of the huge Austin Hospital. Finally at 4.45 p.m. we parked immediately adjacent to the entry to Wards Seven and Eight, the Acute Spinal Ward for the newly injured, and the Readmission Ward for patients with recurring problems.

The doors of the ambulance opened and I was greeted by a long-haired, bearded fellow, who I was to later learn was Dr Joe Toscano, the Spinal Unit Registrar. Joe did not look like your typical doctor. A long ponytail, bright Hawaiian-style clothes, and a loud manner were his trademarks. People new to the Spinal Unit had even been known to mistake Joe for a cleaner. During my time at the hospital he was to become Al and Rosie's trusted source of information and confidant.

Joe leapt into the back of the ambulance and said, 'Oh, you've got a couple of teeth down your throat.' During the accident I had knocked my bottom two middle teeth through my chin, and these were still intact, but pointing down my throat. He cheerily reached in with his hand and, with no warning, grabbed and pulled my teeth back into some sort of alignment. I was fast learning that once you get to a certain level of pain, the body cannot register any more.

After my spontaneous dental work I was unloaded from the ambulance and whisked to the unit's examination room. The room was stark white, and filled with a diverse range of equipment, pots and pans, tables, oxygen bottles, and all types of tube. I felt that I had finally reached the place of some clear diagnosis. However, by this stage of the longest day, my awareness of proceedings was starting to dim due to the consistency of the pain. The room filled with a variety of nurses and doctors, including Joe Toscano, and Dr David Burke, the Medical Director of the Spinal Unit.

The examination began. New X-rays of my back were taken. There were constant questions about what I could and could not do and feel. 'Can you move your right leg?' 'Can you move your left leg?' 'Does this hurt?' 'Does that hurt?' 'Can you feel this? Or that?' and so on. The examination was aimed at establishing a benchmark of what movement and sensation I had in my legs, and measuring the circumference of my legs at various points. I could move my legs, but the degree of movement was nowhere near normal. I was to find out later that muscles are rated from between zero to five, depending upon function. A muscle is rated as a zero if there is no muscle contraction, and five if there is normal, full contraction and strength. Sensation loss is established using a pin to prick the skin, first on the feet and then moving upwards. And for all the above questions I needed to be aware, so I felt justified in my decision to refuse pain killers, despite my desperate desire for the sanctity of sedation.

All muscles below my knees scored zeros. Above the knees my quadriceps and hamstring muscles scored variantly from two to four. In regard to sensation loss, I had no feeling beneath my knees. Above my knees it was patchy up to my groin. Leg measurements were taken so they could monitor muscle atrophy, or identify any possible swelling due to blood clots; after a spinal injury, affected muscles shrink like deflating balloons, while blood clots can occur due to the lack of muscle movement. Once formed, if a clot moves to the heart, lungs or brain, it can be life-threatening.

So, in short, I seemed to be an incomplete paraplegic, with a compression fracture between my twelfth thoracic vertebra and my first lumbar vertebra, as highlighted in all the X-rays. This in effect meant that although I did not have normal leg function, I did have some movement below the level of my injury, making the paraplegia incomplete. The fracture was termed a 'compression injury', since the space between the vertebrae had shrunk significantly as a result of the car's sudden deceleration and impact, and the subsequent force on my body, not to mention the transmission of the impact up through my straightened legs. I was told that this fracture meant I had no function beneath my knees, but would probably be able to walk with the use of below-knee splints or callipers. That was, if my function did not deteriorate due to spinal swelling.

There were other issues to contend with. Spinal injury places all the body in shock and in many cases bowel and bladder function is affected. A urology nurse inserted a long-term catheter into my urethra and up into my bladder, because in my condition I would not be able to independently pass urine.

With the benchmarking of my condition complete, I was willing, desperate and pleading for the pain killers which I had denied myself. Relief arrived as a doctor injected me with pethidine, and wrote up that it was to be repeated every four hours.

And so I drifted from the red raw hell of a pain that only those who have experienced it could understand, to the oasis of a light slumber. Still, my mind raced with the doctor's prognosis. What was spinal swelling? Could you play football at a low-grade level with below-knee callipers? Was this just a dream? Where were Al and Rosie? The questions seemed to be endless, and the answers were not forthcoming, or simply delusional. But as the minutes passed after my introduction to heaven (pethidine), any sort of logical thought, and the myriad of emotions, ceased.

When the examination was finished, it was time to move to

Bed One in Ward Seven. Bed One, I was to learn, was where patients were placed on admittance, or if they were particularly sick and required special attention from a sole nurse. On arrival to Ward Seven, I was lifted from the trolley to the bed by three orderlies and a pack nurse. All lifts were done in a manner to keep the patients' backs or necks straight, minimising pain, and not disrupting healing or creating further spinal damage. One orderly lifted the legs, another the backside and the third the upper body. The pack nurse assisted with holding the patient's head or was involved in stripping or arranging the bed, depending on the injury.

I was vaguely aware of an oxygen mask being strapped to my head, and of the numerous foreign tubes residing within my body, tubes which I was now dependent upon for normal human functions. And then I truly passed out.

Letter from a friend

Of my time in hospital, particularly the initial acute stage, there are huge gaps in my memory and so I have had to rely on Al, Rosie and Cathy to fill in a lot of the detail. For Al and Rosie, the process of recollecting that terrible time is extremely difficult and upsetting. Cathy is now living and working in Sydney and she kindly agreed to write down some of her memories. Her words are divided into various sections, and give an invaluable outside perspective. For her contribution in helping me through that horrible time, and her willingness to add colour in her writings, I am eternally grateful.

The beginning
In 1980 I was completing a TOP year at SMB. In my psychology class one cold, wet Ballarat afternoon, I became aware of an extremely confident phys. ed. student who sat next to me, and afterward suggested we go to a local coffee

shop to talk about the day's class, and chat. I thought this perfectly harmless as we seemed to click straight away, and since it was pouring with rain I appreciated the lift home. This friendship continued for some time, quite innocently on my part, but not so on his. I was seeing someone at the time who didn't have the confidence or the maturity of this Derrinallum boy. One day, when a couple of classes had been cancelled, he invited me to go for a quick trip up the country to see the farm and to meet his folks. During this excursion he asked me if I'd like to drive around the farm and see the sheep. I'm a shearer's daughter, and when you've seen one sheep, you've seen them all, but I guess it was a more original line than some. So on a cold, wet, windy day in a four-wheel drive he kissed me.

This was my first experience of Sandy's drive and focus. If he wanted something he would persist until he got it. Whether it be saving for his first car, representing the state in football, pushing himself to train so hard he was physically sick, or getting the girl. In many ways he had maturity beyond his years, and a confidence that was at times both annoying and disarming. He had a physical presence about him and an air that made him stand out in a crowd. He stood just over 180 centimetres tall, with blond hair and the lean athletic body of an aspiring AFL footballer. There were a lot of things I didn't know then; I was only seventeen. But I did know that he was different, and my life would never be the same.

As friends and buddies we were as thick as thieves. As a couple in a relationship we were volatile, intense and unpredictable. He was driven, highly motivated and very sure of himself. I was shy, insecure and far too intense for my years. So I guess our time together was anything but boring. Sandy believed in testing the waters and taking everything life had to offer. I believed in stability, consistency and loyalty. Our relationship was one of constant break-ups and make-ups. Then one night at the end of the school year in 1981 we had the barney to end all barneys. We parted company on the worst possible terms. I didn't want to see him again and this time I meant it.

The accident
The morning of 23rd November 1981 dawned clear and bright. My mother, Harriet, or Harry, did voluntary work at the Ballarat Base Hospital flower shop and that day she felt very strongly that she shouldn't go, but go she did. Sandy was due to collect some things. I was all fired up for a parting shot at the rat, but when eleven o'clock came and went and he had not arrived I knew something was definitely amiss. Sandy may have been a lot of things, but late was never one of them and I started to worry. A girlfriend came around to visit that afternoon, and by this stage I was getting quite agitated. About two o'clock the phone rang and I answered. I assumed from the background noise that he had gone into Wye River, deciding that because of the argument it was safer to call me from there.

 Then came the voice. All the venom I was ready to spew forth dissipated when I recognised Sandy's father's very quiet voice. And then the words:

 'Cathy, its Allan Blythe here. Sandy's been in an accident.'

 The tone of his voice led me to fear the worst.

 'Oh my God, is he dead?'

 'No, but he is quite badly injured. They think that he may be paralysed. He's asking for you. If we come and get you, would you pack a bag and come to Melbourne with us? They're sending him down in an ambulance now and they don't know how bad the injuries are. We'll come and get you and follow the ambulance down.'

 I was floored, absolutely. The wind knocked out of my sails. Fortunately my girlfriend was able to think for me and packed a small case. In the meantime, Mum came home, then Rosemary and Allan arrived. We all sat, dumbfounded, not really able to take it all in. When we arrived at the Austin Hospital, it was very late in the afternoon, and we were taken into a waiting room opposite the examination area. We could hear them speaking to Sandy, asking him to lift this or that, whether he could feel this or that. After what seemed like an interminably long time, the doctors came in to see us and discuss the situation. What was the car he was driving? Were the seat belts static or inertia reel? Then we were able to ask our important question: 'What is the prognosis?'

'Well, if he doesn't lose anything he has now, he has sensation halfway down to his calves and movement to the knees. If nothing changes he will walk with callipers, but we don't know how much the spine will swell. We could operate to relieve the pressure, but when we're dealing with nerves, we may do more harm than good.'

The decision was made to let nature take its course. Little were we to know that his spine would swell more than anticipated, blocking the blood supply, and basically causing Sandy to lose all movement from the hips down.

When we followed Sandy into Ward Seven, the acute ward of the Austin Hospital's Spinal Unit, we didn't know what to expect. As yet he hadn't been cleaned up; the caked blood on his face, the oxygen mask and the general atmosphere of the ward was quite alarming. He looked very small lying there and, as I took his hand, I thought the sedatives were beginning to take effect. He opened his eyes and with his pupils dilated he looked like a very frightened little boy. His parents had decided they would stay and asked if I would like to stay with them. I turned my head, not wanting Sandy to see me cry. I felt I couldn't stay. I couldn't afford it and I couldn't be a burden.

'Yes, stay' came a muffled, drowsy voice from behind the mask, and stay I did.

The first night a nurse suggested a hotel for us to stay at. We slept very little and were back at the hospital as soon as possible the next morning. The pethidine kept him fairly drowsy and every time he opened his eyes he would panic if we weren't right by his bedside.

The first milestone was Sandy being allowed a glass of water instead of only being able to rub his lips with ice. Each day we hoped for some movement to return to his legs. As the days went by there was no new response, even to painful stimuli. We could see the leg muscles atrophying as we watched.

The ward

In the spinal unit you get to see many things, some tragic, some positive, some uplifting and some plain stupid. At one stage there were five boys in a row all at the tender age of nineteen and all suffering severe spinal injury, most resulting from car or motorcycle accidents. In fact many patients had photos of their accidents above their beds, almost like badges.

There was Sam who was a total quadriplegic yet retained perfect sensation all over his body. He was driving along a country road when the sun shone in his eyes; he lost control of the car. He would need twenty-four-hour care for the rest of his life, probably in a nursing home, and he had no one to sue. He had no family and his girlfriend stopped coming to see him. How those days and nights must have dragged. But if you propped his arm up at a certain angle he could flop his wrist enough to simulate the royal wave, which he took great delight in.

There was Mike who had been a sign writer. He left the unit with a limp and little use of his left arm. He entered the hospital a young man with a broken body and he left an older man with a broken spirit.

Malcolm was a street kid, originally from New Zealand. He could be impish, cheeky and wise. He had no family that we knew of and nobody to rely on. He was a source of confidence for me because no patient's or visitor's expression escaped the mirror above his bed, and whenever we looked a little sad he would call us over one by one for counselling.

Laurie enjoyed telling everyone that he was a wanted criminal. He was covered in tats and most certainly looked the part. He drank copious amounts of Coca-Cola until it was discovered that it was liberally spiked with Bundy rum. He also created a huge furore the time he partook of his conjugal rights whilst in traction. He had ended up in hospital after diving off a friend's shoulders whilst drunk, straight into a toddlers' wading pool. He spent three months in traction, then after some physio, walked away. He was the cause of one of my many arguments with God.

I think young Dean was all of fifteen when he and his mother took a Volkswagon for a test drive. A drunk driver went through a stop sign, fatally injuring his mother and rendering him a quadriplegic. He was an inspiration, and the dedication and support of his family was obviously paramount in his rehabilitation. With limited use of his arms he went from strength to strength.

And there was Dimitri, a non-English-speaking man who, when admitted to the hospital one night, kept screaming blue murder, apparently because he thought the staff were trying to kill him. He had the most wonderful family and a son at college who switched to medicine after his father's injury. I am sure the experience would have made him a very empathic doctor.

Sandy's family
Alan, Sandy's dad, is a very proud man. He had a private education and has in him a lot of the old school, but also is very sweet with a twinkle in his eye. He would often give me little pep talks about Sandy, even though I'm sure he considered us far too young to be serious about each other. He

wanted Sandy to treat me well, but he also wanted him to get out and see the world—an experience which had largely been denied to Al.

The second night at the hotel, Mr Blythe asked me not to call them Mr and Mrs but to call them as Sandy did, Al and Rosie; and from then on that's who they became. They helped me buy my first car. I had only $1,000 and Al said he wouldn't have me being seen in the type of car that I would have got for that price, so he helped me to buy a Mazda Coupe for $2,400. Sandy's grandmother also gave me $500 for tyres and other accessories; I loved that car.

Sandy's family has always been tremendously supportive of him, whether it be keeping statistics at the footy on a freezing cold and wet day, to choosing schools and career paths. Sandy and Al share a very common bond in sport and were exceptionally close. By aiming for a football career after his studies, Sandy would be able to fulfil the dreams that his father had put to one side after taking responsibility for the family farm.

HORROR ON THE HILL

(WARDS SEVEN

AND EIGHT)

Fading in, fading out, fading in, fading out, all to the rhythm of the pethidine injections. This was my introduction to Ward Seven, Bed One. Each pethidine injection took about ten minutes to take effect. A blissful two-and-a-half-hours of sleep or drowsiness followed this. And then the wait. Because I was only allowed to have injections four-hourly, a one-and-a-half hour window existed where the pain took over. And in that window I would sweat, go to hell and back, and wait for the next respite.

However, this window was to become an open door. Due to concerns about addiction, my withdrawal from pethidine injections began on the third day after my entry to the ward. The injections were replaced with oral analgesics, mainly Panadeine Forte. They barely worked. For the next three weeks I was confronted with a pain that made me cry, chew on pillows, or even on my metal bedhead, and grind my teeth. And still these words are inadequate to describe it. Then it simply stopped. I was to later learn that every person with a spinal injury is an individual in that his or her symptoms vary. Some have enormous pain, others none. Following the first week the best way of describing the pain in my back is like a sleeping dog that is more than vicious when awoken. I quickly found I would do anything to keep it asleep. And yet this was not always in my control.

As I lay in Bed One, there seemed to be constant activity around me. The orderlies would come to turn me every couple of hours so as to prevent pressure sores, and my nurse would take my temperature or empty the urine bag on the side of the bed, and so I found I was never alone. With the nasogastric tube in my nose from Ballarat and an oxygen mask on my face, it was difficult to talk to Al and Rosie or Cathy who seemed to be right there whenever I awoke. That is, except for the nights—the worst time in any hospital, the time when the demons come.

Why are the nights so bad for the hospitalised? The reasons vary from person to person. For me, it was because there were no family or friends; my only real company was my solitude, and my frightened, confused and drug-influenced thoughts, all ensconced in a darkened, quiet, yet busy ward. The best time was sleep. It was only there that I could escape the harsh and shocking realities of my predicament, and of course the pain. One change, which had a sense of eeriness about it, was that I had lost the sensation of falling in my dreams. Many of us experience the sense of falling, only to awake with a start—and a huge sense of relief—when we realise it was just a dream. This feeling had always been a constant part of my sleep pattern, but one day after my accident, I realised that the sensation had disappeared. In a way, I suppose I had actually hit the bottom of the abyss. (To this day falling remains absent from my dreams.) But when I awoke, it was apparent that, although

Horror on the Hill (Wards Seven and Eight)

I was not asleep, my life had become a nightmare, and my mind was an open pathway to hell.

The first three nights felt interminably long, and yet there always seemed to be something happening. I remember one of these nights in particular, when the staff member who was 'specialling' me did not know how to care for someone with a nasogastric tube. She was an elderly woman with greying hair. She was from a nursing agency, and apparently did not work regularly in the Spinal Unit. In fact, despite my drowsy state, I got the feeling that she probably hadn't worked anywhere for quite some time! First she attempted to take my blood pressure with the monitor by my bed, and repeatedly couldn't make it work. She gave up on this task and attempted to give me some mixture down my nasogastric tube, from a large syringe. After connecting the syringe she pushed the plunger in one swift motion, forcing all the contents swiftly into the tube and into my stomach, not in any sort of controlled manner which was the norm. I remember a funny sensation. For the remainder of the night I stayed awake, scared of her and her incompetence. Come morning, I mentioned my fears to the nurse who was soon to become known as the 'bran' nurse, due to her habit of force-feeding patients bran to keep them regular. The agency nurse was never again seen on the ward.

Quite quickly, apart from the pain, I found that I settled into the routine of the ward, the constant bustle, and the chat of other patients who were further advanced in their acute stage. I was told that I would spend at least six weeks, probably eight, in bed waiting for my back to heal and that this was not negotiable. Each day in the first week my legs were measured for atrophy and function and compared to that at the time of arrival. My once strong, athletic legs were getting smaller.

My leg function degenerated markedly, and I could barely move my legs at all. The cause of this was swelling within the spinal canal, which was blocking and perhaps killing existing nerves. Sometime in the first week a number of doctors came to see me and shared their concerns. Apparently there was a split viewpoint as to whether it would be wise to operate to relieve pressure on the nerves, as the nerves may have been damaged in any such operation. The decision was made by the doctors to treat my spine conservatively, and to do nothing. To wait and hope that function would return when the swelling subsided. I was told that if function were to return, it would happen three weeks after the injury. If it did not, I would never ever walk again. So I thought and I prayed.

When awake, my often pain-filled hours where spent thinking—thinking and thinking, trying to find answers to question after question, all aimed at coming to terms with my unclear future, and my immediate environment. It was difficult to remember what my leg function had been in the car after the accident, or even in either of the examination rooms, but I knew there had been some movement. But in my groggy state the doctors and nursing staff kept telling me (and intimating) that the muscle function in my legs had changed. To an extent, I knew that my legs' current function—or more specifically, lack of function—meant I wouldn't walk, one way or another. And if I couldn't walk there was no football, no physical education degree, no farm. There was nothing.

For the first few days I was not allowed to eat or drink anything, with my only intake being through the nasogastric tube, and the odd piece of ice I was given to suck. I never knew ice could taste so good, but I'm sure I wasn't the first person to feel this.

Just before I left Bed One, two nurses gave me the good news that my nasogastric tube was to be removed and they were going to do it right then. Taking the tape off my face, and assuring me that it wouldn't hurt but may feel strange, one of the nurses began to pull the tube. Out and out and out, it came, leaving me with a funny burning sensation and an uncontrollable gagging. Finally it was out. The tube was covered in all sorts of grime that one would never expect to see related to

Horror on the Hill (Wards Seven and Eight)

oneself. I was in no hurry to have another one taken out or, least of all, put in.

After four or five days I left Bed One, and began what was to become many shifts in bed numbers over the coming weeks. The further away the bed was from the nurses' station, generally the healthier you were. The reality checks came with the nursing staff every morning, lunch, dinner and supper, and during the drug rounds, when medications were given out. Pills, pills and more pills. They never ended, with my record being fourteen, all swallowed in one gulp, along with my hundred millilitres of water. Later on in my rehabilitation, the number of pills dropped, and it was then that I really felt I was on the mend.

Nursing staff and doctors began to become more than just uniforms, and apart from the odd exception, were superb. But of course they were a mixed lot, and their true colours came out in a myriad of ways.

Lying in bed, day after day, in a ward without air conditioning unable to sit up or roll over, and unable to shower, every patient—be they patients with broken backs, or those with broken necks and accompanying head tongs—craved for their hair to be washed. This was done on a weekly basis, and due to time and staff constraints there was never enough time for that extra wash—that is, except for when Janine made the time. 'J9', as she was known, was an attractive brunette in her early twenties and was a favourite with all the guys on the ward, not only for her sunny nature, but also for her commitment. Understanding the emotional lift a wash and a little extra care gave, J9 regularly stayed back after the completion of her shift to wash patients' hair. She, with her reams of green plastic sheeting, her two buckets of water and her shampoo, easily surmounted the problems of the horizontal bedwash, head tongs or not. And I was just one of the many who readily joined the queue for her services.

But with the good came the bad. Ivan was one of the few

male nurses on the ward. He was of slight build with a clipped beard, and loved any position of power he could attain. Soon after my admission he had a run-in with Rosie over visiting hours. Despite my parents having been told by senior nursing staff that they could come and go as they wished during the early days of my admission, Ivan confronted Rosie and, in an arrogant and short manner, asked her to leave. With the backing of adjacent staff she won the right to stay, but had made an enemy for life. Nor was she alone. A few days after this, there was a heated discussion between Ivan and Brian, an earthy patient who had spent some time prior to his injury incarcerated. With voices raised in the open ward, Brian brought cheers from the other partients and a conclusion to the debate when, in his loud ocker accent, he said: 'When I get out of here, I'm going to stick a knife in you.' There was no reply from Ivan; it was clear he was no-one's favourite.

And then there was the clumsy. Shelly was a homely nurse in her mid-twenties, who was always on hand to meet any of the patients' needs in a helpful, professional and happy manner. However she had one major flaw. In her rush to do her duties or to respond to patient requests she was invariably clumsy, and either kicked or knocked my bed every time she passed. While this generally would have been inconsequential on another ward, with a broken back it had the effect of waking the pain dog. Her clumsy performance improved only after Rosie made a request for less haste and more caution. Anything to let the sleeping dog lie.

But of course all this was seen through irregular means. I quickly discovered the importance of the mirror above my bed. Because I couldn't sit up, it was the only way of seeing anything or anyone around the ward. It feels strange to be in the one room with the same people for eight weeks and not see their faces. As the first days became a week, I was allowed a virtually unlimited diet of hospital food. When my meals arrived they would be placed on my chest; my mirror would be positioned above the plate and I would eat, guided by the reflection. Difficult, but you do get very good at it, or you starve. At mealtimes Al, Rosie or Cathy often fed patients like Malcolm or Sam, high quadriplegics who couldn't feed themselves. Everyone pitched in together. In some ways we all became family.

And often we would all look the same as well. Lying on our backs, we found ourselves staring at the bright fluorescent lights on the ceiling. In an effort to avoid the resultant headaches, everyone would wear sunglasses. So regardless of the weather, or the time of day, the ward must often have looked like a Blues Brothers session.

As a group, and individually, our days and nights were serial and monotonous. From waking to the clang and clatter of a 5.30 a.m. pill-and-pan round, to the regular visits of the orderlies turning all the patients—somewhat akin to chooks in a rotisserie—to the daily visits of therapy staff. With three meals a day, featuring a substance disguised as food, the odd bed wash and streams of empathetic visitors, the days meshed and the actual day and date became irrelevant. That is, of course, except for how long it had been since this life had begun, and how long before it might be over, or at least a little better.

The late-adolescent voices that the vast majority of us patients had often betrayed our bravado. Magazines of all descriptions regularly circulated the ward along with stories of our individual carnage, but so too did our questioning of the future. The topic of suicide was not infrequently raised.

Al, Rosie and Cathy were my constant visitors, however, after the first few days various people started to drift in to see me. The drift eventually became a mind-boggling stream, and, with Al keeping a note of who had visited, we found that the numbers soared well beyond a hundred before the end of rehabilitation. Other key people were Bud, and many and varied relatives who *en-masse* were stoutly supportive not only to me, but also to Al and Rosie. Plus so many old friends from

Derrinallum and new ones from the physical education course. But in his own way one stood out.

Laurie Prosser, from Ballarat College and the pre-season training group, came and kept coming, always to tell me that not only would I be able to get out of bed soon but he believed I could complete my degree in physical education from a wheelchair, which had never been done before. His visits were noted by a number of people because they were different: he appeared to give virtually all his energy to me during his visits, almost in a spiritual sense, and then leave my bedside spent.

Yet in some ways I found visitors a pressure. I knew people were scared of what they would see, worried about what they should say and how upset they appeared to be. It was like being on stage: you couldn't show your real emotions, so you acted and put on a brave, frivolous face, and would then crash after they left. After my discharge from hospital I was to learn of a number of people who came to visit me, but got no further than the ward entrance. They simply couldn't make it through the doors.

From those who did, often something remained after they left my bedside. I soon developed a menagerie of stuffed toys, some attractive and some plain horrible, ranging from a pink pig and a pale unicorn to the obligatory monkey or two. There was also a large array of sweets, chocolates and lollies. And from those who didn't come—the news of my accident had quickly spread on various grapevines—I was inundated with get-well cards, all with a range of heartfelt messages. This at least meant that my battle was not just my own.

But the support didn't end there. At home, a relief effort had sprung into action, with neighbours and friends stripping crops, checking sheep and carting hay on Barbary, all for nothing, allowing Al to be by my side. This went on throughout my stay at the hospital, and even when Al went home for a few days after the initial month or two of admission he would often find the paddock he had planned to plough, ploughed; or the sheep which had needed to be crutched, on his inspection wearing clean white underpants. And all this by people who were pressed to the limit with their own properties and mortgages. We have never forgotten this depth of giving. Al and Rosie needed it, for the stresses were huge. Becoming familiar with a large hospital for the first time and constantly having to change their lodgings were one thing, but seeing their boy broken was another.

Early in the second week after my admission, I got Al to purchase strong springs and handgrips, and had these attached to the end of my bed. The thought behind this was that if I couldn't exercise my legs, I could try to maintain some strength in my arms. So with these rigged up I could lie on my back and do bicep curls. It worked for the first day, but then it woke the sleeping dog. The weights were not touched again until the pain had truly departed.

Lying on your back does have major drawbacks, particularly when you are sick. In the third week I managed to catch a severe urinary infection which, whilst making me feel ill and nauseous, had severely spiked my temperature. In an effort to control it, nursing staff placed wet towels on my chest and directed a fan onto me. Although this was effective in bringing my temperature down, the chill through my body awoke the dog, in no uncertain fashion, but worse was to follow. The next day, although my temperature was down, I still felt sick when lunch arrived. Al cut up the steak and placed it on my chest, despite my protestations that I was not hungry. After a few mouthfuls I realised that I was going to vomit. Al grabbed the tray and ran to get a nurse, who brought a kidney dish and towels. I had to throw up while still lying on my back. The electric bed was tilted to the side as I heaved, and at this point I wondered how low things could go. Al left the ward upset and frustrated, and later I was to learn this was one of his lowest of lows. Mine was just around the corner.

At the end of this week it was crunch time. If I was to regain my lost function, it should have been coming back by then. It was not. Despite the feeling of movement I had when I tried to move, each time the sheets were drawn back and I looked at my feet, there was nothing. And my legs continued to shrink.

Three weeks to the day after my admission, I was visited by all the doctors including Joe and David Burke, on one of their Monday-morning ward rounds. They did a full examination, and then gave me the news that I had refused to consider. The lost leg movement had not come back, and due to the time that had elapsed, the likelihood was that it wouldn't return. Ever. No longer would I be able to walk with below-knee callipers. I would have to use a wheelchair for life. Shattered, I cried, and cried and cried, for oh so many reasons.

I didn't know anyone in a wheelchair. I didn't know what people in wheelchairs were like, or what their lives were like. At nineteen, all I had in my mind were archaic stereotypes, and with these stereotypes came stigmatised images and the associated words, such as 'invalid', 'spastic' and 'handicapped'. With these visions in mind, I was sure these people were cripples; and worst of all, I was one of them.

I was no longer an aspiring footballer, I was no longer an all-round robust son of a farmer, I was no longer 180 centimetres tall and attractive to the opposite sex, and how could I be a physical education teacher? Who was I, and what would become of me? The me who had been developing and dreaming for nineteen years had died by the roadside on 23 November 1981.

The days and weeks immediately after the bad news were very, very low and sombre for me and, I'm sure, for those outside looking in. Moments of solitude, day or night, were still spent searching for answers to interminable questions. The times I spent without putting on a brave face—off-stage, so to speak—were both the easiest and the hardest, since there were no distractions from the realities of my situation. During these times, my overwhelming grief and sadness were for my wet eyes only.

During the fifth week of my stay, one afternoon I received an unexpected visit from a middle-aged lady dressed in dowdy clothes and an ancient leather jacket. She identified herself as a sex counsellor, and drew the blue curtains around my bed, apparently in an attempt to create a sense of privacy, which was impossible in the open-ward environment. With all of my unchosen colleagues intentionally or inadvertently listening on the other side of my curtains, she then proceeded to question me about my sexual experiences. She asked me the age that I had lost my virginity, queried whether I had had any homosexual experiences, and so on, all in the first minutes of discussion. If it had been sex, you would have described her style as light on foreplay. After fifteen minutes of an interrogation-like interview, with minimal answers from me, she departed as suddenly as she had arrived, having garnered from my responses that I was not enamoured with her style.

I was more than interested in what is a pretty important part of life to any nineteen-year-old—and it was a popular topic of discussion on the ward. And at an appropriate time and setting I would address sex, but there and then my priorities were football, defying the doctors by walking again, and the farm. I never saw her again after our aborted conversation.

Letter from a friend

Al, Rosie and I quickly slipped into a routine. Every morning in Melbourne we would get up and head to the Austin Hospital. Sometimes Rosie and I would go via a few shops; we were never popular for that. Every Thursday afternoon Rosie would head back to Derrinallum to her job in the local library and she would drop me in Ballarat for my part-time job at the supermarket. On Saturday afternoon she would come to pick me up and we would head down to the hospital again and stay until visiting time was over. After this we would head back to the flat in Ivanhoe where we would eat, chat and collapse into bed.

Al was determined that nothing was going to hinder Sandy's progress; not the farm, nor the sibling rivalry with Bud, nor the hospital's antiquated facilities. Al would arrive at the hospital the minute visiting hours started and stay.

Sandy and Al had eaten, drunk and slept football, and I did so feel for Rosie in such a male-dominated household. Before the accident, we would live through footy training, then team selection and then the game. Following this we had the post mortem of the game, then we watched the game on TV that night. The next day we watched World of Sport. Food and drinks were served to Sandy and Al on the floor, where they lay on their stomachs watching the game. I could never do this as I got a headache. Rosie said that they were so engrossed in a game of footy you could serve them dog poo and they'd eat it; and she was right.

So in the few minutes it had taken to break Sandy's body, it also broke the pattern of so many lives. Rosie had to come to terms with the fact that Sandy would most likely be in a wheelchair. Al had to accept that not only would they not realise their goal of an AFL guernsey, but also it was highly unlikely that Sandy would be taking over the family farm.

I recall vividly the night it became apparent to Al that Sandy would indeed not be able to return to the farm, and his grief was palpable. It was around the time that Sandy had started to move about in his wheelchair, and Al was switching to Plan B. If Sandy wouldn't be able to get up to open the gates then he would devise a way that the gates would open for Sandy. Al in his turn had been a loyal and dutiful son, putting aside dreams of his own to take on what was assumed would be his role on the family farm. I believe he was very determined that his boys would have all the choices and opportunities that could be afforded them as well as unconditional love and support. A couple of times I inadvertently intruded on one of Al's private moments; once I found him with his head on his hands sobbing: 'Oh, Cathy. Stop me. I'm being stupid.'

I would console him the best I could, but what can a seventeen-year-old say to a parent grieving for their child? What do you say to somebody who has a broken heart? I tried to encourage him to cry, to let the pain out, but he was a very proud man.

This particular night he and Rosie had been talking about Sandy taking over the farm and she was trying to talk him out of it.

'Al, he can't do it. What if he was to have an accident up in the paddock? Who would be there to help him?'

Al was lost in thought about two-way radios, three-wheel motorbikes and all sorts of gismos and contraptions that would make farm work possible for a paraplegic. Finally, in exasperation she turned to me and said: 'You tell him, Cathy.'

Suddenly the spotlight was on me, and I felt as if I had a dagger in my hand. Rosie knew that Sandy and I had talked about what he would do, and that he felt the farm was no longer his direction.

'I don't think he wants to do it Al. He doesn't want to take over the farm,' I heard myself say in a very feeble voice.

I'm not sure if Al physically took a step back, or if that was just my impression, but at least emotionally he staggered, and it was then that he decided he no longer wanted to be a farmer. All the years of sweat and toil, long days, fluctuations in the market, all for the boys, and now pointless. I felt like an intruder at that time. I had been included as a part of the family and involved in one of their most important decisions. I felt his pain and I felt responsible.

The pain became even more vivid when Al and I went to

claim the plates off the Celica at the wreckers. I was stunned that the floor was up at the same height as the gear-stick console.

Sandy's body had very little fat on it, and being flat on his back his muscles atrophied very quickly. It was typical of their lifestyle and attitude not to waste a minute, so it wasn't very long before Allan bought in hand weights and Sandy started back on the road to fitness. Such intensely motivated people can't be held down for long; if Sandy was going to be in a wheelchair then he was going to be the fittest, strongest person in a wheelchair! Besides, we didn't have that long before he would be able to move into the Rehab Ward. This depended on his getting into a wheelchair, which in turn depended on his muscle strength; so we worked with Sandy toward that goal.

It all seemed relatively simple then, to strengthen the body, get into the chair and pick up life as it had been before the accident; however, there were so many things we were still to learn about spinal injury and its consequences. It may have been just under two weeks since his admission; Sandy had a steady stream of visitors and, as was his style, showed people a healthy sense of humour. We had left him one morning to let the orderlies get on with their job. In Sandy's case, his bowel and bladder movements had been paralysed; while he was catheterised to manage urine flow, he had not, to this time, had a bowel movement. This day, to help his bowels along, he was to have a suppository inserted into his rectum. That day we left Sandy a cheeky, jovial boy, to find on our return a humiliated man. He was in tears and we couldn't think what could have caused such a quick change. He was having good and bad days, as was only to be expected, but how could he have been shattered in a matter of hours? Sandy told us that this was his first realisation of the possible long-term effects of his injury. He had had a bowel movement and hadn't felt a thing. We could only sit, hold his hand and wipe away the tears. The rest of that day was spent very quietly.

As time went on, different people came to see Sandy to help him prepare for the possible long-term effects on his life, and to teach him essential daily functions. For example, learning to do intermittent catheterisation and monitor fluid intake: a paralysed bladder once stretched doesn't return to shape as does a bladder that hasn't suffered any trauma. So Sandy had to keep his bladder in good shape through strictly regulating his fluid intake. During this period I recall he had a problem with urethral blockages; after coming back from one examination he informed his mother that he now fully understood how humiliating childbirth must be because he'd spent the entire examination with his legs up in stirrups. We learnt that kidney infections would be a regular part of life if he wasn't very careful in observing hygiene, and that he may never have children. It seemed to me that whenever somebody came to see Sandy he would be in high spirits and then they would leave him shattered. This was very much the case one afternoon when we returned to find Sandy crying until we thought his heart would break. He was devastated that it seemed everything had changed so drastically, at a time when his life should really have been beginning.

There was no privacy on the ward for Sandy and me. Whenever we had a disagreement, and I was giving him a look, I would hear Malcolm call me over to his bed. He would say: 'What's the matter with you? You look like you're ready to kill.' Truly, that boy didn't miss a trick. He was so aware of other people's emotions, and he had read me like a book. I made a mental note to sneak over sometime and adjust the angle of his mirror. It was quite disconcerting to be so easily read.

The time at the hospital was for all of us emotionally and physically tiring. Rosie initially took his prognosis very badly. In her mind, confinement to a wheelchair was the worst thing *that could happen to him. After she got over the shock, she was extremely supportive and protective of him, as she was with me. It was the summer holidays and she thought I should take a break instead of being at the hospital. I thought there was no point, as I'd only worry about Sandy anyway. She drove me home every week and picked me up every Saturday in the blue station wagon, without air conditioning. By the time we got to the hospital she had nearly expired.*

Even though I sometimes felt a burden to them or that I was getting in the way, Al and Rosie never made me feel that way. I think Rosie was secretly happy to redress the hormone imbalance that existed in the family, and now she had a partner in crime. I always felt we got along well and I provided the girlie outlet, even if we would get dark looks from Sandy and Al if we occasionally detoured via a shop.

During Sandy's time in hospital Rosie displayed strength beyond expectations. Her assertiveness was unexpected, and I was quite impressed with the way she took Ivan, a male nurse, to task when he tried to reduce our visiting rights. She took him down in one fell swoop, chewed him up and spat him out. It was pure joy to watch.

Christmas came and went. On the day, a nurse asked me why I wasn't happy. I replied, 'I've got a broken back!' Patients were given the option of two cans of beer to 'celebrate' if they liked. I refused. Malcolm had his two, out of a straw, flat on his back, and was promptly sick. Merry Christmas.

Just before the New Year I was transferred from Ward Seven to Ward Eight, due to the summer rush of new admissions. Ward Eight was depressing, 'the place of no hope'. Many of the people there were regular inmates, in that they were constantly readmitted for pressure sores or other associated problems. Their whole lives seemed to revolve around the Unit, and in fact some were rumoured to try to get into hospital for Christmas, so as to have some people to spend it with.

Soon after my transfer, whilst lying and watching the goings on of the ward, I noticed one of the readmission patients who was a paraplegic having his legs stretched. I was absolutely stunned at how thin his legs were below the knees and I vowed to myself that mine would never get like that. Little did I know that it was not something done by choice or neglect. I was later to learn that my legs looked exactly the same.

Ward Eight, just like Ward Seven, was not air conditioned, so, as the temperature rose outside, the patients cooked inside. And the cooling systems used were pretty basic to say the least: wet towels on the bed, or even the odd water fight—from my stationary horizontal position, of course. There was only one thing that functioned regardless of the facilities, and that was the staff.

In the main they remained a constant positive. Henry, a male nurse who had been blessed by being tall and blond with dimples and a wicked smile, was everyone's favourite—especially the women's—not just because of his nursing skills, but for his innate humour and charisma. With all these patients, predominantly male, all trapped in bed for long periods of time, he shared his escapades, particularly those with women. We lived vicariously through Henry. Rosie fell in love with him because she could see the way he psychologically lifted everyone, including me. To this day I don't know whether he was the consummate actor, or just a fun guy.

I had been in bed for seven weeks, the last four being relatively pain free, whilst I waited for my back to heal. I was told at the six-week X-ray that it had not—that was, not to the satisfaction of the doctors. But one more problem was about to arise. The nursing staff informed me that one of my regular swabs for staph had come back positive. This meant I was placed in isolation, and fed from disposable crockery marked with bright red stickers. All my visitors had to put on gowns before they saw me. This was pretty shattering to what remained of my self-esteem. I was treated as if I was unclean, and many of the people who came to see me did not understand. To be considered clean again, I had to return three negative swabs in a row, despite having recorded only one positive swab. This could not happen quickly, since swabs were taken, from the nasal canal, twice weekly. So, to be clear it would take at least one-and-a-half weeks, assuming three negative swabs in a row were recorded.

On the completion of my eighth week I was X-rayed, and after a few days I was told that I could begin sitting up as soon as I had a brace measured, made and fitted. This was to support my back and prepare me for the introduction to a wheelchair. The brace had two rods, which went from the base of my spine to up between my shoulder blades, and had a large strap at my stomach, and two at chest level. The entire brace was covered in wool, which prevented rubbing. However, this same padding meant that wearing the brace was like having an overcoat on in the middle of summer. But there was no choice—no brace, no sitting, no rehabilitation.

Before sitting up, every patient had to go though a process of slowly having their bed raised, notch by notch, because after being in a horizontal position for such a long time a person can black out or throw up if sat up too quickly. This can take up to a week, depending on the level of injury and other factors.

To assist the body to adjust to sitting up, tight elastic stockings had to be worn by anyone with a spinal injury in the first weeks or months of their rehabilitation. The white stockings, whilst unaesthetic and difficult to get onto non-compliant limbs, limit the swelling of the feet and calf muscles, which occurs because without normal leg muscle contraction the blood can't circulate properly.

Finally, after I completed the sitting-up process, nine weeks and three days since my accident, the moment arrived. On a fine sunny February day with a clear blue sky, a brand spanking new wheelchair was delivered to me. It was chrome, with burgundy upholstery on the seat and back support, and had large curled handles on the back. The tyres had a hard knobbly groove, and the footplates looked inordinately heavy. But it was a step forward.

Getting into the chair was not simply a case of sitting up and jumping aboard. I was like a newborn child. I soon discovered that not only was I terribly weak from the weeks in bed, but that I could also do very little for myself. Any nineteen-year-old man who cannot dress himself, let alone bear his own body weight through his skinny arms whilst coordinating the placement of long unmoving legs, is far from independent. The introduction to the wheelchair was like a film showing highlights of what I had lost, what I had become, and how far I really had to go. Bed, though frustrating, was a place that you could hide in, and not confront all the realities that face you in a wheelchair.

The orderlies arrived and lifted me from my bed into the wheelchair, under the gaze of the physiotherapist, Ros, along with Rosie, and Cathy. (Al was back at Barbary.) This was accomplished without too much drama and I was soon left alone with the family, resplendent in my white stockings, blue moccasins, a stark white drawsheet and a worn grey T-shirt. My catheter bag was hung on the front of the chair, and as I sat with a ramrod-straight braced back, I cautiously began to manoeuvre the chair through the ward to the outside world. I was accompanied on my slow journey by words of encouragement from patients in bed, and some nursing staff who stared, since they had never seen me in a position other than horizontal in bed. I had nearly missed the entire summer and was as pale as a polar bear, and I found that I was blinded by the sun's bright intensity. I didn't want anyone to help me, yet the handles on the back of the chair seemed to be a magnet for people's hands.

During the weeks I was in bed, nursing staff had constantly rubbed moisturising cream into my hands, something that I had never done previously. On the farm I tended to develop the odd callus or occasionally a blister, but in general my hands were tough. Due to the lack of activity and copious amounts of cream, my hands had become as soft as butter. So as soon as I began to push the wheelchair, using the harsh knobbly tyres, my hands basically fell apart. Eventually I gave up pushing myself and we sat under a large gum tree, and I chewed on a red icypole. And all I could think about was what a great day it was for a run!

Everyone who has had a spinal injury is not permitted to sit in a wheelchair for more than a short period of time at first, as their bottom needs to become accustomed to the pressure of sitting. Circulation to the usually atrophied backside is often impinged on by sitting, and can lead to pressure sores if not managed appropriately. And so in a tormented state of mind, and with my few minutes of sitting time expired, I retired back to my bed. Despite all the time I had spent there, I found it a welcome sanctuary.

Shattered and in absolute despair at the reality of the unfolding nightmare, and with the knowledge that there was no chance of awakening, of taking a single step, ever again, I dissolved. Inconsolable, I said again and again to Rosie and Cathy that I couldn't spend the rest of my life confined to a wheelchair. But there were no options.

Each day the staff allowed me to sit for longer periods of time in my chair, initially for ten to fifteen minutes, to allow my backside to adjust to the pressure. To this day, it always seems a little unfair that a paraplegic's most important tool in the world is their backside, and yet they have a significantly greater likelihood of skin problems there than everyone else. It was at this time that I learnt that the general populace walked, sat and lay whilst I simply sat and lay.

Despite still being in isolation (I had obtained only one clear test), the time had come for me to move from Ward Eight, up the hill to the final stop, the Rehabilitation Ward, Ward Seventeen. So with my worldly possessions packed in hospital bags, I made the trip to the turn-of-the-century building that was the Rehab Ward, only to be sent to Siberia.

REHABILITATION

Ward Seventeen was the gateway to discharge and the place where reborn babies became as independent as possible.

The old Victorian building was situated towards the top of the hilly Heidelberg site, and constructed of red bricks. With wide linoleum-surfaced corridors, aged white-painted walls and expansive doors, the building provided plenty of room for novice wheelchair users, however, the sturdy walls were marked from wheelchairs constantly colliding with them. A further addition to a seemingly normal old building were numbers of full-length mirrors. With the vast majority of patients using wheelchairs and having lost musculature and balance, the mirrored images were a simple means of checking whether one was sitting straight, or leaning like the Tower of Pisa. This was more often the case, particularly in early stages of rehabilitation. I came to suspect that the mirrors also played a role in helping patients adjust to their new body image.

But unfortunately the most personal of patient facilities were limited. There were no en-suites, and patients would have to be wheeled the length of the corridor to the bathrooms, which were of open-plan design. It was not uncommon to have four or five patients sitting on commodes together at one time. The bedrooms were rather like open dormitories, with only a blue curtain for privacy and no doors separating one room from the next or from the corridor. With the constant activity of the ward, it was noisy and inconducive to sleep. And again, there was no air conditioning.

The building had high ceilings, but once it got hot, it stayed hot. And in Melbourne, in February 1982, it stayed hot a lot. For many quadriplegics this was serious, as they no longer have the ability to naturally regulate their body temperature. When it was hot they were regularly draped in towels to cool them, and I imagine in winter they would have to be rugged up. They were a little like lizards.

Lizards probably have more in common though than the patients who inhabited Ward Seventeen along with me, as all we shared was our newly acquired disability. I was the only person on the ward who was studying at tertiary level, and one of the few who had been involved in sport. So there wasn't a great deal of depth to our discussions. Malcolm, who had also been transferred to the ward, was now confronting the frustration of his disability. And the frustration was taking over. One day another patient, Clive, dropped his toothpaste onto the floor. He had become a quadriplegic after a motorbike crash overseas, having just reached the top level in speedway racing. And of course he couldn't pick the tube up. Malcolm, also a quadriplegic, then proceeded to run Clive's toothpaste over and over and over until it burst, bringing Clive to tears. No-one was having a good time.

I certainly wasn't, since on my transfer from Ward Eight I had been moved into Siberia. Siberia was a room right at the end of the ward, away from the other beds, where patients with staph were sent. Unclean, unclean. And for company, I had Derek. Derek had supposedly broken his neck after repeatedly, and intentionally, running into a wall head first. Or so other people told me, as Derek didn't talk, not to me, not to anyone.

It was a quiet room and I had no choice. I had to stay in Siberia until I obtained clear swab results, eating my meals away from the dining room, off my disposable plate with the bright stickers.

As I was becoming accustomed to my new accommodation and neighbours, so were Al and Rosie, who had now settled into Melbourne life by taking a unit in East Ivanhoe. They would take it in turns commuting to the farm and Rosie's job at the Derrinallum Library, ensuring someone was always at the hospital. It was to be four months after my admission before I spent a whole day without one of them. Their unit was a small one-bedroom flat with a divan for Cathy to sleep on. It became home for the people who had never come to Melbourne. To help them settle in, they decided to have the *Herald Sun* delivered every morning. After five days of it not arriving, they checked with the newsagent, and were assured that it was being delivered. The chap suggested that perhaps it was being stolen, something they had not considered, being naïve country folk. So Cathy and Al decided to do a little bit of trap-setting. They painted a subtle 'you thieving bastards' on an old newspaper, and then got up bright and early one Wednesday morning, retrieving the newly delivered paper from the letterbox and replacing it with the old paper with the message on it. A little while later the inhabitant of the adjoining flat was seen rushing to the letterbox and taking what they thought was their miraculous free newspaper out. They walked past Al and Rosie's flat opening the paper. It was then that they saw the message. They panicked and made the biggest circuit to avoid going back by Al and Rosie's flat, and skulked back to their own unit.

But back to the ward. The ward was no palace, and the place operated only because of the uncompromising and ultra-committed staff. Yet they were very different from the staff where I'd come from. They all wore casual clothes, with the intent of dehospitalising the place, and there seemed to be far fewer of them. The ward was about rehabilitation, and I was no longer considered sick. In fact I was about to become a gym bunny, like it or not.

The rehabilitation gymnasium was very small, and also housed in a Victorian building, a small distance from the rear of the ward. Soft workout mats covered the floor, ropes hung from the ceiling and various ancient weight machines were available to assist with body rebuilding. A stationary exercise bike sat in a corner, and free weights were propped against the wall. The gym was staffed with five physiotherapists who each coordinated the strengthening of their designated patients. An orderly assisted with bringing patients to and from the ward, and lifting uncooperative bodies on and off the exercise mats. In full swing, the gym provided a chaotic scene, with a number of patients, all with diverse injuries and varying degrees of remaining abilities, sweating for their quest for independence. Or, more importantly, towards being the best that they could be.

Every day the routine was the same. Come morning, I would wait for the orderlies or nursing staff to put my brace on. Without the brace I was not allowed to do anything, and with the brace on I couldn't do anything. The brace stopped me from bending and made me feel more limited than ever. If I dropped something on the floor I could not pick it up, regardless of the strength in my arms. After being fitted with the brace I would either be placed on a commode and taken to the communal toilet, or dressed and lifted into my chair, allowing me to go to the gym. Showers were not an issue; I still couldn't have one because I could not allow the woolly brace to get wet. Some time after I arrived on the ward, a shower brace was designed for me, made and fitted, eventually allowing me to use a mobile shower trolley.

Every four hours, urology staff visited me, as my long-term catheter had been removed virtually on arrival on the ward. Urology nurses who were helping to start my bladder retraining would intermittently catheterise me. As part of this process I was

Rehabilitation

on a strict fluid-intake quota, so at this stage, no matter how hard I worked in the gym, I could only drink the allocated amount.

After the various trials of each morning it was then down to the gym. There was a mirror just outside the gym and it was here that I sized myself up each time I passed.

It was in the gym that in some ways I felt quite lucky. Because my injury was at the base of my spine, I still had full trunk function, and consequently I had a number of muscles to rebuild. Also, having had an active life through sport, weight work wasn't entirely new to me. For people who had very little functioning muscle to work on, and for others who had never seen the inside of a weights room before, the challenge was far greater and much more daunting.

Yet it was at the gym that the real horror of a fresh spinal injury became apparent to me, taking my emotions beyond breaking point and further. Big boys don't cry, or at least nineteen-year-old men are not meant to—but they do. Throughout my time in Wards Seven and Eight, but particularly in quiet moments whilst in Ward Seventeen, I cried and cried and cried. For many reasons. For the things that I had lost along with the use of my legs, such as the dream of playing AFL football and the freedom of running along a beach. For my shattered self-image, which had been transformed back to that of a newborn baby. For my new embarrassments. For all the frustration of no longer being able to do the simple things such as picking something up from the floor, dressing myself or even getting in and out of my wheelchair. I tried whenever possible not to cry, but on many occasions I was not successful. Other people cried more, still others cried less. Everyone who was going through the ward as a patient had lost different things, but each of them had lost so very, very much.

Soon after arriving on Ward Seventeen I had what was called a 'family meeting'. Despite its homely name, the gathering involved not only Al, Rosie, Bud and Cathy, my friends from Ballarat, Ray Mathews and and Laurie Prosser, but also all the staff involved in my rehabilitation. And it was not a fun meeting. The purpose was to outline my prognosis, and my future rehabilitation path. The medical staff gave a synopsis of my injury, and its effects, essentially the loss of lower-limb function, along with altered sensation, and bowel and bladder paralysis. Al asked for an explanation of why I had lost so much movement from the initial time of admission, and was told this was due to initial spinal swelling and consequent blood-vessel damage, leading to death of part of the spinal cord. Walking in any form other than with groin callipers was now out of the question. Nursing, physiotherapy, occupational therapy, and others followed this now believed but still unaccepted news, all outlining the steep relearning curve ahead.

And in a way I was a little like a spectator, the only difference being that I was the one and only subject. Listening to an analysis of one's body's most personal functions in front of an array of people would once have seemed daunting, but after being indoctrinated by the system over the preceding weeks it didn't seem particularly out of the norm. In a way, all hospital patients have to leave their privacy and dignity at admission, and try to pick them up again on discharge. It's just the way it is.

However, after a little while I had stopped taking everything in, because for the first time in my life I nearly fainted. There were fifteen people squeezed into a non-air-conditioned room on a 38-degree February day, with me dressed in a woollen overcoat (my brace). I was more than glad when it was over, and not just because of the heat. There is only so much bad news one can listen to from different people in one sitting, no matter how detached you may try to be.

Letter from a friend

In order for Sandy to be allowed into a wheelchair, he had to prove that he had the strength and stamina to sit up.

For many patients this took a few attempts because after being flat on its back for so long, their body violently objects to being forced upright. The first time most people sat up they turned green and felt nauseous. Sandy was determined to sit up for the required length of time in one hit and I'm fairly sure he did. The excitement of getting out of bed and into a chair was bittersweet though. The movement was great but the reality of a wheelchair as a companion for the rest of his life began to really hit home. We would go for wanders around the grounds but they were pretty dark days for him. However, in his usual gutsy way he pulled himself out of the doldrums and instead we would go to the gym so he could start building up his muscle strength, as this was the first step toward learning to transfer in and out of the wheelchair and a car.

Going to the gym was a test of courage. Sandy had to regain his strength, relearn balance and movement and compensate for two limbs that no longer worked as they should, as they stubbornly refused to stay in place whilst he learned to balance his upper body. In doing all of this he also had to manage the resulting fatigue, bruises and muscle stiffness. The real test, however, was the battle to manage his bowels. During his early rehabilitation they were trying to establish Sandy's bowel routine and his body was refusing to cooperate. No longer being sensitive to regular cues, his body had to be forced into action through the use of laxatives. This was frustrating for all of us and we became aware of how such a basic function is taken for granted. It also demonstrated that under certain circumstances bowels could begin to rule your life, and more importantly your spirit. We would get Sandy up and dressed, he would be transferred into the chair and head up to the gym. Then as he transferred out of his chair, he would have a bowel movement. So it was back into the chair, back to the ward, a change of clothes, return to the wheelchair and back up to the gym again we would go. As if it were yesterday I remember the pain I felt for him; it is still so real. The absolute stabbing of the heart; again, another question to God: 'Hasn't it already been made tough enough? Can't you spare him this?'

Again, as with so many questions I asked, the answer came: 'It is not in making this easy that the true human spirit emerges. This is tough and hard and embarrassing and a true survivor will not be daunted by this trivial matter in the scheme of things.'

I believe this is so true. I saw winners and quitters go through the hospital and strangely enough the quitters usually walked out. The winners triumphed in spirit and when your spirit is strong nothing can get you down.

Many times in the early days I would sit by his bedside and ask: 'Why him?' I'd say, 'God, my legs aren't as important to me. So long as I have my hands I can still work academically.'

I've come to believe that it is there, in asking the question, that the answer lies. I would accept the disability and lay down; people like Sandy refuse to accept the disability, and in doing so create better lives for themselves and greater experiences for others. If it happened to me I would have made just a ripple on the waters of life, whereas Sandy would never be happy with anything less than a tidal wave. I would try to be obscure, where he would make the biggest fuss to get the greatest attention to achieve the greatest good. I have always been humbled by people who have suffered any sort of disability because so many grab life by the horns.

Never did I feel pity for Sandy. I felt sorry that he should have to experience such a life-altering event, but in watching him overcome it, my heart would experience admiration and pride as well as hurt. I was a friend of this man with extraordinary courage. Thank you, God, for letting me learn this at such a young age . . .

At the gym my designated physiotherapist, Yoko, focused on

everything that would make me strong, and that I could do while still trussed in my brace. And that included anything from rope climbing and free weights to working out on the ancient pulley machine. Rope climbing turned out to be incredibly difficult, because once I'd got to the top of the rope I couldn't slither down using my legs. So I'd climb up to the ceiling using only my arms, and arrive at the top, exhausted, but too scared to let go because I'd break my legs in the fall. This was an excellent incentive to climb back down using my arms, despite the overwhelming fatigue. This 'overtraining' was of course aimed at making me strong, not another Tarzan. Although ever limited by my brace, I was regularly lifted onto the floor where she worked with me in retraining my balance and introducing me to transferring techniques which I would use after shedding my brace. One memory of my first day at the gymnasium was of Yoko setting me a task on the pulley machine and designating a certain weight and repetition number. I doubled them both, not because I was disobedient, just because in my mind more was better. The exercise bike became a significant frustration, because Rosie with her blind faith in my ability to recover decided that all I needed to do to get strength in my legs was to work out on the bike. What she could not understand was that with my balance being as it was, I could not sit on the bike without falling off, let alone move the pedals. That took a lot of explaining to her.

I had been in rehabilitation for about three-and-a-half weeks when my birthday came along. There didn't seem that much to celebrate, but during the day a lot of funny things went on.

Cathy was acting strangely. She was not the type of girl to initiate a food fight, and yet in the ward lift she had smeared chocolate on me. Al and Rosie seemed to be conspicuous in their absence. I didn't know it at the time, but Cathy was doing anything to keep me occupied, and Al and Rosie were up to no good. Finally, at about five o'clock Al and Rosie turned up and said there were some funny people down in the autocafe.

The autocafe area was a place with lots of automatic food machines, where people went to escape the ward. So, with their combined urging we went down to the cafeteria. Al opened the door and I saw that all the lights were off in the cafe. I wouldn't go in, despite his urging, and consequently he tried to push me in. A little unnerved, I pushed away from the door, and it was only then that they told me that it was a surprise birthday party.

Ray a mature-age student from my course, and a few other students, had hired a bus and organised the entire physical education year to come to the hospital *en masse* from Ballarat for my party. For weeks they had been in cahoots with Al, Rosie and Cathy, and were waiting for me, in the dark. As I wheeled into the room, fifty or so people broke into a rowdy chorus of 'Happy Birthday', and in that moment what had been a pretty wretched day became the opposite, and my emotions took a giant leap. For the two hours of the party, I was on show since a number of my classmates hadn't seen me since my accident. The party went so quickly; I had fifty people wanting to say hello and have a chat. For each of them my appearance must have been quite shocking and confronting. It's only now, when I look at photos of the night, that I realise that I looked like a skeleton, far from what they had recently known. And yet for me it was wonderful to see that I hadn't been forgotten. More than anything, it showed that there might be a future outside the hospital on the hill.

For someone new to a wheelchair, the apparent fears, hazards and frustrations of the hospital went beyond dark rooms, rope climbing and the lack of independence. A training ground was created just outside the ward for people learning new wheelchair skills. With the Austin and Ward Seventeen being perched on a hill, to get anywhere apart from the gym, you had to go down hills; to get back to your bed, you had to defy gravity and climb the hill. It was not uncommon for a bod in a wheelchair to lose control of their newly acquired chariot and end up in the garden, often upturned. Staff would often be seen fishing patients out of the garden and putting them back into their wheelchairs. One of the saddest and most frightening experiences was had by a quadriplegic who had virtually no arm function. He was sitting at the top of the ramp to the dining room when his chair, with a mind of its own, took off down the ramp and straight into the garden, dumping him deep into a fern. Fortunately he was not injured, but people witnessing this didn't know whether to laugh or cry.

When my rehabilitation was entering its mid phase, one afternoon the physiotherapists organised a game of what could very loosely be described as wheelchair basketball on the asphalt court outside, as a change to our regular routine. With additional players required, Al was one of a number of spectators roped in to participate. Soon after the game commenced, Al, with his long-forgotten competitive juices ever so slightly prodded, discovered he had one significant problem. Every time he went at any sort of pace in his wheelchair and lent forward to grab the ball, he inadvertently transferred weight through his feet onto the footplates, causing the chair to pigroot forward and come to a grinding halt, footplates embedded in asphalt. As for me, the most memorable outcome of the game was a change in perception. This was the first time I'd looked up at a basketball ring from a sitting position and, with the further hindrance of my back brace, the distance seemed somewhat akin to that between Earth and Mars. And when attempting to 'shoot' the ball, only on one occasion did I actually manage to hit the ring. Al survived his basketball debut, but worse was to come for him soon after.

In an effort to understand the functional challenges and feelings confronting me, Al had taken to often sitting in my wheelchair when I was lying on my bed, thinking in his tinkering farmer's mind of potential enhancements to the chair's design. He began conducting some simple manoeuvres in the wheelchair as we talked. About a week after my birthday party, I asked him to go down the hill in my wheelchair to the shops to buy me an icypole. With the challenge set, he readily agreed because, he said, he wanted to learn. For me it was nothing more than a diversion to my day, but to Al it was an important experience. It was about forty degrees in the shade in the middle of the day, and off he went, determined to understand what it was like to push what he saw as a bucking, unwilling piece of machinery. After fifty minutes or more, he arrived back by my bedside, with stories of near misses in the garden, a near-tragic head-on with a white Sigma sedan and many funny looks from passers-by who recognised him, and sad looks from others who didn't and were worried about his unique ineptitude. He arrived the colour of puce, with a very melted icypole, and a new understanding of the difficulties. Despite his litany of challenges, he said that he wanted to learn how to 'mono', that is, to balance the chair on its back wheels. So I told him it was quite simple really—you lean back a little and push the wheels forward (so I'd heard secondhand, as I was yet to complete the feat). If you felt yourself falling, you pulled the wheels back. Unfortunately, in his puce condition, he must have got a little confused. He ultimately got the chair up on its back wheels, was balancing, then felt himself falling back, and pushed the wheels vigorously forward, driving himself into the ground on his neck. At least he had his accident in the right place. He got up after a moment or two, a little shocked and stunned, too hurt to be embarrassed, and has never ever sat in my wheelchair since.

Throughout rehabilitation, attempts were made by staff and patients to keep their spirits up and senses of humour as intact as possible. And there were many funny moments amongst the heavy fog, with the staff often victims of the patients' humour. One day a staff member who was new to the ward brought me lunch in the dining room. Since the food was at times inedible—which is not particularly uncommon with hospital food—I didn't move a muscle when my tray was put in front of me. The new nurse asked me if I was OK, and would I like her to cut up my meal. I took up her kind offer of help. She removed the lid and when she'd finished cutting up my meal, I still hadn't moved. It was then that she made the big decision that I was obviously a high-level quadriplegic and incapable of feeding myself. 'Would you like me to feed you?' she asked, and I quietly answered, 'Yes'. Halfway through her feeding me, and under the watchful eyes of a number of giggling patients, another staff member walked in and saw what was going on. She screamed: 'Sandy, what are you doing?' I quickly grabbed the knife and fork and proceeded to eat my lunch, as the new staff member slid quietly away. I think she was told to assess patients by how big their shoulders looked, not by how little they seemed to be moving.

It was not just the patients who were sensitive of their situations or prone to fluctuating emotions. Bev was a vivacious nurse, initially from New Zealand, who I had become close to. With her dry Kiwi wit and wicked sense of fun, along with her vast travel experiences, she was someone I always looked forward to spending time with, and she was one of the first people that got to know me with no knowledge of my pre-accident life. She knew no other me, unlike the vast majority of people who I talked to. With our discussions taking place with no history, I enjoyed our frivolous repartee. One night we were having a chat when I cracked a joke and she inadvertently said, 'Gee if I did that, I'd break your back.' It went straight over my head. She terminated our conversation and left the ward, only to fret over her words and their impact on me for the remainder of the evening. The next day she came up to me before her shift and started apologising again and again, until I managed to stop her and ask what she was apologising for. This showed how careful the staff were, and it also highlighted how everyone was on eggshells around me.

Now it was a waiting game, waiting to become braceless. The dreaded woolly brace gave me the ability to sit up whilst my back completed its healing process, yet it limited, slowed or stopped everything that I had to learn to do. Finally, after its removal at the end of February, my true rehabilitation could begin. And with that would come increased abilities, the permission to try new skills, and car travel.

Learning to mono was a big thing for me. It would allow me to get up and down gutters, and also is perhaps one of the few cool things you could do in what is a traditionally uncool object, a wheelchair. Patients were not allowed to learn to mono until after discarding their brace. The day after becoming braceless, and after spending a day of learning and practising with Al standing behind me, I had it mastered. Unlike him. I was cool. But as often happens, overconfidence brings on tragedies. Al, who at the time was still smoking, went to place a cigarette in a bin as I did my final mono for the day and my first without my catcher. I lost my balance and fell backwards, landing heavily on the floor, with the wheelchair on top of me. Of course, I couldn't get up. Al, not quite knowing what to do and feeling a little panicked, scooped me up and stuffed me like a sack of spuds back into the chair. It seemed that every time I tried to move forward, and make the best of the terrible situation I was in, I would invariably be brought back to earth and reminded of my limitations.

My first trip in a vehicle after the removal of my brace was on a swimming outing with the physiotherapists to the Doncaster Pool. Being loaded onto a bus and strapped down while still in our wheelchairs made me feel a little like being in a cattle truck. The outing highlighted how difficult simple things had become, such as getting into and out of the pool and getting dressed in my wheelchair in public facilities. My swimming hadn't been particularly impressive prior to my injury, but now I had lost the stabilising effect that my legs had once had; whilst I floated reasonably, the body roll had increased and my swimming strokes had degenerated. My legs were also embarrassingly skinny.

Following the removal of my brace my abilities and independence had grown at a great rate, along with my sense of adventure. But my concept of adventure was significantly different since my accident.

One night, desperately sick of the hospital food and craving some personal space, alone and away from the environs of the sick and the broken, I ventured out. Down through the steeply graded hospital grounds and out onto Burgundy Street I went, in search of a takeaway chicken shop and a sense of being amongst the community. I freewheeled a hundred metres or more down the sloped footpath towards the Heidelberg shopping centre. With the majority of shops on the side opposite the hospital grounds, I then had to cross the road, something which had always been simply a matter of course and completed with a minimum of fuss. This had now changed. With my monoing skills unusable for obstacles such as kerbs, I searched and found a kerb ramp onto the roadway and crossed the road. I was faced by vehicles travelling at seemingly enhanced speeds, and was struck by my new cumbersome being. With no corresponding kerb ramp on the opposite side of the roadway, I was forced to wheel with the traffic flow, keeping as close as possible to the parked cars on the verge, but still on the road, until a kerb ramp gave me an escape back onto the safety of the footpath. Relieved and slightly chuffed, I found a chicken shop, which fortunately had a flat entry and an open door, entered and ordered dinner. I placed the chicken in my lap and wheeled over to an adjacent table and gorged myself on real food. Well satisfied, I then began the return journey across the road, up the street and through the hospital to the top of the grounds. However, this time it was all uphill. The trek back in my 25-kilogram chair took me more than an hour, and I arrived at the ward in a lather of sweat. Yet in many ways it was a little beginning.

My first weekend leave was to the Ivanhoe flat, and it was then that I realised things had altered in the most personal of ways, at least for a time. After not doing much for the day, apart from a drive around the city, we went home. After some takeaway and television it was time to go to bed. For the sleeping arrangements, I was to share Cathy's divan, and after the constant sterility of the starched white hospital sheets and the plastic-lined pillows on a single hospital bed within a group ward, the thought of lying next to my partner was a welcome one. Despite having been affronted by the sex counsellor during the early days of my Austin stay, I couldn't help but wonder what the true consequences of my spinal injury were. After being helped into bed, and the lights being turned off, I did what most nineteen-year-olds would think about doing with their girlfriend, with a mixture of wonder, desire, fear and renewal. And whilst I was keen in spirit, certain other parts of me were still asleep to a fair degree. I was to learn much later that spinal shock, a consequence of spinal injury, takes a significant time to resolve, and one of its impacts is impotence to a range of degrees and time frames. After having bowel accidents, bladder accidents and now another part of my anatomy not performing, I was pretty shattered. Thank God it was to be only a transitory stage. My sex life, however, was not (and is not) of significant interest just to me. It is still amusing that over the years many members of the general public have felt as though they have the permission to ask the very personal question, 'Can ya do it, mate?' in a whole range of settings barely minutes after introducing themselves. Mind you, children at a number of my school visits have been equally direct. They are all quickly stymied when my answer comes straight back: 'Like a champion!'

The following weekend, again on leave from the hospital, Al and I decided to go to the football at the MCG. Football had always been such a part of our lives, both separately and as a unit, be it playing or spectating, live or on television. The day was not a success. Rather than simply watching the match I was doing what I would continue to do for many years, virtually transposing myself into the game and the positions that I played, visualising my movements in response to the ball's location. Yet, whilst doing this, I knew all I ever would be from now on was a spectator in the truest sense of the word. While the fans roared in response to their team's goals or the umpires' decisions, my mood was a stark contrast to the atmosphere surrounding the contest. Al and I sat mutely through the first half, each of us trying to enjoy a day out, but both failing miserably. With barely a word required, we left at half time. We quickly resumed our passion for the game in the insulated world of the print and electronic media, but it would be more than ten years before I would return to the ground to watch a match and be able to view it as a true spectator. Al's time of abstinence was even greater, and even now he goes to games only occasionally.

The desire and will to walk never went away. The gym focused on two things. One was to make me strong enough to transfer independently in and out of my chair and cars, off the bed, and up and down from the floor. The other, which was the preferred option of course, was to walk one way or another. After receiving my clearance to remove the brace for all activities in the last six weeks of my rehabilitation, I was assigned a physiotherapy student from Royal Melbourne Institute of Technology, whose primary assessment was to be based upon teaching me to walk again. So for her, it was nearly as important as for me. But walking didn't mean walking in the manner I had always taken for granted. It meant being measured and fitted with callipers, which went from my groin to my ankles; or, in other words, metal rods which made my legs stiff, like sticks. With the use of crutches, I relearned to 'walk', in a fashion. After weeks and weeks of practice, to get even as far as fifty metres took me half an hour or more, and would leave me lathered in sweat and extremely frustrated. All the time, I needed someone standing in front of me, ready to catch me should I topple over. This technique of walking was known as 'swing to'. This involved swinging both feet forward towards outstretched crutches, regaining one's balance, moving the crutches forward, and swinging the legs again, with all the weight for movement being borne through my arms and hands. Ultimately the goal was to learn the advanced 'swing through', or 'four point' technique. On one particular day, I was strapped in my callipers and had spent fifteen minutes trying to get up off the floor unaided, battling with stiff legs and handicapped by my poor balance. Dripping with sweat, I had then 'walked' from the gym into Ward Seventeen. As I rounded a corner in the main corridor I slipped on the shiny linoleum and fell into the ever waiting arms of my enthusiastic but inexperienced student. This caused both of us to fall to the floor, with me assuming the missionary position directly on top of her. With mutual embarrassment at an all-time high, I set a record for the fastest log roll ever performed by a paraplegic. This event did not strengthen my belief that 'walking' was either functional or aesthetic, not to mention safe. Despite having specialist callipers made, I was never to pick them up from the hospital after being discharged. To me it was blatantly obvious that I couldn't walk.

With my inability to walk now seemingly set in stone, and with my strength continuing to improve, my physiotherapist set about teaching me some of the intricacies of truly independent wheelchair use. One of these skills was learning to come down stairs. Using a flight of twenty or more external stairs adjacent to the gym, I was taken on a circuitous route to the top, and then encouraged to approach the stairs backwards! Watched by a disbelieving Neil and his new wife, neighbours from Barbary who were actually on their one-day honeymoon, and an extremely nervous Rosie, I was then told to grasp the stairs' handrail with my left hand and then ease the chair down the first concrete step, whilst gripping the right wheel. With Neil acting as a backstop, I slowly progressed down the stairs, step by step, because once started down the stairs, there was no going back. With each movement came the rhythmic thud of my footplates hitting the preceding concrete step. It seemed that my chair might fall apart with the repetitive impact. Finally I

Rehabilitation

reached the bottom with a mix of relief and a sense of achievement; I had the very basics of a skill that would allow me access to areas without lifts. Obviously though, it was a skill that needed to be practised with a degree of caution, since any mistake would have dire consequences. And with gravity the only thing bringing me down, it certainly didn't solve the problem of getting back up the stairs.

As my rehabilitation progressed, it became more and more apparent that all of my previous sporting pursuits were no longer possible. In their place I became aware of sports available to people in wheelchairs. I suppose even then it was clear that my passion for sport had survived the accident. The sport that had most appeal was wheelchair basketball, a team sport with a strong physical nature.

Wheelchair basketball is a direct derivative of the able-bodied game, with a few subtle rule changes and different interpretations. The major rule change is the travel rule. A player may have two touches of his wheels and then must dribble the ball once again before pushing or turning the chair. The player can roll as far as he likes with the ball; if a player has speed up on receiving the ball he can go quite a distance without pushing the chair or dribbling the ball, making the game very fast. Any chair contact is ruled as pushing, holding or charging, as in the 'upright' game. However, due to the speed of the wheelchairs, the game is often rough and aggressive, with spectacular spills.

Having heard that there was a local wheelchair basketball competition played at the stadium in Preston every week, I decided to go and inspect what I thought would be the closest thing to football that I could still play. In an attempt to stretch my independence, I ordered a taxi to take me to the stadium. I was dropped at the entrance, and I wheeled in the front door alone. I was immediately confronted with the vision of two matches of wheelchair basketball in progress, and I instantly thought: 'Shit, I don't belong here, everyone's in a wheelchair.' In my mind I was still a 180-centimetre tall footballer. And then

I looked down, and saw that in reality I was 110 centimetres, and sitting.

Recovering from this shock, I found a position courtside, quickly becoming absorbed in the spectacle of the game nearer to me, struck by the cacophony of sound emanating from the colliding wheelchairs, loud voices and the bouncing ball, all interspersed with the occasional referee's whistle. But as much as the sounds, the innate aggression of the game stood out. The players were using their chairs at times as weapons, whilst the fear and inherent danger of falling out had obviously been long forgotten. And what's more it was genuinely competitive. Amongst all this, one player stood out above the rest, for a number of reasons. I was in awe of his wheelchair and ball skills, his speed, his aggression, his passion and his athletic physique, and because he was an athlete, wheelchair or no wheelchair. And I wanted to be like him.

At the end of a night which had been both interesting and confronting, a couple of the players who I had met and chatted to briefly offered me a lift back to the Austin. I thanked them but declined. I had seen a telephone box a little way up the road from which I planned to call a taxi. It was only when I got there that I realised that my big hospital wheelchair was never going to fit into the phone box. Not to be deterred, I saw a McDonald's restaurant on a nearby corner and made my way to it. Feeling a little self-conscious after my attempt at independence had been interrupted by an access barrier, I entered the restaurant and nervously approached the counter. Asked for my order, I responded with 'Two cheeseburgers, and a small fries,' and then asked if someone could call a taxi to take me back to the hospital. And soon, 'home' I went.

Despite the tribulations of the evening, I soon went back to the stadium, and during my last weeks as an in-patient at the Austin played my first games of wheelchair basketball. In my heavy hospital wheelchair, with little strength, appalling balance and certainly no wheelchair skills, I made my debut, at the most basic level with a development team called the Hombres. But there was an early highlight. In my first game I was going at a speed that was for me at this stage fast, but definitely somewhat out of control, when someone passed me the ball. As I careered toward the end line of the court, about to go out of bounds, I threw the ball in a panicked and unplanned long-distance hook shot from the right side of the court. The ball went straight through the hoop, without touching the sides or the backboard, and brought the house down. (I was later to learn the correct call for such a shot was 'all net'.)

Quickly, however, my football background came to the fore, both in a positive and negative sense. Whilst I could catch the ball well, I invariably ran into trouble: having never played basketball, the direct approach to the ball I had learnt in football did not amuse the referees. I would rack up an impressive foul count each week, and that would usually be my only statistic on the score sheet!

Discharge time was getting closer and, to me, an important part of my true rehabilitation was to get back on the road as a driver. Despite my injury having occurred through a motor-vehicle accident, with me at the wheel, strangely, the only fear this had given me—and to an extent this is still the case—was of being a passenger. But I had little trepidation about driving myself.

I was in the unusual position of not having lost my licence, yet having to prepare for and sit another practical test, this time driving with hand controls. With an instructor and adapted car organised through the hospital, I was introduced to the new method. I was later to learn that there are a range of hand-control types and arrangements, with the type I learnt with being intrinsically simple. The car was a standard automatic, but an additional lever had been added to the right-hand side of the steering wheel. I accelerated the car by pulling this lever towards myself, and braked by pushing the lever away from me. When released, the lever went to the neutral position. The only other addition to the car was an attachment known as a spinner, a knob on the steering wheel allowing me to turn it with my left hand only. After a number of lessons where my initial response was to think of braking with my foot, I became quite accustomed to the new techniques, and to the traffic, which was a little different from the country areas I was used to. So, with regular driving-test nerves, enhanced by my instructor telling me that he had never had a hand-controls driver fail a test, I sat and passed first time, while still in the hospital. Soon after, I bought a yellow Ford Laser (called 'Larry'), and had hand controls fitted, ready for my discharge and a surge towards independence.

Such independence with my car, however, relied upon my learning to get my wheelchair in and out. To do this I transferred myself to the passenger seat, then folded my wheelchair and lifted the front of it, placing the footplates onto the doorsill behind me. I then transferred across to the driver's seat, leant across and clicked and slid the passenger seat forward, and then pulled the wheelchair into the car—all the time hanging onto the steering wheel with my right hand so as not to lose my already poor balance. To get out, I reversed this procedure. This took two minutes or more when I first began. A lot of work for such a simple task.

Al and I had made a pact. The night before I was discharged, we were going to steal a sign that had taken our fancy. 'General Manager—Don't Even Think Of Parking Here', which was the best sign in the hospital. It was big and it was bold, ninety centimetres long and sixty centimetres wide with black writing on a white background. It was our bottle of champagne and we had to have it. Being a farmer, Al was always good with a shifting spanner, so he loosened all the bolts and we pinched it. Like two naughty schoolkids. To this day, the sign has never been replaced and until now no-one knew where it went. And yes, I'm banking on possession being nine-tenths of the law!

Discharge day was one of mixed emotions. Whilst I was

desperate to leave the confines of the hospital, in some ways it was safe and secure. Wheelchairs were the norm, not the unusual or the unaccepted. Still, I couldn't wait, because I was going back to university. This overrode the feelings of doubt and the leaving behind of those staff members who had over the previous five-and-a-half months become friends.

Letter from a friend

I believe Sandy came through the whole hospital process due to the support of many people and his unswerving drive.

By the time he had reached the middle and later stages of his rehabilitation, I was back at university and into my second year of a Bachelor of Arts. My lecturers allowed me to alter my timetable to give me Monday free, so I would go down to the hospital on Saturday afternoon with Rosie as usual and come back on the train Monday afternoon. This meant that I was spending less time with Sandy, and he in turn was becoming stronger and clearly more independent. One day, while driving home from the hospital, Rosie asked me what I planned to do. I told her that it was very clear to me that I would stay with Sandy for as long as he needed me, and when he didn't need me anymore, I would drift away. It sounds twee, but I felt very much like Mary Poppins and I knew that one day the wind would blow down Cherry Tree Lane, I would put up my umbrella and be carried away, which is pretty much what happened. On his release from hospital, he and I went back to university, where he took on the next challenge, to complete his physical education degree. This was a battle that Sandy shouldn't have had to fight, but he took to the challenge in his typical take-no-prisoners style. The rest, as they say, is history.

Sandy quickly established a group of friends that he would go out with. And we drifted apart. I guess he felt as though

I was part of the old life and he had to start anew.
  Well that's it.
  Fond regards,
  Cathy

Austin Postscript

Leaving the Austin, I knew there was no going back—having left, I would never be a new patient again. Any hopes, no matter how distant, of walking again went with my discharge.

Al and Rosie went back to the farm and tried their darndest to pick life up where they had left it on the morning of 23 November 1981.

My relationship with Cathy ended two or three months after my return to Ballarat. Despite the ups and downs of our friendship, we have remained close buddies and still keep in touch over the phone.

BACK TO BALLARAT

1982

From the hospital I drove home to Barbary in my new yellow Laser, following Al who played out the role of the protective herding parent.

Nothing had changed about the drive home through Geelong—apart from the compulsory stop to take the weight off my tender bottom, and the need to sit on a soft cushion—but it was quite quickly apparent that things at home were different.

The farmhouse at Barbary had undergone a number of modifications to assist me with my independence. A long ramp had been installed at the rear of the house, the floor of one of the rooms raised to remove a step, and the toilet and shower redeveloped. All these things highlighted how much else had changed. Gone were my abilities to go for a ride on the motorbike, check sheep in the Land Rover, or cart hay, to name but a few losses. I felt that from then on I would just watch the world go by. Any intention to come home and take over Barbary from Al and Rosie was history.

It had always been my intention to get back to college as quickly as possible, because it was something I could do, rather than sit and look out the window. As soon as I heard that the modifications to enable wheelchair access to my accommodation in Ballarat had been completed, I decided to move back to Ballarat, only three days after being discharged. Al and Rosie were not enamoured with this decision, but they knew that I had to live my life the best way I knew how. So I got back in my little yellow Laser, pulled my wheelchair in after me, and drove back to Ballarat to begin again.

A maelstrom of emotions accompanied the fifty-five-minute drive retracing the route I had taken on 23 November. I was nervous as to how I would cope without Al and Rosie, unsure of what the accessibility at the hostel would be like, scared that I would fail in any of a number of ways, wondering how people would respond to me—and on and on in a jumbled never-ending flow. And of course on the outskirts of Ballarat I had to pass the site of the accident. Its appearance, like mine, had also changed. As I rounded the corner I was stunned to see that the council had cut the grass that had blinded my vision, so now the creek was clearly visible. Perhaps my accident had led to this change, but I drove right on by, and soon arrived back at my Ballarat home.

In the year prior to the accident I'd lived at Beaufort House—better known as Bowie—which was hostel-style accommodation for seventy to eighty students predominantly from the country. It was situated near the Arch of Victory on the outskirts of Ballarat, and comprised a large National Trust building and a number of moveable units, each sleeping about eight or ten students, two to a room. The modifications to facilitate my return included the installation of a ramp at the front of the Trust building, along with the development of another ramp to my unit. A bigger, more accessible shower facility was created in the bathroom by the removal of a partition and the provision of a plastic outdoor chair and a plastic curtain. In addition, a grab handle hung from the roof like a trapeze. Aesthetics were obviously not a high priority in the development, but it looked as though it would work, and it did.

Because of the extra space required for my wheelchair, I had been allocated a room to myself. I told the other inhabitants that there were some advantages to being short: much to the other blokes' chagrin, I now had my own bachelor pad.

Yet some of the modifications were not to turn out to be a great success. Whilst being given the grand tour I attempted to push myself up the two metal ramps leading into the National Trust house in my 25-kilogram, hospital-issue wheelchair, all the while trying to appear to the people who hadn't seen me since my accident, to have it all together. Mr Independence. However, the second ramp from the landing to the door was too steep due to the poor design and lack of space. I had little experience in identifying steep gradients at this stage and did not recognise it as a hazard. I consequently fell straight out the back of my chair. I landed on my back and, unable to control my legs against the force of gravity, I kneed myself in the lip. So there I was, lying on my back with a bloodied lip and with all my friends standing around not knowing what to do. Some were embarrassed and some rushed to help. Me, I was embarrassed, I was angry and I was confused. I didn't know what to do, since my recovery skills were inadequate to say the least. But we got the wheelchair turned upright and I managed to get back into my chair, albeit pretty slowly, and we stemmed the flow of the blood from my lip. It was apparent from this practical demonstration, that further modifications needed to be done. The small metal ramp was soon removed and concrete was poured on the National Trust landing!

And yet in some ways this fall was helpful. It showed all the students that I was vulnerable, but that I had the ability to get back into my chair, and that I wouldn't break should the incident be repeated. I suppose some of my wisecracks at the time also showed that I still had my sense of humour, despite how I really felt inside.

In regard to my room, two main problems reared their heads, one immediately and one a little later. The first was that I did not have a 'pigeon perch'. At the Austin, to assist with mobility when on the bed, most patients have a metal bar with a sling arrangement above their bed. Over time one comes to rely on this sling to move quickly and freely around the bed. When settling into my new room I felt lost without my perch. In a flap, Rosie rang Terri, the charge nurse of Ward Seventeen, asking where such a piece of equipment could be purchased. Thankfully Terri advised her not to buy one since she felt that I would become more dependent on it, and so whenever I stayed anywhere else I would not cope. Advice that proved spot on, as I quickly forgot about my hospital-type equipment.

During my time at the hospital it was identified that since I had fair skin, I tended to mark easily. This had been alleviated with a waterbed made up of three water pillows and a border, which had an internal heater and lay on top of a standard bed. One night, a month or two after moving back into the hostel, I returned late at night and got into bed only to find the heater wasn't working, and the bed was freezing. Thinking about sleep first and skin second, I hauled the three large pillows and the border onto the floor and returned to bed for a good night's sleep. This was the end of my special bedding requirement, so the failing of the heater was also actually a positive.

The return to Ballarat was the culmination of a goal of Laurie Prosser's. Laurie's support had been absolutely unstinting throughout, and for him to see me back at his college was a dream for him as well; but that was not a dream shared by all of the physical education staff.

On my second day back at the college, and my fifth day out of hospital, I ran into one of the lecturers. This chap ('My Friend') welcomed me by saying, 'I'm yet to get it into my mind that someone in a wheelchair can teach as well as someone with legs.' Although stunned at hearing these words so soon after my discharge and return to college, I told him that I didn't want an MM (a Mickey Mouse degree). In life only the gutless kick someone when they are already down; or worse, when they are trying to get up. My Friend maintained this attitude throughout the majority of my time at Ballarat. This was to be my first feeling of discrimination due to my disability. An experience I would unfortunately encounter many more times before the completion of my degree.

Many of the physical education lecturers said hello in the days after my return. Generally they appeared comfortable, but of course had some queries as to how things would develop. Thankfully I was to discover that the vast majority of the academic staff were passionate supporters of education for all, and saw my wheelchair as no barrier in the quest to teach physical education, so long as all practical elements of the course were met, albeit at times in an adapted version. Areas such as gymnastics, soccer and aerobics were obviously going to be amongst the most challenging units, or so I thought. Whilst I had never had great ability as a floor gymnast before my accident, I would have the potential now to reach even lesser heights. Soccer? Well, my header wouldn't be too bad but my left-foot cross would need a lot of work. And as far as aerobics was concerned, I'd never had any rhythm anyway. But in reality, I simply needed to *teach* physical education, not master every single sport; and there were many areas that I still felt my skills could be applied to. I'd grown up with football, so that was the least of my worries. For other sports such as badminton, I felt particularly confident due to the slow-moving shuttlecock. How wrong I was to be!

Since I had returned in May after the completion of my first year of study the previous November, I had in fact three years' course work still to do, and really only two-and-a-half years in which to complete it. That was, if I was to attain my goal of completing my degree on time with my supportive classmates.

Over the first two weeks I organised a mass of meetings with lecturers and found that most were flexible and were prepared to let me do a little bit of work even though I had actually returned midway through the first semester. So bits and pieces could be done, but once second semester started, I would have to overload my study units. Normally a full-time has twenty-four contact hours a week, but if I was to begin making up for lost time, I would have to take on thirty-one contact hours. Meanwhile the medicos from the Austin said I should not return to college for the entire year. But my mountain awaited.

My mountain to climb, the focus of my personal challenge, had moved from football to my course. My study still existed, footy didn't. And there were other reasons too. Unless I graduated with my original classmates, I would have seen my decision to go back to college as a waste of time. If I didn't graduate with them, I may as well have sat the remainder of the year out at Barbary and resumed second year at the beginning of the following year with the next undergraduate class. And sitting the year out on the farm wouldn't have had any positive outcomes, so it really wasn't negotiable. I was going to catch up!

Each weekend was a time to recharge the batteries, and pretty much throughout the year, I went home every Friday evening to do just that. On one of these early visits I found a further addition to the television room's decor. Al, having witnessed the use of ropes in the hospital gym, had hung a thick rope from a ceiling joist in the middle of the room as a means of assisting me in transferring to and from my chair, and up and down from the floor. This aid, whilst not doing much for Rosie's interior design, proved invaluable as it allowed me to practise my green and immature transfers into and out of beanbags.

Another idea of Al and Rosie's that came to fruition was a piece of foam covered in brown corduroy, which they left near the university gym. This was for me to lie on between classes should I have needed to get off my backside during the extra time I would have to spend on campus to catch up. It quickly became the place for anyone looking for a comfortable siesta, wheelchair user or not!

Second semester arrived, and along with it, the thirty-hour-plus workload. This consisted of attending all classes with my year, along with picking up one unit with one of the other year's students. With it came regular contact both with students who I had known prior to my accident and with those I hadn't, and they all seemed unfazed by my 'change'. Whilst I was sure that this was not necessarily the case, it was not something I gave much thought to. They just treated me like everyone else. However, I knew just how hard it was—for them and for me—and how thin my coping skin was. And one day it did crack.

Beaufort House had provided me with my own designated car park in the often crowded student parking area, and the odd-job man had painted 'Sandy' in white paint on the pine posts at the front of the bay. When I arrived back at the hostel one evening I found that another student had parked partly in my designated area, and with no other parking places available I squeezed my car into the remaining space. Without the extra room required to fully open my door, I found it difficult to get my wheelchair out of the car. And so with my skills still green, and my attitude and inner strength still developing, I mentioned my problem quietly to the hostel supervisor. She, with all good intentions but not much tact, stood at the front of the dining room at dinner that night and raised the issue, emphasising that no-one was to park in my bay. I could have crawled under the table with embarrassment. I had been doing my utmost to be inconspicuous and to be the Sandy of last year and not to be the centre of attention. A couple of students called out, 'Ah, you've been sooking, Sandy!' and 'You've been whingeing.' I quickly finished my dinner, threw the remnants in the scrap bucket and went to my room. I slammed the door to my unit, transferred onto my bed, and started to cry. I resolved that I would never again be that person who sank into obscurity. After a few minutes there was a quiet knock at the door. It was

Mary-Lou. She and I had been very close since living at the hostel the year before, and had seen my quick exit. She sat on my bed and cried and cried with me. We cried over the way last year had gone and what the future held, and because we both felt so sad. We had been chatting and crying for about half an hour when a further knock at the door disturbed us. Another student opened the door and blurted out, 'Does anyone want to come to the pub?' As the word 'pub' came out of his mouth, he was stunned to see these two very red-eyed, sad-looking people. He left very quickly, a little embarrassed, but that he had come to ask me did show that I was accepted. Mary-Lou and I did not find any answers, but all my friends were still rallying. Beaufort House soon became my new sanctuary, a place that I could just be.

I settled back into college life and felt a little stronger as the first months passed, despite still being dreadfully thin—a sight which constantly confronted me in an unfortunately placed mirror in my room. Lecturers seemed to accept me, and all the staff and students—even those I hadn't met—knew who I was, because I was different. But the real battles were soon to begin.

One of the classes I had to complete was Physical Education Curriculum 1, and My Friend ran this class. The unit was based on giving students the skills and ideas to organise and prepare classes for when we went on teaching rounds and later became qualified teachers. The only problem was that I wasn't seen as a future teacher.

Essential to the class were practical activities, which demonstrated effective, and sometimes novel, drills and teaching techniques. Yet when the practical activities were set up I was not included. One day during an activity, My Friend instructed me to sit in the corner and count how many times each participating group caught the ball. It was one of the activities I would have been able to participate in successfully, since I could of course catch a ball. But down to the corner I went, and simply sat there, not counting and not participating. I was a wallflower. Soon after that session a large number of my classmates went and complained to our year coordinator. It didn't seem to make much difference, but it was nice to know that they knew what was going on, and that they cared.

One of the practical units I was enrolled in was badminton, 'taught' by another lecturer, 'O'. The weekly sessions started off unspectacularly, but it was apparent early on that he had a significant problem with my continued drive towards my degree. After a few weeks, O came up to me halfway through a practical session and asked me to play with other students instead of just the same one or two, saying that my partners needed to get some practice that they were not getting from me. As he walked through the adjoining gym doors I threw my racket against the adjacent wall to the door. He did not look back, and it bounced off the wall next to his head. I was furious, since the week before I had been ranked eleven out of twenty-one in a skills test; it was blatantly obvious that not only was I a reasonable badminton player, but my skills were not too bad. This tension remained over the weeks up to my practical assessment, and when I arrived for my final practical test, O would not assess me because I was in a wheelchair. It was eventually agreed some time later that to complete the unit I had to make a teaching video on badminton. One moment he refused to assess my skills because they were different and then he wanted them for broad exposure on videotape. I made the video, yet because I utilised an ex-state representative as the demonstrator, and didn't actually hit the shuttlecock on tape, I was again denied a pass. Enough was enough, and I lodged a discrimination complaint with the Equal Opportunity Commission. This complaint had years to go before its conclusion.

As the academic year drew to a close, each student had a compulsory teaching-round placement. To me, this was the next giant hurdle. To obtain a teaching degree, I had to complete and pass many teaching rounds. Every time I thought of the prospect, my brain was inundated with questions such as 'how were the kids going to take being taught physical education by someone in a wheelchair?' and 'where was I to find an accessible school to give me a chance in my placement?'

After much investigation I found that Mount Clear Technical High School was reasonably accessible, and was just down the road from Beaufort House, thus removing the need to find short-term accessible accommodation. Prior to the beginning of my placement, I went to the school to introduce myself, and to work out all the accessible routes and paths of travel. These turned out in the main to be pretty good. The staff I met during this visit were friendly and appeared to be looking forward to my placement, which was pleasing; there was no doubt that they would have felt challenged as well, having never had a physical education teacher in a wheelchair before.

On the first day of the teaching round, I arrived early and parked in the teachers' car park. This was the moment. It seemed as though I would be able to complete the majority of the academic aspects of my degree, but how was I going to teach? Over the preceding weeks, I had worked out that I was certainly going to have to be pretty careful with the way I used my communication skills. I had to become the communicator's communicator, and on occasion use students to demonstrate activities as I talked them through it, using their bodies and my knowledge. Equally I was going to need to show that I was still a pretty fit, physical and active person to gain their respect. It was going to be a funny mix.

After I had settled in and observed a number of classes, the first class that I was actually going to teach was a large group of Year Seven students who were a typical noisy, boisterous group of kids. Year Seven students had had their physical education curriculum broken into segments to enable them to be introduced to a range of sports. At the time of my placement they were participating in, of all things, badminton! I felt that I could demonstrate badminton pretty well. Introducing myself, I explained to the students that I would be their teacher for the coming weeks. A small buzz of surprise emanated from the class. Just as I was about to launch into my demonstration of the underarm serve, I received my first excuse letter from a student. A girl presented me with a note from her mother which claimed that she had her period and asked that she be excused from PE. I readily gave permission. For the remaining time of my placement, at the beginning of each class she would present me with a letter saying she had her period. So together she and I were setting two new precedents: I was the first physical education student teacher in a wheelchair, and she was the only thirteen-year-old student to have her period every week!

The initial class went well and I demonstrated serving skills to the students. As I moved through the range of courts, I quickly built rapport with individuals, and also beat a number of students in rallies, which helped my standing. It was important to win a few points to ensure that respect was quickly earned.

My placement continued uneventfully. My supervising teacher, Tanya, was supportive and directive, and constructive with her criticisms. In her eyes I was simply a student teacher, keen to learn, enthusiastic, but prone to naïve teaching, just like anyone else. As for the students, they quickly accepted me as their teacher. I really enjoyed my placement at Mount Clear, because the teachers were relaxed and the kids were down to earth. This was one of the most uplifting experiences I had had in the twelve months since my accident. Having made friends with a number of the staff, in particular the physical education department, I went back to the school each week to play social badminton for the next year or two. I was to go back to teach at the school in two years' time, yet the tenor of that stay was to be very different.

During my first placement at Mount Clear, Tom Prior, a well-known sports writer from the *Herald Sun* (who has since 'ghosted' a number of biographies) came to visit me. The media were starting to show some interest in my story because it was a different and positive one. His article focused on me being the first person in a wheelchair to aim to complete a physical education degree, and on how well the kids accepted me. It made page three of the *Sun*. Tom was a great bloke and was my introduction to the genuine interest that the media has taken in my somewhat unusual career paths and passions. Good stories, and bad (well, embarrassing), were to follow over the years.

Quite some interest was generated by this article, all of it positive. I received a number of letters encouraging me in my quest for success. One of the letters was from David McPherson's mother. David had become a paraplegic a number of years previously, yet had made a great success of his life both professionally and in a sporting sense. I had seen a video about him during my stay at the hospital, which I had found particularly inspiring. So her thoughts were most appreciated.

I also received a request to speak at a Catholic Convent School in Melbourne for half an hour, on the subject of 'Hope'. After some thought and with more than a little trepidation, I accepted. On the day of the presentation Al and Rosie drove from Barbary to the school, and to this day they still talk of how I did not appear to be very nervous. My response then, as it is now, was: What is the worst thing that can happen? If I stuff it up, the sun will still come up tomorrow. At that time, with the memories and the smell of the hospital still in my nostrils, I had a renewed understanding of the fickle turns life can take, and with it a new perspective on what aspects of life are worth fearing, a perspective which is still with me today.

The topic was an interesting one, because 'hope' is a term that means different things to different people. I focused on always moving forwards, grabbing any opportunities within reach and not wasting your life. The students and staff received my address well, with the streak of humorous stories being particular hits. This was my first taste of public speaking—something that would become a regular feature in my life, one which I enjoy both for the pleasure and motivation that I can impart, and for the people that I meet.

After my successful placement at Mount Clear, I returned to college and completed all my academic units and practical subjects. I passed all of these, with the exception of badminton.

And with that, I now had summer holidays to look forward to. Most of these were spent at Barbary, where a three-wheel motorbike had been purchased to allow me to get around the farm independently. The bike was good, however I needed to be careful when riding alone at the back of the farm and well away from anyone. There was no reverse on the bike and if I had put myself in a situation where I had to back out, I would have been stuck. Al and Rosie decided to go for a two-week break to Point Lonsdale in a friend's caravan. They had rung the caravan park to check on their facilities for people in wheelchairs and were told that they were accessible, so off we went. On arrival I checked out the communal shower and toilet facilities and found that there was no way that I could use either since they were too narrow for my wheelchair. The owners of the park, when approached about the misinformation that they had given to Rosie, replied, with blank expressions, 'We never get many people in wheelchairs, and we've never had any complaints before.' It was pretty obvious why that was the case. We packed our bags, and were lucky enough to get a beach house for a similar period of time as we'd planned to stay at the caravan park. Al organised two pieces of four-by-two timber as a temporary ramp at the front of the staired house. It was not a ramp to test in the dark, but apart from that the house was good enough.

1983

I returned to Beaufort House and again overloaded my course, still chasing the units that I had missed whilst I was in hospital. By now, though not enjoying my situation, I was far more in control of my emotions and was inwardly feeling much more positive. The year was to prove to be desperately busy due to the additional units, yet also fun, as there were a number of social functions both at the hostel and at the college.

Soon after the beginning of the academic year, I turned twenty-one and held a large party at Barbary in March. More than a hundred people came, with the vast majority of students from my year attending, along with Cathy and numerous other close friends and family. The night in many ways was more than a twenty-first; it was a coming-out-again party. Laurie Prosser proposed the toast, closing a number of chapters which had been written over the past eighteen months.

The football season was approaching, or at least as close as I was going to get to it. Football was one of a vast range of practical units that I had to participate in and complete during my degree, and was of course the one that I had felt most confident about. I was so wrong; My Friend taught the unit. Despite managing to get twenty-nine out of thirty on the theoretical exam and gaining sufficient marks in the remaining areas of the grading criteria, I failed. Throughout the unit I participated in all the practical handballing sessions and could demonstrate all activities except for kicking the ball and some bumping and tackling techniques. As an alternative to these, I was requested to prepare a lesson plan on football, which was failed. Despite all my other marks, I was deemed to be of not an acceptable standard. The following year I was asked to prepare another lesson plan. Understanding that I was fighting an uphill battle, I obtained a friend's lesson plan from a previous year that had received a grade A. I copied ninety-five per cent of it and submitted it as my own. It came back graded with a C.

With the various stresses of my studies being all consuming, my goal of becoming a competitive basketball player had been put pretty much on hold since leaving hospital. My main sporting activity focused on the social games of badminton each week. On a couple of occasions I did drive to Melbourne to play basketball. Yet it wasn't all smooth sailing. At the start of the year I had bought a new wheelchair that was significantly lighter. It was made of light alloy, rather than stainless steel, and had a special folding mechanism and cable structure. With the chair being less than half the weight of my hospital-issue wheelchair, it made life a lot easier but did take some getting used to, not only when using it for mobility but also loading it into and out of the Laser. In fact on the first occasion that I pulled it in behind the passenger seat, I nearly threw the chair straight through the other side of the car! There were more serious disadvantages to the change: the chair was far more susceptible to breakages, and when I played my first game of basketball in it, it didn't survive the battering. After I'd driven the hour-and-three-quarters to the stadium from Ballarat, one of the stabilising cables broke within the first five minutes of the match, and that was that for the game. I decided it wasn't worth the hassle at that stage, so basketball was once again put on the back burner. I was sure though that the opportunity would come when there was time for me to mount a no-holds-barred attack on the game.

Outside the onerous hours of study, I did have to fit in a little bit of a social life. David Stevenson (Stevo), was doing the same course as me in the year below, and was one of the people at the hostel who I spent quite a lot of time with. One particular evening in the dining room, he was cleaning his plate into the scrap bucket (using both hands) when I rolled by and grabbed his trackie pants and pulled them (along with his undies) down to his ankles. Defenceless, he threw plate, cutlery and all into the bucket and retrieved his pants, to the cheers of the rest of the dining room. But he always found a way of exacting revenge.

One night in the middle of the first semester, Stevo promised to take me out and 'look after me'. The physical education students had organised a function at the Sporting Tavern and since I had not been out for a while, Stevo had been at me to lift my game and come out, saying that no matter how hard I worked I needed a break. And so the night unfolded. Stevo drove my car and offered to get all my drinks. I was told that all I had to do was to have a good time and drink the drinks provided by him.

His skulduggery began to surface when he bet me that I could not drink ten Galliano liqueurs. Being a frustrated sportsperson with too little competition in my life, I immediately took up the challenge: 'Not a problem.' So I cruised around the room, and whenever my glass was empty, another would appear. I had two jobs, one was to drink them, and the other was to count them. One, two ... six, nine and ten. 'There's ten,' I slurred.

He replied, 'I bet you can't drink fifteen.' Again: 'Not a problem!' Slurring more with each increment, I ploughed on. 'Eleven, twelve ... fifteen.' At this stage it could probably have been argued whether I was counting in English or in French. I lifted, and the competitive side of my nature took control of what remained of my senses. I suggested that twenty was a round number. Stevo, concerned about my health and poor drinking record, informed me that the bar had closed. I spied my five watches, and all of them said it was only 8.30 p.m. So on I went: 'Sixteen, seventeen, eighteen, nineteen ...' I reached my gold medal of twenty and said to Stevo 'Thhaaat's twenty. I dddonnn't wwwannnt aaanny mmmorrre.' Unfortunately the story does not end there.

A girl came up to me, and appeared to my drunken eyes to have a smile like Luna Park. She said, 'Sandy, you bought me a Galliano last week, here are two more.' Now, not being in a condition where I could recognise a gift horse, let alone look one in the mouth, I promptly said, 'Two,' and scoffed them both. 'Twenty-two.' Some time after that we left with a fellow Bowie-house girl sitting on my lap. It was a long and fun night, but when Stevo had persuaded me that I could afford to have a night off, I'm not sure he planned for me to have the entire next day off as well!

The hostel was going through its own dramas, as it had suffered funding cuts and was going to be ordered to close at the end of the year. Using any avenue they could, the management approached me to assist them with a media campaign to save Beaufort House. I went as far as saying that I wouldn't be able to stay at college if the hostel closed. The local television station ran a story, focusing on me as the student spokesperson for a couple of minutes in a tight shot, and then going to a wide-angle, highlighting the wheelchair. It was the first occasion that I was to gain a real grasp of the power of my chair as a tool.

In the middle of the year I got to go back to Derrinallum and do a teaching round at the high school. This was in some ways to prove that, whilst I had changed physically, I still had the same fire in my belly that the people of the town had seen on the football field. I wanted to prove that I was not dead, as rumours in the pub had it. The few times in the two years since my accident that I had been to the local pub, I would hear people speak about me in the past tense. Something akin to: 'Here's Sandy; he was one of the best footballers that the town had ever seen' or 'He would have made league football'. It really was as though I had died. Going back gave me a chance to prove that I was moving forward and that although my football career was over, I was still hanging in there.

This placement predominantly focused on my second teaching subject, English. This part of my degree needed no adjustments. The placement was no different to the norm, with the children again responding to my dry sense of humour and friendly nature. The most interesting moment came at the end of the three-week round, when in my last class with a Year Nine group I threw the last session open to the students for questions—including questions about what it was like to be in a wheelchair. Boy, that opened the floodgates. After forty-five minutes they were still going strong. The questions ranged from how did I get dressed to how did I drive a car, from how did I go to the toilet to my favourite from the rowdy red-head up the back: 'Can you have sex, sir?' I promptly responded with: 'Yes, like a tiger, can you?' All the students cracked up. This was not only an important educational opportunity for the students, but also for me. It was then I realised most people probably didn't have a very positive image of disability, and frankly knew very little at all. I had now become educated first hand. At the conclusion of my placement, I was sure that, via the unerring country grapevine, people now knew I was very much alive. And with that the semester closed.

The second semester of the third year started with a setback, this time one of my own doing. One night, feeling a little tired and emotional and in a hurry, instead of going to the car park the long way around a road, I decided to take a short cut down a steep grass embankment of ten to fifteen metres. Inevitably losing control after a couple of metres, I fell from the chair, which immediately rolled to the bottom of the embankment, with me following it in a semi-uncontrolled fashion. I got back in my chair completely unconcerned, much to the amusement of onlookers (my friends?), and I continued on my journey without another thought. In the clarity of the morn I was to find that I had knocked a layer of skin off my sacrum, at the base of my spine. I'd only lost a piece of skin the size of a ten-cent piece, but it was below my line of sensation, and this meant the injury was serious. The healing of my most valuable asset, my backside, is poor due to lack of circulation and the constant pressure of sitting. I had no option but to go home to Al and Rosie where I could lie on my stomach and be cared for, and not sit in my chair for anything more than a minute or two each day. After a week of lying, frustrated and impatient, face down in a beanbag on the floor, the skin on my sacrum was healed and I was able to return to Ballarat. This week highlighted how careful I had to be with my skin. There were obviously different rules applying to my life now.

Making up the time lost in the beanbag was not that difficult since it was only the beginning of the semester and there were not enormous amounts of work to be submitted. After the early excitement of the embankment, the semester seemed to be passing relatively uneventfully. However, this was about to change.

O was my 'guiding light' in the practical unit of tennis. Prior to my injury I had never played tennis, but having played a lot of ball sports, I felt that I would quickly adapt. The assessment for the unit was broken into a number of areas, including a workbook, lesson plans, and a practical examination of skills to be performed by all students and assessed by selected elite players within the year. When I came to the completion of the unit I thought things had gone quite well. I had practised and practised, and in the practical exam I served into all the designated areas to score maximum points and had reasonable stroke production. So I passed the practical component. I had filled in my workbook and I'd written my assignment and passed both of these. Yet at the completion of the year when I went to check my results posted on the results board, I had an X mark next to tennis. An X mark meant incomplete, so I went to see O and queried the result. O said, 'Sandy, you didn't come and see me before the unit began, for alternative assessment.' I said that I hadn't required alternative assessment, as I was able to complete everything that the other students did. He replied simply, 'You should have come and seen me, I now want a thousand-word essay on wheelchair tennis.'

I refused point blank, somewhat aggressively, and stormed to the office of the head of the physical education department, Peter Fryer. I yelled at him: 'You must be able to do something, you're the head of the school for God's sake!' He said, 'Yes, Sandy, yes.' And then I am sure he went off to O and said, 'Yes, O, yes.' After some weeks, I was the victor; since O hadn't told me that I had to do the essay at the beginning of the term, I received a pass grade for tennis. And the badminton issue was still yet to be resolved.

Not all the practical units provided dramas, and some were challenging and unique in their adaptations. In the apparatus gym unit, taught by Laurie, I found that I had some advantages. Due to my injury, and the related wasting of muscle bulk, I had little weight in my legs. This, along with my now well-trained and strengthened upper body, helped me to be a full participant in the activities of the class, including rope climbing to the top of the gym, almost being able to perform the crucifix on the roman rings, and putting together a detailed routine on the parallel bars. With the bars set a little lower than usual, I began my routine sitting in my chair at one end of the bars. From here I went into a straight lift, followed by turns, presses and even a somersault. Olympic judges may not have scored me with nines or tens, but the classes were challenging enough to give me a buzz; they really stretched the boundaries, and in a way I was more able in some areas than my 'weak mates'!

My final teaching round for the year was in October and saw me being placed at a Hawkesdale High School, a small school in the Western District. I had in fact played interschool sport against Hawkesdale students whilst I was attending Derrinallum High School, and had visited the school once during this time. The school had been made accessible since two brothers with muscular dystrophy who were wheelchair users had been attending for years. Under the influence of its Principal, Ian Findlay, the school strongly supported the brothers, and had developed a strong integration policy. For accommodation I had arranged to stay with people who had an accessible house. The placement was great, the kids were country open and fresh, and my supervising teacher Glenn was down to earth and encouraging. This was my third placement since the beginning of my degree (and the second since my accident) so I had to plan and coordinate all my own lessons. Glenn felt that on the whole students responded well, with my techniques to get around my limited demonstrating abilities working well. However, the placement was to create an explosion which was felt all the way back in Ballarat.

My Friend from the college came to assess my teaching

performance. He arrived and sat at the back of my class. I wasn't happy, but what could I do?

Yet he was about to make his biggest mistake. At the conclusion of my class, and without my knowledge, My Friend dropped in to see Principal Findlay. During their discussion he intimated that someone who was in a wheelchair had no right to teach, and aired other disparaging thoughts to that effect. At the completion of my teaching round I returned to college knowing nothing of their meeting. Meanwhile Principal Findlay had written to the college complaining about My Friend and his attitude. He also had sent a copy to my father. This set off the big bang! Findlay made it obvious in his correspondence of his concerns regarding the attitude that My Friend held against me. Al was livid, as he had a fair inkling how hard life was for me at the time. He rang Jack Barker, a fiery character who was the Principal of the university. Jack quickly went on the defensive when Al questioned the actions of a member of his staff; however, he became conciliatory when Al told him to shut up and read Findlay's letter. Jack saw the situation for what it was. (In fact, in later years he was to see Al and Rosie on a personal level.) For my part, I confronted Peter Fryer again, and told him that if My Friend appeared at any of my classes, he would be the one teaching them, as I would walk out of the classroom, so to speak. He no longer attended any of my classes. Suddenly a few people's heads had been pulled in.

I returned to the college and completed my year, and was now only three units behind the rest of the students. That is, except for badminton, which was still outstanding. Both the physical education department and myself had had discussions with the Equal Opportunities Commission, but it was still to be resolved.

During my placement at Hawkesdale, the civil action against Phys Eds Stay On Top was settled. To get to a situation from which a potential settlement could be reached, I had had to visit three members of the medical fraternity, whose role was not to improve my health, but to assess on behalf of the defendant's insurers whether or not I was malingering—or, more bluntly put, faking my injury. During each of the interviews I was put to the test, from being asked to transfer onto impossibly high benches, to the least subtle doctor who requested, 'Please stand for me'! All avenues of defence were being explored, and despite my severely atrophied legs the medicos had to ask the questions. After being prodded and poked in each of these 'consultations' for more than half an hour, all the learned doctors came to the startling conclusion that I was a paraplegic. After each of these sessions I felt a mixture of disbelief, anger and humour at the ludicrous examinations, and at the insinuation that I would choose such a means for financial gain. But if nothing else, they brought the closure of the case nearer, the importance of which my representatives had stressed for two reasons.

Firstly, any potential achievement on my part was likely to have a detrimental effect on the size of the settlement if put to a jury. Since I was getting on with my life and was not seen to be sitting broken in a corner, the further I progressed the less compensation I would receive. In fact, over the previous two years I had been advised to not be an achiever prior to settlement. The law is an ass in this regard; it discourages anyone with a disability from becoming a participant in life instead of just a spectator.

Secondly, because of the clogged legal system, my case would not get to court until late 1984 or 1985. The settlement would need to be substantially more than if it had been achieved earlier because of the effect of inflation and potential lost investment earnings.

So, with all the above in mind, I settled for a sum of money that, whilst compensating me for my accident, could not begin to replace what I had lost. No amount could ever do that for me. However, there is no doubt that I was lucky to have had someone to take action against, and receive at least a small payout to cater for my now unclear long-term future.

I have often been asked about my feelings towards Phys Eds Stay On Top. I have no anger in regard to his driving error, as we are all human and we all make mistakes.

As for my own actions in attempting to overtake vehicles in a situation where there was a net benefit on my journey of approximately two minutes, I obviously regret my decision. I would have been far wiser to chug into Ballarat. However, one doesn't expect the situation of my accident to occur; and when it does, one would expect evasive action from all involved. That that didn't happen, and for the consequences of that moment to last a lifetime, is a fluke of almost the worst kind. But there is little purpose in looking back, and it is not something I do a great deal of.

Back home at Barbary over the summer I did some long-distance training, akin to my pre-season football days, but this time in a racing wheelchair. Near the end of the year I had purchased a racing chair so as to participate in many of the running activities at the college in my final year. In an effort to get stronger I went for long pushes on the country roads near the farm. I had also thought it would be a good way of finding some solitude and independence. The only problem was Rosie. After my discharge, like any parent having had the type of experience she had with me, she wanted to keep me in cotton wool. On my long pushes she insisted that I had her for protection as my support vehicle to stop me from getting run over. So for anything up to sixteen kilometres I would push the chair, moving with the traffic, with Rosie immediately behind, hazard indicators on, asking whether I had had enough yet, and could we go home. Greater love hath no mother! Unfortunately she wasn't there when I needed her the following year in Ballarat: I was pushing towards the oncoming traffic when a car went one side of me, and a motorbike the other, on the gutter side.

1984
My accident had, as so eloquently described by Cathy, changed the direction of not only my life, but also of Al and Rosie's. One day, whilst going for a drive with Al around the paddocks, I looked into his eyes and made a spontaneous comment on what I'd seen in the windows to his soul. I said, 'You don't love this place anymore do you?' He answered, 'No, I don't.' I asked him why was he still running the farm and he said, 'In case you want to come home.' In all this time we had never really discussed this. He had simply gone back to the farm after my discharge from the Austin and got on with farming. He now says that for him these were very heavy-hearted days, but the only ones he shared this sadness with were Fred and Ding when well away from the farmhouse. Al of course already knew in his heart what my answer would be. I told him that I was never going to come back to try and run the farm, and that he should sell Barbary. Around this time Bud had made the big offer of taking the farm over, but everyone knew this was not his true vocation and that it would not work. Two days after my discussion with Al, the farm went on the market and was sold privately two days later. The hope of Barbary staying in the family was gone, and for Rosie it was a time of mixed emotions. On the one hand she wanted to leave the land because of the hardship and the inevitable loneliness, but on the other hand it was her home and was where she had spent a large portion of her life.

Selling the property also meant leaving the neighbours and people who had shared the ups and downs of their farming life. These people had of course been intrinsic in allowing Al and Rosie to spend so much time at the Austin during my rehabilitation. They were like an extended part of the family, and have never been replaced.

After the selling of Barbary and prior to leaving, the traditional clearing sale day had to be held. Clearing sales in the country are many things, from a social occasion giving the often isolated farmers a chance to catch up with long unseen friends, to an opportunity to pick up a much-needed piece of farm machinery at a reduced price. However, for the people conducting the sale it is an emotional time. They see their prized possessions picked over by vultures—or so it seems—and the carnival atmosphere of the prospective buyers is in stark contrast to the mood of the sellers. Any tool or piece of machinery which has spent long lonely hours with its owner has an emotional worth unequalled by its monetary value. So on the day, with all the machinery and equipment lined up in unnatural lines, everything was sold—from tractors to ploughs, to shearing hand pieces, to welding sets, and even the rabbit traps and specialist hammer and digging implement I'd used as a small boy. With the crowd swarming to the location of each item being auctioned, it was difficult to believe that all of these possessions that were a part of Barbary would be leaving her through our choice. The clearing sale day was the exclamation mark that confirmed that everything had been broken up.

Since the sale had occurred in such a rush, little planning had been done as to where Al and Rosie would go and what they would do. They had enjoyed a couple of holidays at Point Lonsdale, which seemed to be the right choice. After looking at a number of properties, they purchased at auction a large house called 'Bryngola', which was on three blocks in the town. We all felt that the size would assist with the transition from the farm to town living, and would also provide space for Fred and Ding who would go with them, but who were now unemployed.

Rosie and Al did not want to join Fred and Ding in the unemployment queue, and so upon settling in Point Lonsdale opened 'Barbary Antiques' in the adjoining town, Queenscliff. Suddenly good stock was not sheep or cattle, but Georgian and Victorian furniture. And whereas on the land they had sometimes gone days seeing no-one apart from each other, now they both had to learn how to sell to and deal with the public. Having worked in a menswear store for twelve months prior to my accident, I became their coach whenever I was around. Whilst Al had no trouble chatting to prospective buyers, he had no understanding of how to close a sale. He was just so happy to have a captive audience to talk to, selling was irrelevant, and was sometimes forgotten! On the other hand Rosie had great trouble with the intricacies of credit cards. Finally, feeling confident she had the trials of the plastic mastered, I left her alone for a couple of hours. Upon my return to the shop she told me triumphantly that she had sold a small fruitwood cabinet on Bankcard, and that she had had no problems. But when I queried her as to how she had gone seeking authorisation for the sale, she paled significantly. She had forgotten. The sale was in fact honoured, but over the next twelve months it was to be a particularly steep learning curve for them both. The rumour that it was a *Fawlty Towers* antique shop was only true occasionally!

Following one of my visits to Point Lonsdale, on the drive back to Ballarat I was to face a challenge of a different kind. Driving through the middle of Geelong, I went to accelerate to complete a right-hand turn from the middle of a busy intersection, when the cable on my hand controls snapped. This resulted in me being able to brake, but not accelerate. Since I was stuck in the middle of the intersection, somewhat stunned, I quickly bent down and pushed the accelerator pedal with my right hand, allowing me to clear the intersection. Pulling to the side of the road, I regained my composure and considered my options for a few minutes. With mobile phones a thing of the future, no accessible phone box in sight and a burgeoning desire to overcome the inevitable obstacles of life, I decided there was only one solution to my predicament, and that was to drive back to Point Lonsdale for repairs. So, having been blessed with long arms, and deciding that my novel technique was a safe one, I did a U-turn and drove back the half-hour to Point Lonsdale. On the dual carriageway towards home, all the time driving with one hand on the accelerator and my eyes peering out just above the steering wheel, I became accustomed to my hunched position and passed a number of vehicles. I'm sure it looked a sight to the occupants of the other cars, who must have wondered if there was anyone driving the bright yellow Laser. Where there is a will there is a way, no matter how lateral the approach!

Having lived for a year-and-a-half at Beaufort House since my accident, and for all of the time that I had spent at college, I felt the need to spread my wings. Using the money from my settlement, I bought a small house in Lylia Avenue in Mount Clear, which was only five minutes from the college. The house was of a basic design, but did require modifications including an entry ramp and the inevitable bathroom alterations, which were completed in January 1984. The house had one unique characteristic: in its backyard two large gum trees were occupied by two koalas! And that was not the only accommodation I provided. Since my culinary skills were yet to mature, and since I was still overloading my course, I convinced two students in my year, Christine and Trish, to live with me. The deal was subsidised rent in exchange for the provision of edible meals, and some sort of maintenance of the house. Over the year this worked very well. However, Chris being Chris did once serve me cauliflower and white sauce with a condom hidden within! A particularly 'safe' meal.

My mid-year teaching round was back at Mount Clear, and as I had had a lot more experience since my previous placement at the school, I felt a little more confident than before. This time, however, I had a different supervisor. No matter what I did, it was not good enough. No matter how well I planned a class, it did not work according to him. Whether he asked me to move a video recorder from one side of the school to the other a mere five minutes before my lesson was to begin, or arranged for my lessons to take place in inaccessible classrooms, he was prepared to do anything that would highlight my disability, not my ability. At the end of the first week, after getting on well with the students, and appallingly with my supervisor, I spat the dummy. I felt that I had nothing to lose because the way the placement was going I was going to fail anyway. And, yes, I'd seen all the signs before.

One of my classes was scheduled to start at 1.50 p.m., and at 1.40 p.m. the argument to end all arguments began. I feared that the supervisor was going to fail me anyway on unfair grounds so I made a decision to go down on my own terms. 'You have a problem with me don't you?' He denied this of course, and so it escalated. 'Every class you organise is at an inaccessible venue. You make it as difficult as possible for me one way or another.' Again, denial. 'You're just not coping with the wheelchair. I'm different but that doesn't mean that I can't teach as well as anybody, with a little more organisation and a fair go. You just won't give me that.' Denial. 'Well, you tell me why it's been so bloody difficult. You tell me what efforts you've made. I suppose that won't take long.' And so it went on and on and on. 1.50 came, and neither of us went to take our class. At 2.00 p.m. the argument continued, until finally at 2.10, one of the other physical education staff, who had been hovering embarrassed in the background, volunteered to take the class.

I fought and I fought and I fought. And I was to find over the weeks after our 'discussion', he gave me a go. It was a pity that it had had to get to this, and there is little doubt that if I had not confronted him, the remainder of the teaching round would have been horrific and I probably would have failed. Amazingly he turned his prejudice around, was hard but fair, and we developed a good, friendly working relationship. To this day I don't know why his attitude was the way it was. At times I have wondered whether it was a permanent change; in my experience it takes courage to admit you are wrong and then to get on with things positively.

The germ of an idea to do further study came in early 1984. The University of Western Australia (UWA) had the reputation of being the best place to do a Masters Degree in Education (Physical Education). The thinking behind my taking on further study was based on three simple premises. The first was, I hated study so I thought I had better do some more! Translated: since I recognised that I hated to study, I knew that once I stopped I'd never do anymore, so it was a question of continuing the slog and keeping my momentum up, or resigning myself to probably never gaining any further qualifications. Secondly, due to the extra work I had had to do in Ballarat, I felt that I hadn't had the time or the emotional strength since my accident to live the tertiary social life to the fullest. The third reason was that living in a major city would give me the opportunity to play basketball.

After corresponding with the university in the middle of the year, I paid for my friend Rob, who was also doing physical education, to fly to Perth with me, both for company and also to act as a chauffeur, because at this time portable hand controls were not available, or at least I wasn't aware of them. At Tullamarine Airport, we checked in and then proceeded to the departure lounge in preparation for boarding. However, on arrival at the door of the plane, we found that my wheelchair was too wide to fit down the aisle to my allocated seat. At the time there wasn't the now common purpose-built narrow aisle chair, specifically for passengers who couldn't walk to and from their seats, so we had to be inventive. I transferred out of my chair and then wheelbarrowed down the aisle, with Rob holding my legs and me walking on my hands, exactly as last done in novelty races in my primary-school days. Whilst this method of boarding a plane was effective and original, it was not at all dignified, but at the time this seemed only a minor inconvenience. After an uneventful flight, on arrival in Perth we reversed the loading process and made our way to Rent-A-Wreck, where we hired a very old and battered blue Ford Falcon, which was to suffer a severe decline below wreck status after Rob had driven it for a week. Rob, as a lost and confused tour guide, executed U-turns without ever worrying about bouncing over kerbs and knocking the wheels out of alignment; and this was the most gentle thing he did to the car all week.

We visited the university, which was old and beautiful, with sandstone buildings and classic architecture, but appeared to be particularly accessible. Secondly, and just as importantly, all the lecturing staff appeared to be supportive and keen. They saw no reason for me not to complete a Masters degree like anybody else, if I was granted a place in the course. At the time it appeared that the UWA physical education department might play fair.

Over the week, Rob and I continued to get lost, whilst inspecting the basketball courts, looking for possible accommodation, repairing my constantly breaking chair at a cable factory, and even visiting one or two alcohol dispensaries. At the end of my week in Perth I decided that I would apply for entry to UWA to study for a Masters of Education.

Rob had been a great travelling companion, but he had had an unusual time. It was at the end of the week that he brought to my attention something that I was becoming less and less aware of. We were sitting in the middle of the Hay Street Mall in central Perth, when Rob looked at me and said, 'Sandy, how do you put up with it?' I asked what he meant. 'Everybody stares at you,' he said. I replied that I tended not to notice, or I only noticed if they had made it particularly obvious or had stared for an overtly long time. But then the week had been pretty hard for the poor guy from surfside Frankston due to a number of encounters. We had been confronted twice by Satanists who had said I was in a wheelchair because of Satan; whilst I found this an interesting philosophy, Rob was a little unnerved. We had also been confronted by a variety of other religious zealots who said, 'Praise the Lord and forgive and I can make you walk again,' which became a tad amusing, at least for the first four or five times.

Above left: Al, big brother Tony and me at eight months checking the taste of my toes. Stretching those hamies for my future football career.
Above right: Growing up with Polly, the fattest labrador in the Western Plains, who came to Barbary whilst we dogsat her for a neighbour.

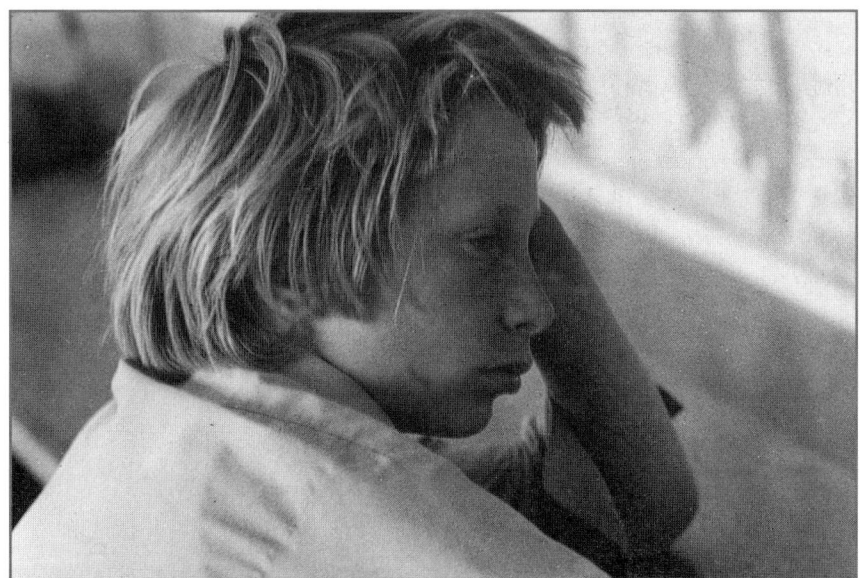

Above: Bored, disinterested and dreaming about football during a history class – age 12.

Above: Playing football for the School of Mines, Ballarat. I seem to have lost the ball and am focussing on an arm lock on my unfortunate opponent.

Above: All dressed up with somewhere to go. Leaving to represent Victoria in the Teal Cup Under-Seventeen Football Championships – August 1979.
Right: Knackered at the end of winning the interschool 200 metres championship – age 17.

Above: Crash. Leaving the car with a lot of assistance and beginning the trek up through the grass to the ambulance. All under the gaze of the other driver. (Photo courtesy of *The Ballarat Courier*)

Below: My bent beauty. It's amazing how little damage there seems to be when you look at my car. But notice how far back the front right hand wheel is. For me, in the background, it is the beginning of my journey. (Photo courtesy of *The Ballarat Courier*)

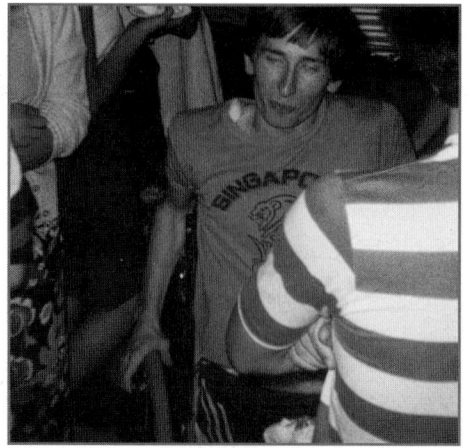

Left: A skeleton version of my former self. This photo was taken at my surprise 20th birthday party at the Austin Hospital. Under the t-shirt is my ever present brace keeping my back straight and rigid.

Below: In the first few months after my return to the newly ramped accommodation at Beaufort House. Notice the groovy hospital chair.

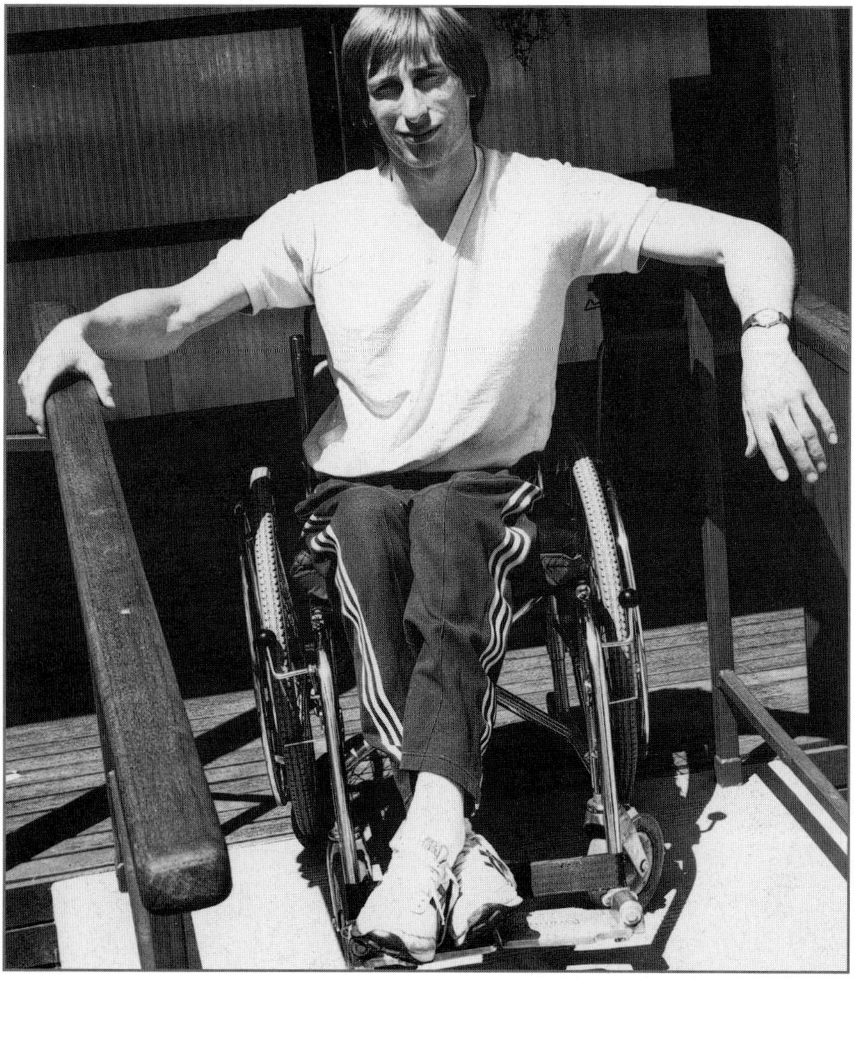

Above: On teaching rounds at Hawksedale High School demonstrating stretches during a Physical Education Class – 1983.
Below: Taking Year 7 students for a run in my track chair during teaching rounds at Mount Clear College – 1984.

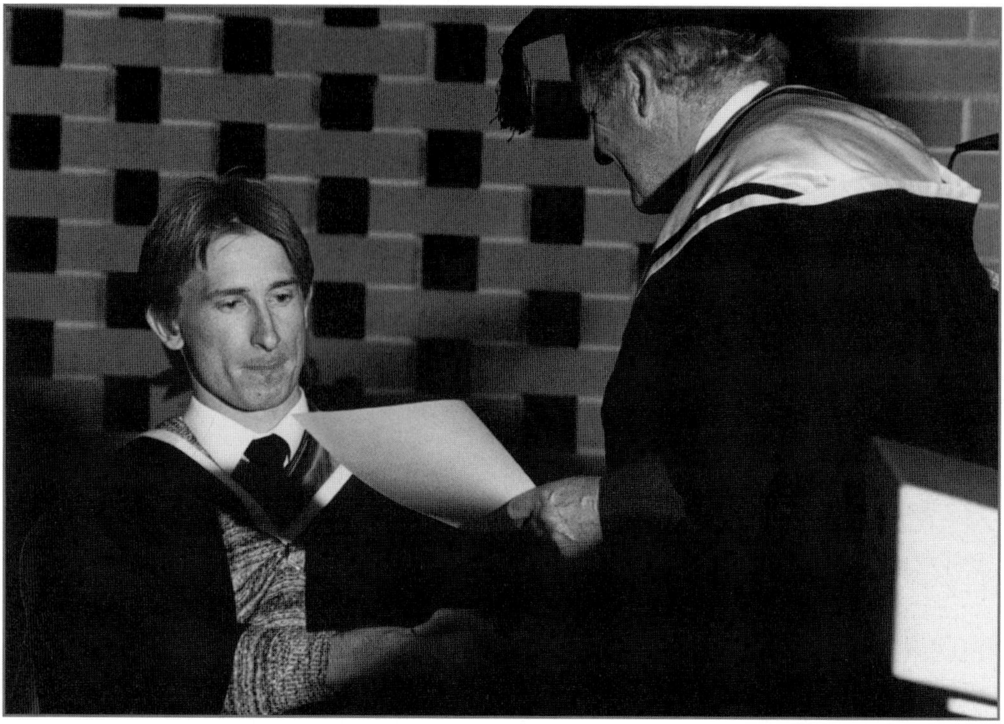

Above: Receiving my hard-fought for Degree of Physical Education from Peter Fryer – Ballarat University, 1984. The look says it all.
Below: The clearing sale and the breaking up of everything. Even the wire cutters were sold.

Right: Al and Rosie.

Below: Camping at Kangaroobie during my work at the Austin Hospital.

Above: A sweet beginning on the gold medal journey. Receiving the gold medal from Mr Phil Cravin, President of the International Wheelchair Basketball Federation, after winning the Paralympic Qualifying Tournament in Yamagata, Japan – 1995.

Right: In pursuit with Nick in the background as a more than interested observer – gold medal game, Atlanta Paralympics. (Photo courtesy of John Sherwell.)

Left: David Gould making a bounce pass – gold medal game, Atlanta Paralympics.

Below: A big play. After making a steal I'm about to pass the ball to David for a layup. In the process of making the lay up, he was fouled making it a 3 point play – gold medal game, Atlanta Paralympics. (Photo courtesy of John Sherwell.)

Above: In the zone of zones and pumped up. Troy Sachs acknowledging the crowd during his superb gold medal game at the Atlanta Paralympics.
(Photo courtesy of John Sherwell.)

Left: The buzzer having sounded, Nick Morris, all muscled-up, expresses the passions held within – gold medal game, Atlanta Paralympics. (Photo courtesy of John Sherwell.)

Below: As one. Linked with David Gould on my right and Ben Cox on my left, we celebrate our victory.
(Photo courtesy of John Sherwell.)

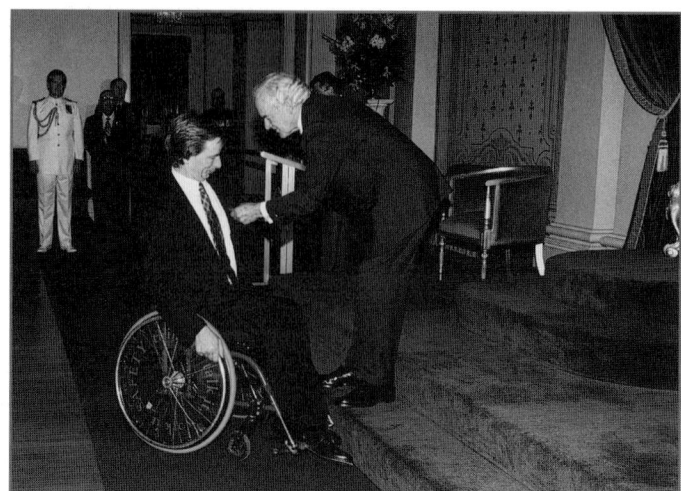

Left: Receiving my Order of Australia medal from the Governor General, May 1997.

Above: Putting a down payment on a medal in 2000. Participating in the handover of the silver for the production of the 2000 Olympic and Paralympic medals. Presenting me with the silver is Paul Anderson, Chief Executive Officer of BHP, keen to get her hands on it is Gill Rolton (dual gold medallist 1992 and 1996, equestrian) all watched by a proud Sandy Holloway, Chief Executive Officer, SOCOG. (Photo courtesy of *The Australian*.)

Above: Me the business executive. Telling a tale during a presentation, 1998.

Above: With Mark Seymour, lead singer of Hunters and Collectors whose song The Holy Grail became something of an anthem for the team. This was at the One Year To Go function in Sydney.
Below: Presenting at the Derrindlum/Lismore Football Club. June '99.

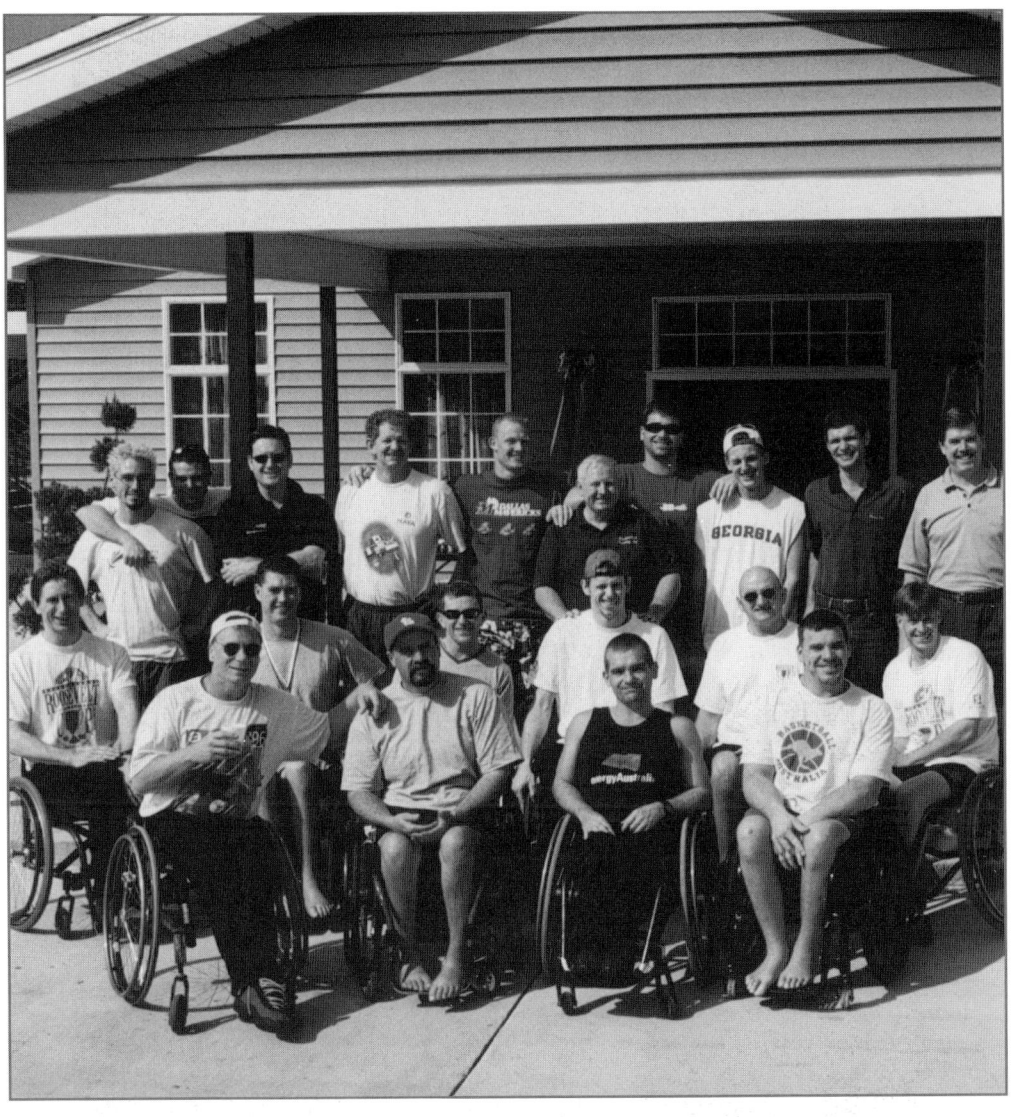

On tour at the Roosevelt Cup, 1999, as part of our Paralympic preparation. The boys in a relaxed mood.
Back row (left to right): Brook Quinn, Greg Warnecke (Ass. Coach), Fred Heidt (Team Mgr.), Graham Gould (mechanic), Troy Sachs, our USA host, Brad Ness, Shaun Groenewegen, John Camens (Physiotherapist), Bob Turner (coach).
Middle row (left to right): Sandy Blythe, Adrian King, Gerry Hewson, Shane Porter, Michael McFawn, David Gould.
Front row (left to right): Richard Oliver (Ass. Coach), Michael Walker (Ass. Coach), Troy Andrews, Nick Morris.

During the photo shoot for the book – Paula trying to get her head on to the front cover.

My faith from meeting those idiots didn't change, but I think Rob's humour was stretched. He had never been approached by so many weirdos.

With my next goal set, it was back to Ballarat and the final units of my degree. One of the practical units I had to complete was Individual Conditioning. I'd chosen this unit for two reasons. Firstly because it was run by Laurie Prosser. Laurie had lectured me in a range of subjects over the years of my degree, however it was his unstinting support and idealistic values that set him apart from many members of the department. He had played representative football and been involved on a fitness advisory level with a number of AFL clubs, so he and I had a lot in common. And from the time of his support during the foggy days at the Austin, he continued to stand up for me. He simply wanted me to be the best that I could be. In moments when the frustration seemed overwhelming, Laurie always made himself available and provided all sorts of motivation, and encouraged me to continue to fight. Secondly, the unit itself held some interest for me because of its varied and challenging physical activities.

In Ballarat, the running mecca is around Lake Wendouree, where Steve Moneghetti has invested many a kilometre. Early one morning a race was organised for the students partaking in the unit. However, the track around Lake Wendouree was not sealed, so I had to complete a larger course around the bitumen roads circling the Lake. So I was sent off first in my racing chair, only to lead all the way, fade in the last kilometre and be beaten in the last ten metres to the extended finish line by Ray. This loss meant he had bragging rights for ever!

As the year drew to a close, the final activity for the Individual Conditioning class was running from the college to Mount Buninyong and back. Again, with much of the terrain unsuitable for my track wheelchair, I participated in a unique manner, as much a means of celebrating nearing completion of my degree. I organised a lift up to the top of the mountain, transferred into my track chair, and strapped my hands in preparation for the impending descent, all with a wry smile at the thought of my classmates toiling and sweating their way up the mountain. As the first of the runners reached the top I pushed off, gaining speed as I flew down through the twists and turns of the mountain road surrounded by the natural greenery and trees. Exhilarated, with the wind rushing through my hair, enveloped in the odours of the bush and with tyres screeching on the damp bitumen, it was a moment of the utmost freedom, and for once I had the advantage! I made it to the bottom invigorated, glowing and alive!

The last unit, which was still outstanding on my academic record at Ballarat, was badminton. Having received a letter of apology from the entire physical education department after my complaint to the Equal Opportunity Commission, I was not altogether satisfied. My complaint had not been directed at the whole department. Yet I received a letter of apology from the physical education department as a whole.

And to pass the unit? I had to be assessed by Peter Fryer in a game of badminton to prove that my skills were up to par. After a few minutes of quiet observation he said, 'Sandy, you're a good badminton player,' and with that I dropped my racket to the ground and replied, 'It's a pity it's only taken me two bloody years to prove it.'

I had finished all my academic subjects on time, finally catching up with the rest of my year. The badminton assessment was on 23 November 1984, three years to the day since my accident. I had achieved my goal!

With that, it was celebration time. A big dinner was organised at the Mid City Motor Inn with the entire year attending, all thrilled that the course was finally over. There were two choices on the menu: chicken or fish. I chose the chicken, which was the wrong choice. After dinner everyone retired to a private house for a party and eventually I made my way home, still relatively sober, and not giving the dinner much thought. The following day I went to Point Lonsdale to visit Al and Rosie as I was going to a twenty-first birthday party in Geelong. After saying a brief hello to my parents, I went to the party, and after the main meal had fresh strawberries with a large dob of cream. This was to be my second bad move. As the evening was coming to a close, I was starting to feel quite ill. Driving home took me only twenty minutes, but I wondered if I was going to make it. On arrival I rushed into the house and through Al and Rosie's bedroom into the *en suite*—the only bathroom in the house that is accessible to me. I promptly vomited in the toilet. As I made my way back through my parents' bedroom Al asked, 'Do you think you have finished?' Groaning, I said I didn't know. Al went and found me a bucket from outside and I retired to my bed with this for company. This was just the beginning of the evening from hell. As I staggered through their bedroom on one of my many trips to empty my donations into the toilet, my mother asked me to 'Please vomit quietly.' (This she still denies.) Come morning, I'd thrown up at least eleven times and was a very sick boy. Rosie, lifting her caring rating immensely, rang the doctor who did a house call and injected me with maxalon to stop the heaving.

Meanwhile my friend Ray, who had also been at the college dinner, had arrived at Point Lonsdale overnight. When he saw me in the morning he commented on how crook I looked. Whilst I returned to my sick bed, Ray went off with Al to paint one of the shops that Al was doing up in the local shopping centre, and after a while indulged himself with a large ice cream. For Ray, that was not a good move. Sure enough, within half an hour he went a dark shade of green and the painting was abandoned. He went down like a tonne of bricks and began throwing up. We were soon to discover that the fifty per cent of the year who had had the chicken at the college dinner had been violently ill with salmonella poisoning, and the dairy products that Ray and I had eaten had set off the reaction in our stomachs. Thirty people had been violently ill, and one girl had ended up in hospital. This incident reinforced the idea that perhaps fate does exist, as the poisoning had occurred on ... 23 November.

A couple of days after the unforgettable 'last supper', I received notification of an offer of a place at UWA. And of course the date on this letter was ... 23 November.

Ballarat Postscript

Looking back on Ballarat during the research for this book, it seems inconceivable that what was always a difficult task, but also my human right, was made so terribly much harder than it should ever have been. The questions as to how and why it occurred, along with why I persisted, require some consideration.

One would never have expected that the behaviour I experienced could occur immediately upon my return from the hospital. But it did.

I believe that whilst this may have been through ignorance of my abilities, it must also have been due to a perception that all physical educators should be of a kind: 180 centimetres, 80 kilograms and able to run the hundred metres in seven seconds! Perhaps a basic premise was forgotten. And that is the role of the degree was to teach people to teach and participate, not perform.

Whilst the head of the physical education department was a personable and charming man, my many discussions with him as to the problems I was facing never led to the outcomes that I felt they should have. Apparently, as I have now found out, Rosie and Al regularly rang him encouraging him to take control of the situation. To do that he would have to have made some hard calls, not say yes to everyone, and perhaps discipline staff. If he did, the staff didn't respond. Neither my parents nor the head of the department should have been put in that situation.

Throughout all the times of feeling low and alone due to O and My Friend, I was always aware that if I failed in my attempt to graduate as a person with a disability, no-one else in a similar situation may ever get the opportunity. I felt in a sense that I was paving the way for others to follow. Since my graduation, a student with cerebral palsy, and another with a lower-limb amputation have graduated from Ballarat College.

In 1997 I was asked to return to the college to be the guest speaker at the conferring ceremony for physical education graduates, which I accepted. I am led to believe that I am the first graduate from the physical education department to receive this honour. The ugly duckling had grown into a swan.

PLANE TO PERTH

The time came for me to move to Perth and take up my place at the University of Western Australia, studying for a Masters of Education. I had organised accommodation by phone, at a residential college which was sight unseen, as it was not one of the places Rob and I had visited during our investigative tour the previous year. I had also packed my Laser full of my worldly possessions and loaded it onto a train bound for Perth as I was going by plane. My sense of adventure had grown somewhat since my days at the Austin.

February 15, 1985 saw me at Tullamarine Airport with Al and Rosie, who had driven me from Bryngola. For the entire journey from Point Lonsdale they had looked particularly glum, yet had tried to be talkative and upbeat, as parents do. They realised that this was my final effort to re-establish my total independence. Their little boy who had grown from being a reborn baby three years ago was making the attempt to leap the chasm, to become a man again.

Our final goodbyes were said after I was called for boarding.

To get to my seat from the door of the plane I again wheelbarrowed down the aisle as I had done with Rob, but this time with a stranger. Whilst not comfortable or pleased with the situation, again there seemed no alternative to get to where I wanted to go, so do it I did. I was happy to make it to my seat, plus it was a good way of introducing myself to the airline staff!

Meanwhile Al and Rosie stood in the departure lounge and cried. They felt fear. They assumed that the battles of Ballarat would continue in Perth, but this time they would be too far away to provide support.

After arriving in Perth, I was unloaded via the food truck since the Perth Airport did not have aerobridge facilities. I followed the yellow line from the tarmac to the terminal, collected my bag, and then caught a taxi to Saint Columba Residential College, which was to be my new home. Sitting in the taxi my primary fear was that the information I had received from St Columba indicated that the college was accessible, but then again, so had the information from the caravan park at Point Lonsdale two years ago. And if it wasn't, where was I going to go?

I also had many moments of wondering if the move was a wise one, and whether I would be able to handle the challenges. Worries about not knowing anyone in the entire state, loneliness, how I would be received by the other students, and how I would get around, all weighed heavily at times. But it was an opportunity to have the experience of a lifetime, so entangled with these negative emotions was keen excitement!

St Columba College provided accommodation for 170 UWA students, and was located on Stirling Highway in the leafy suburb of Nedlands. I went to the reception and met the Principal, Richard Craig, who took me to see my new lodgings. It was a tutor's flat, not a normal student's room. The flat had a large bedroom, and when Richard asked me whether I wanted a single bed or a double bed I answered, 'A double bed of course, for medical reasons.' With my own toilet, shower, lounge and kitchen, the flat was fantastic, and it was also accessible enough. I was in clover.

The college, as I came to learn, provided much more than simply a roof over my head. Located amongst trees and manicured lawns, it also housed a library, tutorial rooms, and function area, with staff presenting three meals a day to the inhabitants, who created a wonderful built-in social life.

Since I had arrived a little before the start of the academic year, the college was only partially full. Many of the new students arrived the same day as me, but students from previous years tended to drift in over the next few days. Everyone that I met seemed pretty friendly, but that may have been because they all thought I was a tutor and were trying to get in my good books. This facade was lost the moment a 'real' tutor explained that I wasn't, I just had the flat of a tutor. That was the first of many assumptions to arise, because for the first time I carried no baggage from my previous life.

Everyone thought I had always been in a wheelchair until I told them that wasn't the case. And everyone thought that I was an academic; I told them that this was the case, even though it wasn't.

My car arrived a few days after I did, covered in red dust from its trip across the Nullarbor. So with independent travel, I proceeded to spend the next few weeks getting lost, and then finding my way home. The university was located on the opposite side of the Stirling Highway from the college. Entry to the grounds from St Columba was via a crossing of the busy four-lane highway (plus median strip), or along the streetscape and then through a tunnel under the highway. For life preservation I usually chose the tunnel. However, one day when heading to the shops across the highway and in the opposite direction, I had a near miss. Having safely crossed the first part of the highway and bounced up onto the median strip, I checked the traffic. Deciding that there was plenty of time to safely cross, I bounced off the median strip, still looking at the traffic, and straight into a grate. Due to the width of the spacings, my wheels went straight through and right down to my axles. I was stuck, with a wall of traffic now fast approaching, and my options limited. In a quick, but planned move, I intentionally fell out the back of my chair, back onto the median strip, and then hauled my chair out of the grate up with me, and out of harm's way. Whilst not the most dignified solution, it worked, and so I remounted and continued on my way, avoiding the grate. That incident was to encourage me to use the tunnel, and quite literally look before I leapt!

The university's architecture was very different to that of Ballarat College. Whilst Ballarat had been built in the seventies and eighties using rendered concrete and plain bricks, the university had both heritage and aesthetic charm. The physical education department was located at the other end of the campus from the college so it was a ten-minute push down to the rooms or the lecture theatres, winding my way through the sandstone buildings. It was not a chore.

The first day of classes was momentous for many reasons, but primarily due to the heat. The temperature was 43 degrees, a real change from the weather back home. Ballarat is often overcast and even had snow on the odd occasion; Perth is the home of the perennial blue sky. Perth is significantly larger, yet still gave me the feel of a big country town.

On my first day I met James Bridle, who was to become one of my best friends while I was in Perth. Since he hailed from Canberra, he was coping equally badly with the heat. James had come over from the east specifically like me to enrol in a Masters of Education. In many ways we were the new boys, and had a lot in common. Apart from a differing opinion about the ranking of the various codes of football, we quickly became close. James had been a quality rugby union player, and many avid discussions were had over the merits of rugby and football. But as I told him repeatedly, the argument was clear to me:

rugby was a wanker's game and football was made in heaven. On this we did not see eye to eye.

A week after arriving, I went to the local wheelchair basketball competition, which was played in Shenton Park, a suburb just around the corner from St Columba, which was in Nedlands. There were eight teams playing in the local competition and, despite the stadium being less than salubrious, the skill level seemed pretty good. This time when I rolled in the door I was not shocked. The intensity of the game was as I had first seen it, only here due to the heat of the mid-summer evening the players seemed to be sweating a lot more!

The coaches and players seemed pretty excited to see a new player, particularly one with a football background, who was keen and looked strongly built. I had many offers to join different teams, despite trying to assure my range of suitors that I had had very limited game experience, which I knew would become apparent once I joined the fray.

I was soon to join a team led by Mark who was a resident international player and whose excellent chair and ball skills left me a little in awe. Over the coming weeks Mark proved to be supportive, since my basketball career didn't exactly take off with a bang. The team I joined had been premiers for three seasons in a row, so I quickly got used to sitting on the bench; and when I wasn't on the bench, I got used to being fouled back onto the bench, due to my football legacy making its presence felt. I was a footballer playing basketball like a footballer, and as such still tended to go straight at the ball, accidentally running over anyone in my path. The referees were horrified. It was to take a deal of time before my aggression was slowly tempered to become a skill rather than a hindrance.

Well-honed aggression in wheelchair basketball plays the same role as in a lot of sports. Basketball is termed a non-contact sport, but it is that by name only. I had to adjust my hunger for the ball and my intensity in defence to an acceptable level, just above the line of fouling. And the more I played the more I learnt what constituted a foul. In wheelchair basketball, the wheelchair is considered to be part of the player and the general rules of regular basketball apply; charging, holding and blocking are all fouls. My problem was that any sort of basketball was foreign. Fouling has far more serious consequences than simply giving away a free kick as in my football days, as once you earn five fouls you are out of the game for the duration.

The other major hindrance to me was the lack of a specialist basketball chair. Like a good pair of distance-running shoes for runners, the right equipment for any specific activity is paramount to the likelihood of success. Wheelchair basketball is no different. I was using my day chair with its knobbly tyres, low back and no camber, and so in some ways I was beaten before I started.

A basketball wheelchair is a fine-tuned piece of sports equipment made of light alloy, weighing around ten kilograms. Usually the chairs are individually measured and made, and have high-pressure tyres for decreased rolling resistance, cambered or angled back wheels for increased turning ability and stability, along with a variant seat height (to a maximum of 53 centimetres) to suit the players needs. The width and axle placement are also individual choices. Finally, many players use strapping to hold their feet on the chair or across their hips to assist with lateral stability. All the above tends to lead to

increased balance, and hence performance. This is because to do any activity well and in a controlled manner, you need to be balanced. Yet the terms 'balance' and 'spinal injury' are often somewhat of a contradiction, because when muscle function is lost, so is balance. And whilst my day chair was like a comfortable pair of work shoes, as soon as I tried to do anything dynamic in it, I lost my balance. The results were often spectacular.

After many discussions with Mark I eventually ordered my first basketball chair—a blue Quickie, all the way from the USA.

With a higher back support, a 7.5-centimetre angled seat (also known as rake, which is higher at the front than at the rear to assist with balance) and 10-degree camber, to name but a few design characteristics, the chair would give me a better chance to play.

With the West Australian wheelchair basketball fraternity being a small pool, I quickly became known and was invited in March to train with the state team, which was soon to be travelling to Melbourne for the National Championships. Whilst not being up to standard, I provided an extra training body, and had an opportunity to improve my inadequate skills.

But officially basketball was not why I was in Perth. My Masters degree involved a preliminary year, followed by a Masters year. To prepare students for thesis work in their second year, one of the compulsory subjects was Research Methods. This course was held every Monday evening from 6.00 pm to 9.00 pm, and since it meant a lot of computer work and advanced algebra, I hated it. Every time the class finished, all the eastern-states students would leave the study room feeling like catching the first plane home, and yet each following week everyone would turn up for more.

I was homesick since everyone was a new friend, but a little like everyone did with Research Methods, I persisted. At the end of the term I found that I had actually settled well, was enjoying myself, and doing well in all my physical education subjects, but not of course in my nemesis of a course. So during study week at the end of the first semester, I called on the help of another student, Cindy. She seemed to have a good grasp of the subject, but after sitting with her for an hour in my unit at St Columba I became more and more depressed. Her broad comprehension made it blatantly apparent that I had the opposite—in other words, no idea. Sure of this, and never one to look a gift horse in the mouth, I bet her that she would do better than me in the exam. She disagreed, so we decided whoever did best should take the other out for dinner and commiserate. After agreeing on the bet we quit studying and went to the pub to salvage my morale. Thankfully much of the unit was ongoing assessment because when the examination results were published, I had attained only 30 per cent and she had received 90 per cent. So I won the bet and got shouted out.

In late April I went back to Ballarat College for my graduation, catching the red-eye special from Perth, departing at midnight and arriving at Tullamarine at 5 a.m., and feeling somewhat second hand. Initially when the issue of graduation arose I had been a little blasé. But Al and Rosie, and my friend Ray all insisted that I must attend; they said it was my moment in the sun. So after catching a few hours' sleep at Ray's house, off I went to the ceremony, only to find that I could not join my classmates in their procession up to get their degrees from their seats, because there was no ramp at the front of the stage. The only means of entering was to go up sets of stairs at either side of the stage; consequently I had to access the stage from the rear. Whilst this was definitely not my ideal means of gaining my degree, there was no other option. The plan was for me to wait out of sight behind the curtains during the ceremony, and then when my name was called to enter the stage, collect my degree and then bounce down the six red-carpeted stairs, where I would join the audience. Simple in theory! But as I waited, I noticed that my cushion cover was catching on the pushrim screws on each wheel, resulting in one wheel or the other suddenly stopping as it caught in the fabric. This normally minor inconvenience became something more than that for someone about to attempt to mono down a number of stairs in front of a packed auditorium. As I waited I fiddled with it and worried. After my fellow graduates had individually filed up to the stage, received their certificate, and then departed via the stairs on the opposite side, the time came for me to be presented with my much fought for degree by Peter Fryer, the head of the physical education department.

In that moment of accepting my degree from Peter, accompanied by his best wishes, so many feelings were so near to the surface. All the drive I had needed and the extra work I had done to catch up became worthwhile. The railing against the unfair treatment by a couple of staff members was absolutely over, and I had paid back a little to all of the people whose support had been unstinting. I then proceeded to the top of the six stairs leading from the stage to the seating area, with the certificate secure on my lap. Tucking the cover under the cushion I monoed my chair onto the back wheels and prepared to descend the stairs. On the second step the cover caught on my left wheel. The left wheel stopped, and my right wheel continued to roll, immediately creating a usually catastrophic situation for a wheelchair user going down stairs! In front of around 600 people, I was about to do a face plant. In a desperate instantaneous reaction to save myself, I gave the stuck wheel an almighty push, tearing the rim free from the cover. I skated down the steps, in only vague control, as an usher tried to grab me. On arriving at the bottom of the stairs, and regaining full control, I was to find all my fellow graduates doubled up laughing. The common theme of their comments was: 'Sandy, you've done that hundreds of times, you've never stuffed it up before now.' What a moment to pick.

Following the conclusion of the ceremony many of the students, along with their families and staff, adjourned to Craig's Hotel for a graduation function. At this function Rosie was to have *her* moment in the sun. With a lot of students chatting to one another and various lecturers, she saw My Friend. Before my accident she had been a little shy and reserved; but not anymore. She strode up to him, and in front of a group of people said: 'That Sandy has graduated tonight is not because of you, it is in spite of you.' His response was that she had ruined his night, to which she replied, 'I couldn't be happier', and with that she flounced off. I wasn't within hearing distance, nor was I aware of her intention, but her comments brought acclaim from surrounding students.

The next day it was back to my new life in Perth, which I was settling more and more into for a number of reasons. My basketball chair finally arrived from the US in June, and with my bright blue rocket came my first taste of control on a basketball court, albeit limited. The transition felt akin to what an athlete would feel when changing from day shoes to running spikes: alive and far more conducive to action. With the angled seat assisting my balance, in conjunction with the rear-wheel camber, I immediately found that I could turn the chair immensely quicker. So within a few days, helped by one or two adjustments, the chair became like any piece of good sports equipment—it was one with its owner. And with this came the ability to concentrate on just the game and improving, rather than spending a fair degree of my attention on struggling to control and trying not to fall out of my unsuitable day chair. Whilst my scoring didn't necessarily improve, I found that I was being less of a court sweeper, which meant I could be more use to my team.

At the conclusion of the year, not only was my basketball on the up, but I had also completed the preliminary year of my degree, and though I hadn't exactly got straight A's, I had passed. However, towards the end of the year I was becoming more and more tired. All I ever wanted to do was sleep. I had been trying to sleep all day and then train, but it hadn't been really working. I was diagnosed as having glandular fever, and due to the summer break I was able to go home for a month and sleep it away. On one of a number of visits to the family doctor during my recovery in Point Lonsdale, I was also to mention that I had a black toenail which had been injured playing basketball sometime. Examining it, the doctor asked whether it was sore, and quickly followed up by asking whether it was throbbing. In exasperation, and quite some mirth, Rosie said: 'He is a paraplegic, if you haven't noticed.' The doctor went a bright shade of red and mumbled that he wasn't having a very good day, and was very aware of my relatively recent injury. As he finished his podiatry duties, I was to remark that there really were some advantages in having lost my sensation. After recovering from the glandular fever, I returned to Perth to train with the state team, when fate intervened and a flashback occurred.

I was driving the Laser along Stirling Highway away from the college. I approached a set of traffic lights and as they changed to green I entered the intersection. In the prior light sequence, oncoming traffic had had a green arrow, allowing them to cross my path and have right of way. A P-plate driver had noted this arrow whilst he sat well back in a queue of traffic, and then assuming that it was still green, entered the intersection and tried to turn right directly in front of me. With nowhere to go, I locked the breaks of 'Larry' and ploughed into his car. We hit hard, and after coming to rest, I limped the car from the intersection in a virtually undriveable condition. As I began to get out of the car a policeman on a motorbike arrived, and said he had seen the whole incident. He then proceeded to question the other driver, who, after getting over the shock of seeing me get out of my battered car and into my wheelchair, was grieving over his car, because it wasn't his. He sheepishly told us that the previous week he had been driving his car when he saw a dog hit by another vehicle and whilst looking in his mirror at the dog, drove off the road and into another car. So he had borrowed his uncle's car. Both the policeman and I were thinking the same thing, hoping for everyone's safety no-one else gave him another set of wheels to demolish.

I was not injured, apart from a stiff neck. But the major fright was as in my original accident: if you are put in a certain situation there is nothing you can do.

My Masters year was more memorable for my extracurricular activites than my studies. I was lured into standing as the Student President of St Columba and was duly elected. The year as President culminated in me being asked to attend the other five college end-of-year functions. Not a particularly onerous task. The position did have some commitments, but it also came with its year-long perks. I was granted a master key to all rooms at the college, so when any of my mates got too cheeky, or were up to no good with the fairer sex, I could keep an eye on them. Unfortunately, James, by now having moved into the college and become a tutor, also had the same privilege, and at times I was concerned at hearing the lock turn at my flat in the middle of the night. It was difficult to keep anything quiet.

Throughout the year I had worked at my skills and understanding of basketball. Grasping the small nuances and subtleties of the game continued to be a slow process. But I was still training with the state squad, playing domestic league and beginning to hone my game. My skills, though still unrefined in their form, continued to improve under the specific tutelage of two people. The state coach, Bill Mather Brown, had contracted polio at an early age and had been a more than physical player in his early days; I'm sure he was another frustrated footballer, and we established an early rapport. I was also assisted by Mark, the ex-national player who initially took me under his wing as I tried to emulate his silky skills. I focused on enhancing my chair skills and trying to learn to shoot the ball consistently, or at least lay the foundations for a technique that would assist this. The on- and off-court training throughout the Perth summer, both at the squad sessions and individual workouts, had resulted in me in getting as fit as I had been since the day of my accident. Come selection time I was rewarded with a place in the Western Australian team for the 1986 Australian National Championships in Adelaide, along with a number of veterans. But my first championships were not to be smooth going, due to my classification.

Before players can compete at a basketball championship, licensed classifiers must medically examine them. This is to establish their physical ability in terms of a points value. Each team of five players is allowed a maximum of 14 points on the court, thus ensuring the two competing teams have an equivalent physical ability. Each player is given a medical classification card between 1 point and 4.5 points, with half-point increments. One point players usually have paralysis from the mid-thoracic region, or belly-button level, with no leg function; 2.5 players have full trunk function, with little or no leg movement; 4.5 players have a limited deficit in one leg, or a below-knee amputation. And of course all players must use a wheelchair throughout the game, no matter what their point classification is. Though this may sound complex, in practice it's quite simple. The higher the point classification, the less the functional loss, resulting in the player having greater balance and agility in a chair. The upper-point players tend to dominate games in regard to scoring and rebounding. The lower-point players' major role is screening, picking and helping the high pointers; a thankless unglamorous job, but just as important. Obviously if a 2.5 player can play like a 3.5, or guard someone of a greater points value, it's of great importance. Sadly, low-point players don't get much recognition. The coach needs to be a numbers person when substituting, since it is not necessarily a case of swapping players of the same points value. And so to my classification.

A player's classification is not only important to their team, but also to themselves since it can mean the difference between playing a lot of time or very little. Since I had not previously competed, I didn't have a classification. Leading into the competition and having no idea what points I would be, I based all my assumptions on what I was told. That information seemed to indicate that I would be classified as 1.5, and so in my mind that is what I was. This classification fitted neatly into the team's player and points requirements, and I would play a lot of minutes. I was shattered when at the conclusion of my physical examination, I was notified that my classification was 2.0 points. I was nowhere near being any less, and I was later to become a 2.5. Whether the Western Australian people didn't know or had been kidding themselves, I'm not sure. But come the championships I cut up a lot of oranges!

As the week went on and the team performed below expectations the coach increased my court time as part of his effort to blood new players. This resulted in me playing a reasonable number of minutes, and while being far from spectacular, I showed that I had that mysterious characteristic: potential. Coach Mather Brown implored his players to be and play of the same ilk as himself. Before every match we would get together and chant 'GTOD'. Being the new boy, it took me a while to summon the nerve to ask the coach what the acronym stood for. He looked at me with steely blue eyes and said, 'Get Tough or Die, son.' In fact, of the sixteen matches I played for Western Australia, inclusive of the 1986 and 1987 championships, due to a dearth of talent, a lack of regular elite competition because of the distance from the other states, and an outdated game plan, I died every time.

At the end of the week in Adelaide at my first national competition, I was selected for a novice team to compete in the Far Eastern and South Pacific Games (FESPIC) which were to be held in Indonesia. With the national team having other commitments and the reserve team going to a tournament in England, the FESPIC team was made up of young novice players who were seen to have some future in the game, fortified by the odd veteran or two. Surprised at my selection, I immediately saw it as a great opportunity to get a taste of basketball outside the confines of Western Australia. This trip would define to me how high my true basketball aspirations would be, and what an experience it was.

The FESPIC Games are basically a development opportunity for Asian countries' up and coming athletes. Australia has used these games over many years as an opportunity to send athletes identified as future senior Australian representatives, however the athletes at the Games generally have a diverse range of abilities. To get to the Games the development team departed from their individual states and flew direct to Jakarta, and then took an internal flight to the host city, Solo. The internal flight was, to say the least, interesting. Without an aerobridge or hoists, all the athletes had to be carried individually up the plane stairs and down the aisle to their seats by the accompanying team staff. After the initial shock they quickly worked out a plan which involved taking the lightest athletes first, and placing them the furthermost from the plane entrance. This in principle seemed a good idea. However, in the humid conditions, the human hoists were dripping wet with sweat and exhausted by the time they reached the last, particularly large athlete. That was just the beginning of the fun. The plane crew then informed the team manager that all the equipment would not fit, despite some of it being loaded along the aisle inside the cabin. Their suggestion was to leave some of the wheelchairs behind to be brought on a later flight. After some urgent and direct explanation, this idea was shelved. On approaching the city of Solo the plane crew were obviously on overtime, since from approximately twenty feet above the ground, they dropped the plane in like a brick. I was later told by staff, after our safe arrival in Australia, that when they had assisted ground crew in Solo to load the plane at the end of the tournament, they had seen the inside of the plane where the luggage was stored, and it looked particularly rusty.

The actual Games Village was an old army barracks and of basic design. However, it did not so much feel like an army barracks but a prison camp, since all entries and exits were secured by armed guards. Once when I tried to leave the grounds I had a large rifle pointed at me. This tended to put one off unauthorised excursions.

The games were played on a soft court, which was not exactly appropriate for wheelchair basketball. All of the games were slow, and when the players stopped pushing they certainly didn't get much free roll. Even what in basketball is called a fast break was in fact a very, very slow one. Mind you, anyone chasing couldn't catch up because they were going at the same speed.

The teams were of varying ability, like us. We quickly found ourselves in the final, having thrashed Hong Kong, Malaysia and India, to name a few. But our glory was to be short-lived. The Japanese team had sent their full national squad since a good showing at any Asian Games was of paramount importance. With a packed crowd of more than two thousand people hanging from the rafters in the small stadium, we went to battle. The strategy, due to the Japanese team's tight full-court press, was for me and one other player to 'bust into the front court and receive the ball over halfway'. After doing this for four or five minutes, as I puffed by my fellow 'bustee', I said to him 'We haven't got the ball over halfway yet.' The Japanese team kept pinching the ball and scoring down the other end. Perhaps they were more used to the soft court. Things marginally improved, and I was lucky enough to score 12 of the team's humble total of 16, compared to Japan's 72. We were humiliated and it was as though I'd been running (so to speak) in quicksand for forty minutes. I remember thinking how far I had to go to really be able to compete at international level.

But if nothing else, this trip allowed me to experience overseas travel for the first time, and also introduced a new advantage to being in a wheelchair. When we escaped into Solo, we quickly identified the potential of the rickshaw. By grabbing hold of the back of one, we got a free ride and could travel great distances. Often the poor unfortunate rickshaw rider would be pedalling along, thinking that they were doing it hard that particular day, only to look behind them and see up to ten wheelchairs hooked on the back, all for free. They weren't happy, but they generally recognised how ludicrous the situation was, and smiled. Besides, how could they get us off? But the 'freewheelers' had their own pitfalls. For the inexperienced rickshaw rear rider, tragedy was never far away. One particular day someone new to the game hooked on but forgot to look constantly at the bitumen ahead and therefore did not see an approaching pothole. As the front castor of their wheelchair disappeared into the hole, they too disappeared from the back of the rickshaw, and became disassociated with their wheelchair. Messy business, that!

I returned from my first international competition inspired, because I felt that I still had the innate abilities of an athlete, regardless of the fact I was in a wheelchair, but I obviously still had a lot of work to do. My wheelchair was a piece of sports equipment on the court, not a disability aid. And with this attitude I applied for and was awarded a 1987 Western Australian Institute of Sport non-residential scholarship, being the first wheelchair athlete in the state ever to receive one. The scholarship was for an annual amount of money along with access to the Institute's facilities, including the weights room and associated support staff, such as sports doctors and sports psychologists. This was the first time that I felt anyone other than my fellow participants took my sport seriously. The intrinsic sensation felt the same as my football aspirations had previously. I was hungry for success, and because I had finished my Masters and was looking for a job, I did not have any major time constraints. I was able to be a full-time athlete, training every day and shooting the ball.

With this training base my game made a huge leap. I was lucky enough to win the Best and Fairest Award at the domestic competition, and also played far better at the National Championships in Perth. Following the championships I was chosen in a squad, from which the Australian team to play in the Stoke Mandeville Games in England was to be selected. I attended the final selection camp in Melbourne with fifteen other players from throughout Australia, but I did not have a good camp. Being the only player from Western Australia in attendance, I felt a little on the outer, and produced a horrible training performance over virtually all the sessions, which resulted in me missing out on selection. I was very disappointed. I had no-one else to blame for my omission but myself; I had choked, stricken by nerves at the prospect of genuinely representing the country, and overawed by other players. Following my return to Perth, some of the people around the Western Australian basketball scene did not believe me when I told them of my non-selection; having witnessed my in-state form, they had thought I was a sure thing. I simply told them I hadn't travelled well, which was definitely the case, and inwardly vowed if given the chance, that it wouldn't happen again.

But having obtained my Masters degree it was never my plan simply to play basketball. It did not provide an income, apart from the Institute's scholarship money, nor perhaps enough of an intellectual challenge. Because of the university's reputation with regard to Masters degrees in physical education, it seemed that everyone who went to Perth to study stayed. So it seemed there were more Masters of Education sweeping the streets in Perth than anywhere in the world. Though I was officially a real tutor at the university, this was not full-time work. And whilst I had been doing part-time fitness testing and a range of odd jobs, nothing appropriate of a full-time nature seemed to be around. Things were so desperate that I even applied to be an education officer at Fremantle Prison.

Probably the most interesting position that I held was working at Potter Partners, one of Perth's leading stockbroking firms. I had called them on my own initiative and talked my way into an interview, and had secured a part-time position there, despite no job being advertised. With two degrees in physical education, I felt well qualified for the money market (not). And of course, during the phone call I had conveniently forgotten to mention that I was in a wheelchair. At the time, one of my mates suggested that I go to the interview with a rug over my knees and perhaps they wouldn't notice, or alternatively, put both legs in plaster and say I had had a skiing accident in Aspen, Colorado. I didn't think either would work, so at the interview I simply wheeled in and talked my way into a position. My job involved collecting bad debts and a little bit of time on the dealing floor. After a period of three or four months, I had had enough of the experience of hounding people who didn't wish to pay for their share purchases. I decided to leave and did so on good terms.

Then, out of the blue, in October 1987, Ray rang from Ballarat and said that the Austin was advertising a new position called Recreation Officer, which was to be specific to the Rehabilitation Ward. Until that point in time I had no plans to go back to Melbourne. I had fallen in love with the Perth lifestyle, and had even bought a house, of which I was yet to take possession. I rang the contact number at the hospital anyway, and was told that the position was about to close. I convinced them to extend the date by a day or so and promptly packaged up my application and sent it off. Quite a bit of time went by and eventually I called the employment officer at the hospital. I was duly informed that I hadn't been granted an interview. Saying, 'You have got to be joking,' I asked him to reconsider my application. He then rang me a couple of hours later and granted me an interview. It pays to be assertive.

Since I was the only interstate candidate, my initial interview was to be by phone, while the other six contenders had face-to-face meetings. For the interview they had organised a speaker phone, so at that end there were four or five staff members, with a photo that I had sent propped up on the phone to give some sort of idea about the person on the other end. The interview seemed to go quite well, but it was hard to get a real feel over the phone. Within a day or two of the phone conversation, I received a call confirming that I was to receive a second interview. Since Doug Brown, the Spinal Unit medical director, was coming to Perth for a conference, there was an opportunity to meet one of the main voices from the phone interview. I organised to pick Doug up from the airport in my new car. (Larry never was quite the same after his shunt.) My only concern with this particular arrangement was that I had not had the opportunity to train at driving the car at only sixty kilometres an hour. I reasoned that it would not look good hurtling Doug into Perth City at about eighty-five or ninety kilometres per hour, as I may have done once or twice when on my own.

Meanwhile, Al and Rosie were airborne about this event. They thought that I might be coming home again. This brought on a number of haranguing phone calls from them asking me to be on my best behaviour. After picking Doug up I managed to not frighten him too badly, and subsequently I was flown to Melbourne for my final interview. The interview went so well that on leaving it I said, 'Shit, I've got that job.' And that was how it came to pass. Within three or four days I was out of Perth and back to Melbourne, and within a week working at the Austin, never to live in my beautiful house on a lake in Perth. But then you must grasp opportunities when they present themselves. And this was one, not only in a professional sense, but also—just as importantly—in a basketball one.

Perth Postscript

Sometimes in life we make decisions that we regret, and thankfully other times we make those that lead to everything we hope for. My Perth experience was the latter because it allowed me to grow up again in so many ways. Since I had no history when I arrived in Perth, there was no pity about what I had lost, or what I couldn't do anymore. It was just about who I was there and then.

My Masters degree was gained with no issues of discrimination raised in any shape or form. This was a huge relief. St

Columba College certainly gave me the opportunity to live university life, unencumbered by the restraints of an overloaded study program.

Living in Perth, whilst not enabling me to play in a strong state basketball team, gave me a chance to learn the basics. Certainly the intensive base that I was able to put down during my last year was invaluable. But as importantly, it showed me that the game had the intrinsic element of a sport that I genuinely valued and was passionate about, while my scholarship intimated to me that the sport was slowly growing in the administrators' values as well as mine.

The way I obtained the position at the Austin taught me that if you really want something, go after it with passion and self-confidence. I wanted the job because I thought it was an opportunity to show in-patients that life does go on after spinal injury no matter how hard.

BACK TO THE AUSTIN

Returning to the Austin Hospital to work in the rehabilitation of patients with spinal injuries and to establish a Recreation and Leisure Department, was something that I had never envisaged until contacted about the position. The day I left the hospital as a patient had been, in my mind, the end of the hospital's role in my life. Yet my time in Perth after the completion of my studies had come to a little bit of a dead end, and perhaps fate had again taken a hand.

I obtained temporary accommodation in one of the hospital flats immediately over the road, and the night before I was to start my job I went for a wander through the hospital grounds, eventually finding my way to Ward Seventeen. It was an emotional visit, since a number of staff who had actually nursed me were still around, and the dreaded hospital smells and visions that had confronted me as a patient six years ago still existed. This job was to be more interesting, fulfilling and challenging than I ever could have imagined.

How do you create a new position that provides appropriate opportunities for people still stunned at their individual life scenarios? A position which, having been mooted for a long time, has attracted diverse and strong opinions throughout the staff ranks as to what a leisure coordinator should actually do. These were my dominant thoughts in the first days in the job, as I settled into my new expansive office, which had in fact been the cleaner's closet! In an effort to let both patients and staff know of my existence, I had rung the maintenance department and requested that the term Leisure Department be signposted on the office door. I went out and returned to find 'Leasure' printed on the door, and it was then I knew I had a long way to go in regard to educating about my work. Quite quickly someone added a 'P', and so the 'Pleasure Department' was born, and began the business of bringing smiles to faces that had little reason to smile.

My initial work strategy was to put my feet up on the desk, stare out the window and ask myself, 'What can I do with these people who have just had their life changed?' The patients didn't really know what I could offer. I talked to people, and more people and even more people.

But the greatest challenge of the position was that the patients wanted to know nothing about recreation, and everything personal about me. How did I do this or that, how did I pass urine, were my bowels affected by my spinal injury, how did I have sex, what did I find the best position . . .? The questions went on and on and on! I was meant to have all the answers, because I was seen as one of them, being the only spinal-injured person employed on the Unit. And while all these questions were a means of understanding and learning something to help them with their own situation, for me it was like losing every vestige of privacy, and going through rehabilitation again. This seemingly incessant interrogation, mixed with the feelings of missing the people of Perth, made me wonder if I had made the right choice in going back. And worse, I had an acute awareness of a hospital that had the same smells and sounds of a nightmare I'd long since put to bed. So, one Friday, six weeks after beginning at the Austin, I resigned. However, after a weekend in Point Lonsdale discussing my options with my friend Hague, who was from Perth but based in Melbourne, I went back to the Austin. I sat in the courtyard for half an hour considering things, then went to see Doug Brown and withdrew my resignation.

With renewed determination I decided that I was simply going to have to get a thicker skin, and handle the questions in a less specific and at times evasive manner. By being generalist in my answers and evasive about personal details, I found that I could help patients on their road back whilst still retaining the amount of me that I chose to. In essence, no matter what I was asked, I still had control of the inner me that I chose to withhold. And over time, my responses to the continuing and natural queries of patients became second nature, and it changed from being an unnerving experience to an unnoticed occurrence.

I established short-term 'pick-me-up' activities such as group trips to the movies, concerts or sport events. Whilst these were only brief, they aimed to bring a little fun and normality back to patients' lives, putting them in a better humour to help them with their rehabilitation. Yet this was nothing like organising a 'normal' day out.

After convincing and regularly cajoling patients to go, purchasing tickets if required, organising enough nursing staff to attend (often in their own time), and checking each patient's needs with urology staff, the major remaining issue to be addressed was how to get to the function. The mode of transport depended on the make-up of the patients attending and the stage of their rehabilitation, since spinal patients have to wait a period of time before they can travel by car due to the complications that would follow an accident and further injury. We also had to take into account whether or not the venue was near a train line (patients do not have to wait to travel by train due to the smaller risk of an accident) and who (if any) of the patients could transfer in and out of which vehicles. And through all this, constant adjustments would have to be made to cater for the inevitable withdrawals due to illness or simply black days. It was not easy, and you always worried about something going wrong, or a patient becoming unwell or injured; anything from hypothermia, to falls from chairs, or even a patient being dropped during a transfer were distinct possibilities on an outing. But if all went well, the complicated and time-consuming organisation and preparation was worth it.

The problem of finding attendants—able-bodied people to push and lift patients who were either unable to do one or both of these activities for themselves—was a constant issue that never went away. Over the years I seconded everyone from a volunteer group called the 'White Ants' from Banyule Football Club, who became my main pool of fit and strong manpower, to loitering personal friends. John Simpson, a feisty coach and motivator, who always said he could lift anybody, coordinated the White Ants. Yet one day John was to meet his match. A young chap had had a fracture to the neck, leaving him a quadriplegic and severely dependent. Whilst this in itself was not uncommon, what was, was that he was 205 centimetres tall, and heavy! One day John lifted the young fellow into a car in preparation for an outing. On completion of the lift he walked over to me with a wry smile on his face and said that he didn't think he would ever be able to get him out. Another time a different Ant thought he had drawn the long straw, when in fact he had got the short one. The patient he had been assigned to was using an electric wheelchair, so all the volunteer had to do was help with activities such as feeding and the like. That was until the battery in the chair went flat, and consequently the patient and heavy chair had to be pushed back to the train station, and then up the hill to the ward. Judging by the state he arrived in, it was obviously harder than any football training.

A friend of mine was to have a far worse experience. Hague was roped into coming to a sports event at the tennis centre (later named Melbourne Park). I had convinced him that it would be a good night out, and assisted by the lure of a free ticket, he had 'volunteered'. I assigned him to a relatively independent patient, who required only minimal assistance with steep hills and gutters. The night unfolded with no apparent dramas, and Hague finished the evening feeling positive about his experience and his ability to assist, though mentioning to me his patient had been very quiet. A month or two later, Hague was stunned to learn that his companion had committed suicide soon after discharge. It was the end of his volunteering.

One of my main roles was to spend quality one-on-one time with patients, be it soon after admission or on readmission. These interviews, or often informal chats, were about many things, from simply building rapport, to organising attendance at activities, to investigating long-term leisure goals. I got to meet some weird and wonderful people, and hear how they had been unfortunate enough to end up at the Unit. There were of course the plethora of car and motorbike accidents, diving and surf injuries, plus a lot of falls in a range of settings—work, leisure or home. These were the norm, but there were exceptions.

Peter had bought an ultra-light flying machine, which for years remained in storage and not constructed. After finally putting the machine together he had run into an instructor who agreed to meet him at the take-off zone. The instructor was short of time, so told Peter to simply run the ultra-light up and down the runway a few times, without exceeding a certain speed. The air-speed indicator was wrong, so on his third or fourth run down the airstrip Peter took off, having never flown before and yet to receive any instruction. Ultra-lights gain altitude quickly, so in desperation Peter had pulled every lever to stop the ascent and crashed. Heavily.

Jeremy was a keen middle-aged triathlete, who as well as

working as a professional builder, spent many hours training on the roads on his racing bike. One day, riding in a speed-enhancing streamlined riding posture, Jeremy was flying down a hill, with his head down and his arms resting on the Allen handlebars of his bike. Excitedly noting that the speedometer was registering forty-five kilometres an hour, Jeremy had drifted a little to the left of the roadway. He ran straight into the rear of a stationary council truck parked on the side of the road. Jeremy had crushed his black helmet as he used his head to stop, resulting in high paraplegia, and the end of his days as a triathlete.

But tragically not all accidents were accidents. 'Y' had had a history of psychiatric illness when he was admitted to a hospital for institutionalised care. One way or another he managed to remove himself from attending staff and launched himself from the seventh floor of the hospital in a desperate suicide attempt, only to crash through the roof of an annexe cafeteria on the ground floor in the midst of a hospital function. Y dropped in, resulting in a high level of paraplegia and a long stay on the Unit. A function not to forget!

And with this eclectic population, came a range of attitudes and interests, family support and moods. My main job was to raise patients' spirits. However, my actual role was far broader than this, since having been through rehabilitation myself, I had an in with patients frustrated with the system or process.

Graeme was an ex-bikie who had ended up at the Unit as a paraplegic after being shot in a bikie feud. Though he had a heart of gold, this red-haired, bearded fellow could on occasion be fiery. One day I got a call from Ward Seventeen saying Graeme was pretty angry, and in fact was about to tear the place apart, bit by bit. After a few moments' thought I rang the ward back to check that they had some beer in the fridge. (Patients after being in rehabilitation for a period of time could be 'prescribed' a can of beer with their evening meal.) I went and found Graeme on the ward, with appropriate refreshments in hand, and we retired to the sanctity of an adjacent tree. There we talked about the frustration of his situation, the reasons for his particular annoyance, and averted a blow-up, all over a cold beer.

Neil had been a truck driver and was involved in a horrific accident, resulting in severe injuries. Though many of these had healed, he was angry and frustrated and often refused to cooperate with staff. During his rehabilitation, Neil's occupational therapist would ring the ward to enquire as to his whereabouts, only to be told that he was still in bed and refusing to get up. The ward would then ring me. Armed with a wet towel I would go to his room and toss it in his face to drag him back to reality. After this, and at times harsh words, he would get out of bed, get dressed, and then we would have a coffee, discuss his interests—girls, motorbikes and footy—and then he would head off to therapy. Strange but effective rehabilitation.

Steve had been a particularly wild country teenager, living a life of leisure based entirely on the next high, whatever it may have been, before he was injured in the inevitable car smash. Despite his accident, one way or another during his early days of rehabilitation, Steve still managed to wallow in a haze of dope. I had built a relaxed mate-like relationship with him, and one day I found him 'floating' in the dining room. Confronting him, I said that I knew he was constantly 'stoned', that it was apparent that he wasn't doing anything towards getting himself out of hospital, and if things continued he was most likely going to spend the rest of his life in a nursing home. In short, it was up to him. I challenged him to go pushing in his wheelchair with me, with the long-term aim of developing fitness and strength. Steve was a low-level quadriplegic of a thin weedy stature, but I felt he had untapped ability, which due to his being 'relaxed' was being smothered. The following afternoon I met him on the ward and took him for a thirty-minute push throughout the hospital grounds, turning his normally pallid complexion green and leaving him whingeing and apparently exhausted. He was not happy, but I arranged to repeat the medicine the following day at the same time. Come the next day I was running late, and was stunned to receive a phone call from someone on his behalf asking where I was. The fire had been lit, and when I got to the ward I found him ready and waiting. After discharge, Steve has never lived in a nursing home.

I'd used a similar approach with John, who had been in the army, and had done a little bit of boxing in his leisure time prior to the accident which had left him quadriplegic. The gym, since my days of rehabilitation, had been relocated to a position down the hill from Ward Seventeen. Consequently, on the completion of gym sessions, patients had to either push themselves up the hill or be assisted back to the ward. One day I was chatting to John as he left the gym with his father, and I asked him whether or not he had ever been able to get back up the hill independently. He replied, 'I'm a quad, I can't do it'. With that, I laid out a direct challenge to him, and as he began his struggle up the hill alone, with his father alongside, I exhorted him to work, questioning many of his personal attributes. On cresting the top of the hill in his breathless state, he thanked me, realising I was trying to get him angry enough to give him a reason to push himself further than he had to. In my time at the hospital no other patient with an injury as severe managed to accomplish this feat. John proved that the inner strength and drive that I had seen in the way he spoke, in his perseverance at mastering tasks once so menial, and in the glint in his eyes, was no mirage.

The Austin was also home to one of the supercharacters. Oz Tennis funded weekly tennis lessons for patients, and it was during one of these sessions that 'our hero' was exposed! Greg, the coach, was approached by a new patient who on first inspection appeared to be somewhat knocked about. The coach proffered his hand and said, 'Hi, I'm Greg.' The patient responded with, 'Hi, I'm Superman.' Asked by Greg how that came to be, Superman replied that he had stopped a train, explaining to a somewhat bemused coach that he had in fact fallen under the wheels of a train, with the resultant loss of one arm and the 'gaining' of permanent spinal paralysis. But throughout his traumatic experience and consequential extended hospitalisation, the one thing that Superman retained was his sense of humour, allowing him to try to alter the things he could, and learn to live with the things he couldn't.

These stories highlight the judgement calls which often had to be made whilst working in rehabilitation. Sometimes square pegs (or even Superman) don't necessarily fit into the round holes of hospitals. Amongst the diverse and constantly changing patients, some special relationships developed. Danni was thirteen years old at the time of her injury. Though not a swimmer of any great talent, she had attended her inter-school swimming carnival to support her schoolmates. As she tells the story, the day unfolded with her somehow becoming the swim team's mascot, with all the winners pinning their ribbons on her favourite purple bathers. Suddenly a brick wall collapsed onto a spectator area, trapping Danni and other students for only a few minutes, and leaving her with a damaged lower spinal cord, whilst every other classmate escaped with no permanent injury. And so she came to the Spinal Unit, bringing with her an inner strength, first shown in an extreme way. Danni refused to have her fave bathers with attached ribbons cut off, but insisted on taking them off herself, despite a broken back, setting the benchmark of her will so high at such an early stage. From my first visits to this kid with the big buck teeth, olive skin and sparkling eyes, lying in the acute ward, I soon got a feeling that whatever positive experiences and advice I could give her would have a multiple effect. After a few weeks of my telling her about the possibilities of an uncompromised life that still lay ahead, and that her hopes and dreams had not died under a rubble of bricks, she emerged from her bed for her first days in a wheelchair, accompanied by an ever-supportive family, and a similarly supportive back brace. From her early days, despite the intrusion of the media due to the nature of her accident, she simply tried, listened and absorbed every skerrick that she could from all and sundry. My role ranged from making her laugh from behind the photographer snapping shots for the *Herald Sun*, to towing her up the hill from the train station to show her how able she could choose to be. She now says that she gleaned from me that one day she could still drive a car, hold down a job and do all the things she had imagined herself doing post-adolescence, but pre-accident. My aim was not to rescue her but simply to show her the way. And so as her rehabilitation progressed I introduced her to anything and everything. From city outings, to tennis lessons with Greg, and latterly a debut at wheelchair basketball, I watched her blossom despite her moments of introspection. More quickly than most, she was ready to go back to her school, her wonderful family and her still intact dreams.

At the moment of writing, Danni now sits atop of the rankings as number one wheelchair tennis player in the world, and has recently won Paralympian of the Year honours. In addition to this she holds a behavioural science degree, and works with an organisation focusing on kids in crisis, sharing her now matured inner strength which was seen far earlier than anyone would have wished.

Of course sometimes I didn't get it right, with what I said to patients, old or new. One day a regular readmission patient was lying in his bed, out in the sun. I asked him how things were going, and he replied that things were not good, since due to circulation problems the medicos were likely to amputate one leg. Trying to lift his flagging spirits and feeling that he may be exaggerating the graveness of the situation, I told him that I was sure things would improve. When I saw him a couple of days later, lying in his regular spot, I enquired of his health and he responded, 'They took my leg off.' I virtually patted the bed where his leg should have been in disbelief, thinking he was joking, only to hear him say that they were thinking of taking the other one too, which they did.

Before seeing a new patient, I would always review their history, so as to gain an understanding of them by learning where they came from, what they did prior to injury, the type of injury, and most importantly the mode of injury. That was the plan anyway. One day a physiotherapist was taking a quadriplegic, whose history I had not read and who I hadn't met, for his first tour of the gymnasium, when she ran into me. Suddenly being called away, she asked me to explain what the leisure department did, and what things this patient could in fact do. Whilst there were many activities a high-level quadriplegic could do, in the hospital it was at times limiting. As I chatted, in my mind I was scrambling for positive sounding events. I announced that once he could travel in a car, if he was interested, we would be able to take him to the newly developed air-weapons shooting group. As I said the word shooting I had a sinking feeling that this patient's injury had been caused by a shooting accident. I slunk back to the office and confirmed my fears.

Neither of these two patients may have noticed my lack of tact, but I certainly did—just as the nurse who had joked about breaking my back in the days of my own rehabilitation. Having moved from the internalised perspective of acute spinal injury to a more mature understanding of the often exposed emotions of in-patients, the last thing I wanted to do was increase the likelihood of the patient reliving the trauma which saw them admitted, or the worst of what was happening to them whilst admitted. You could never be too careful.

With my clear intent and passion still being the development of my own wheelchair basketball career, there seemed to be a natural opportunity to blend my professional position with my basketball skills. On arriving in Victoria I immediately joined a team in the domestic basketball competition, as well as training with the state squad for the coming National Championships, since my ambitions and aspirations had been ignited by the Western Australian experience. I knew where I wanted to go. I was aiming at selection for the Seoul Paralympic team. I also established and entered a team with the unimaginative title of 'Austin' in a competition that had a very different agenda. Each week, for season after season, the team—comprising myself and one or two able-bodied staff playing in wheelchairs—joined patients in the hospital or those who had been recently discharged, with the aim of providing a range of opportunities: meeting other people in wheelchairs, developing individual wheelchair skills, seeing other players who had established relationships after injury, and, often lastly, learning to play wheelchair basketball. Week in, week out, we would invariably get flogged, since there was only one division at the time, with my team pitted against established state and occasionally international players. One of the saddest and most frustrating things throughout these years was that 'Austin' was not recognised for what it was by some of the other teams; and that was, simply, a vehicle for rehabilitation. These people who were green, and had no wheelchair skills or confidence and little strength, would play only to be full courted, pressured and belted by would-be champions. It was very frustrating, and regularly I would have to remind players of how far they had come, or, on the odd occasion, physically liaise with opposition players to get them to play in the right spirit. When I went overseas to compete internationally in later years, I'd come back and find that my team had been beaten 65–2 or 65–4. To this day I am amazed by some people's attitude in the sport. When a pool of participants is relatively small, one would think every effort should be made to enhance potential talent and allowing the sport to truly grow. But on a more human level, one would have expected anyone undergoing rehabilitation to have been encouraged to have a positive experience. Whilst every team should want to win in any sport, the question must always be asked: when does competition end, and humiliation take over?

Yet this seemed beyond some people's comprehension. Despite many of the dominant players having gone through the frailties of rehabilitation themselves, memories were short, and human nature will always make some people bignote themselves at the expense of the defenceless. It is not one of the more attractive aspects of competition.

Despite this, and the loss of some participants because of it, the involvement of more than fifty players made the frustration well worth it. Although limited numbers continued to play over an extended period of time, many said the experience was fulfilling in various ways. An in-patient who experienced constant severe pain told me that the only time his life was free of it was when he played basketball. Another, who had attempted to take his life after being discharged, found his commitment and connection to the team helped him start to put the pieces of his life together again. The team also had some players who simply stood out. The Austin provided rehabilitation for patients from New Caledonia, and at one stage I had two players from this country with a somewhat limited sporting pedigree, who on nearing the end of their rehabilitation, played three games. Tall and lean, with dark skin and huge smiles, their background had been that of villagers, essentially gathering food, including climbing trees for coconuts. Basketball was not something that they had encountered. Undeterred by this and the small fact that they spoke virtually no English and I spoke no French, they simply played. With the interpreter stranded courtside, communication challenges took on a whole new meaning, with much pointing and waving taking precedence over talk. But through the smiles on both faces, their enjoyment was plainly understood, and when they each scored a basket in their last game, after many attempts, it was wonderful to see. Their major disappointment on being discharged, and going home to New Caledonia was that it also meant the end of their basketball career. They'd fallen in love with the game and they weren't alone.

The profile of the Spinal Unit and the Austin team received a boost when the Harlem Globetrotters basketball show came to town. On hearing that a tour was planned, I rang their promoters and issued a challenge to them, to play the Austin, in wheelchairs. After much negotiating, they agreed, and so it came to be. With a few hundred school children in attendance, the match was played at the Melbourne Glasshouse. With every patient who was able to get leave from the hospital in attendance, along with a copious number of hospital staff, it was a great success. The Austin players loved the game, and actually won. It made a lot of people feel good!

But this was not the end of the frivolities of wheelchair basketball for the patients and staff of the hospital, for they were to witness the funniest occurrence that I've ever been involved in on court. A demonstration match had been arranged, again at the Melbourne Glasshouse, preceding a National Basketball League match. I had arranged for a number of patients and staff to attend the game. The demonstration match was uneventful until the end of the first half. With fifteen seconds left on the game clock I was near the halfway line of the court, attempting to head towards my basket with the ball being held by one of my team mates on the opposite side of the court. Attempting to flash to the basket, receive the ball and lay it up, I found myself hindered by my opponent, who was leaning all over me. I gave him a gentle push, and he lost his balance, but still had me locked with his wheelchair. Another little push from me saw him fall out of his wheelchair, only to lie on the court grasping the footplates of my chair. This particular opponent was renowned for his defensive intensity, and of course it's difficult to move a wheelchair anywhere with someone hanging onto it like an anchor. In frustration, and not wishing to ruin the friendly spirit of the demonstration match, I reached down and grabbed his tracksuit pants and swiftly brought them to his knees. But that was not all. In sympathy, his underpants went down to his knees as well, exposing a particularly hairy bottom to the spectators. He immediately released his grip on my chair in an effort to rescue his dignity, but he'd done his job, as time had run out for me to score. At the half-time break, the opposition coach was laughing too much to address the team, my opponent was thinking of wearing braces, and the hospital patients, with tears in their eyes from laughter, had seen my more flamboyant side.

Of course, sport wasn't everyone's bag and so with the intent of reintroducing fun and regrowing shattered confidence, I set about developing two types of camp experience, one based on recreation, and the other with a focus on active leisure pursuits. After much searching and many inspections of prospective venues, and together with a drive down the Victorian west coast on a forty-degree horror day with no air conditioning, I found 'Kangaroobie', a site for the recreation camps. Kangaroobie, situated a few miles from Port Campbell, was a large host farm with reasonably accessible facilities, and was set up as a camp, catering for schools and other groups. The camp building, on the top of a hill, provided a serene outlook over adjoining land and was a perfect setting for dehospitilisation, and whilst the accommodation was basic, it appeared as though it would serve its purpose. The sleeping area consisted of bunk-style accommodation and some accessible toilets and showers, and a large dining hall featured a sunken pit and fire as its centrepiece. And so after a second visit to Kangaroobie, with a nurse from the Unit to ensure the facilities were up to standard from a medical perspective, the camping program came to fruition.

Every three or four months saw the hospital bus and various cars being loaded for the three-and-a-half-hour drive to Kangaroobie, with the huge amount of equipment that invariably accompanies long-term hospital patients on leave. With the usual eight or nine patients and family, crammed in alongside a range of staff from various disciplines, the weekends began, with a keen focus on anything dehospitalised. From stopping at a particular hot-doughnut van on the journeys to the camp, to partaking in activities on the farm such as archery, target shooting, spotlighting, fishing or farm tours where one would meet Ralph the donkey, the weekends were about growing. And, of course, with a mostly young group, we had the compulsory night out at a local pub.

For me and the staff, the weekends would be the longest shifts of our lives. Camp staff arrived at work on the Friday morning and signed off on return to the hospital on Sunday night. We were all on duty throughout, since there was only one member for each discipline, apart from a total of two nurses. My role on the camps was last to bed and first up, apart from the nurses, the coordinator, urger and worrier for what may or actually did happen. Every camp was different, as the individual successes and failures, along with the roulette factor of moods, made everything unpredictable. And it was often the staff who would have to lift themselves, hoping the patients' moods would follow.

One particular Kangaroobie camp stands alone in my memory for the depths of despair experienced by the seven or eight patients in attendance. By some sort of fluke, all the patients over this particular weekend all reached absolute lows, in one form or another. From one battling to control the emotions of being near the sea for the first time since a water-related spinal injury, to a high-level quadriplegic who failed at one activity too many and whose spirit plummeted in a strong downward spiral. Another was struggling to come to grips with his own situation when he had learnt of the suicide of a close relative, only moments before we left the hospital. The remaining participants each had their own story of individual angst. Amongst this group of wailing patients, the staff—each with official roles as nurse, orderly, physiotherapist and so on, along with unspoken roles of listeners, confidants, motivators and organisers—mixed and moved. Come two o'clock Sunday morning, when everyone else had gone to bed drained and spent, I sat with the only staff member still awake, Justine. We talked until four, trying to debrief. We successfully negotiated the Sunday, which included a trip to the Twelve Apostles and a walk out onto London Bridge (natural rock formations on the West Coast) and everyone arrived back safely at the hospital. But only just. The narrow path to London Bridge was to collapse two weeks after our visit. On the Monday morning back at the Austin, I asked Justine how she had pulled up from her weekend away. 'I went home and cried,' she said. Rehabilitation is hard, not just for the patients.

But the highs far outweighed the lows on these weekends away. We used anything to create an upbeat mood and a sense of mirth. One camp, my partner at the time, Lisa, was assisting under the guise of being a leisure student under my tutelage. The whole weekend was based around me potentially failing this poor innocent-looking girl, and Lisa played the role of a recalcitrant student oh so well. On the farm tour, which was part of the program for every camp, we had left my wheelchair behind. I sat (stranded) in the back of the trailer and Lisa, with all the patients being aware of it, rubbed sheep manure all over the pushrims. Eventually a huge sheep-manure fight broke out, starting with dry ammunition but quickly deteriorating to 'the wetter the better'. After this incident the patients thought Lisa was definitely going to fail, since it is generally not preferable to have to push a poo-encrusted wheelchair anywhere.

An incident while organising the farm tour on another of the camps led to ultimate ignominy for me and hysteria for everyone else. Sitting outside in the yard adjacent to the camp building, I was busy ensuring all patients were secured safely on a trailer behind the farm vehicle, when unbeknownst to me, a farm dog made my chair his target. Sidling up to me from the right, the big red kelpie suddenly stopped, and in one motion, did as dogs do when spotting a wheel that takes their fancy. Cocking his leg he let fly at one of the rear wheels of my chair, just as I became aware of his presence and intentions. I instantaneously pushed away, sending expletives in the direction of the dog, while the assembled audience dissolved into laughter at the impromptu shower.

Naughtiness of the human kind also appeared without warning, arriving in many shapes and forms, with regrowing confidence at times getting just a little out of hand. One camp, a decision was made to have the standard Saturday-night dinner at a different hotel from our usual. We dined at the quaint and intimate Boggy Creek Hotel, and the next morning the host of Kangaroobie told me that she had had a phone call from the hotel. Being small, the hotel had quickly noted on our departure that some of its drinking glasses were missing. After I'd managed to overcome my embarrassment, a brief reading of the riot act followed to all camp attendees. The said glassware reappeared, left by unknown subjects at an anonymous drop-off point. It paid to keep on my toes.

Each time I took a group away, the major priority was to get everyone home safely, because this was never easy. One camp saw me spend much of an evening at Terang Hospital after a patient took seriously ill with a bowel obstruction. Since the facilities at Kangaroobie were not of medical-centre standard, accidents were always lurking, and occasionally they happened. One morning a nurse was showering a patient who had limited sensation, in a shower without a thermostat control. She noticed steam coming from the patient's groin and found that the water had become scalding. The man's groin was burnt, as was his accompanying appendage. It healed, thankfully, after a week or two in bed.

Legends of camp weekends developed, of which the unchallenged champion was Dennis. Dennis was fifteen at the time of his admission after an accident which had left him with high quadriplegia, limited arm movement and minimal balance. He had red hair, freckles, and the constantly cheeky demeanour of the cartoon character that shares his name. Dennis was both a favourite and a nemesis of the leisure department in so many ways. One night summed him up. Going into Melbourne on an outing with patients, friends and some volunteers, we went by train to Flinders Street Station and then walked and wheeled our way to the Olympic Park Greyhound meeting which we were attending. Dennis, cheery and boisterous in his heavy electric wheelchair, drove himself independently to our destination some two to three kilometres from the station. After a fun night, with both winners and losers amongst the group from their betting endeavours, the time came for the long trek back to the train, and it was then that Dennis found that his chair had a flat battery. A pair of volunteers sweated profusely as they pushed Dennis back up the graded footpath to the station, making the last train by barely a minute. Exhausted and lathered in sweat, the two pushers slumped into their seats until we arrived in Heidelberg, where the real hill awaited. And through the loss of his independence and the groans of the volunteers' effort, Dennis simply laughed and smiled with a twinkle in his eyes.

Somehow, in the two years after his injury, Dennis always managed to be in hospital having further surgery whenever the time for a camp arose. His determination to partake in every opportunity and his refusal to concede to his limitations almost led him to a most unusual sticky end. Returning in my own car from a camp with Dennis for company (by then he was almost family), I had left him sitting in the car while I got some takeaway food with the remainder of the group. Dennis, always trying to do something he couldn't or shouldn't, had tried to lean forward and change the channel on the car radio and had lost his balance. He couldn't sit back up without assistance, so he was left hanging with his head under the glove box and the seat belt across his throat. Arriving back at my car some ten minutes later, I was greeted with the back of his little red head peaking out from under my glove box. Because Dennis was Dennis, I grabbed the nearest protruding piece, which happened to be hair, and pulled him upright in his seat. In a gasping voice, he said 'Sandy, I couldn't breathe; I nearly choked myself.' Yes, we'd nearly killed Dennis. But of course he still came on the next camp.

Soon after beginning my work at the Austin, I had noticed that many people went home after discharge never to venture back into active pursuits, consequently limiting their fitness and increasing their risk of readmission. In an effort to redress this, I initiated annual sports camps, with often sport being the least of the issues touched upon. These weekends were coordinated with Wheelchair Sports Victoria. We scoured old records looking for lost souls, and sometimes found them. After these weekends, some special people in fact found themselves.

One camp was attended by a girl who was a dazed spectator in her own blurred life, due to a regular intake of Valium since her discharge from the Austin. The drug was initially prescribed as a muscle relaxant to assist with controlling spasm, which is a common side effect of spinal injury. Her medication had never been modified, despite her condition stabilising and her life changing. The girl, who later professed to being nervous to the point of nearly withdrawing from the camp, fronted for the weekend. She participated in anything—tennis, basketball, ten-pin bowling and more—but as importantly, she talked. She talked to other spinal injury patients, she talked to professionals in the rehabilitation industry, and through other people she saw a mirror of her own potential to make the step. With her self-confidence nudged and her horizons broadened, over the next year she grew, partaking in wheelchair netball, wheelchair basketball, and sky diving. She found a new job, which came with a new car. Soon after, I received a phone call from her mother saying that I had changed her daughter's life.

The sports camps were directed solely at spinal-injured patients. However, a week before one camp I received a phone call from Bethesda Hospital, enquiring as to whether two patients with acquired brain injuries could attend. I was hesitant, but eventually I accepted. For their tennis session, the two patients used wheelchairs, although both were partially ambulant, and placed them at one end of the tennis court and Greg, the coach, up the other. Although Greg had a seemingly bottomless basket of balls to hit with the two, I ended up sitting behind them and hitting the balls back to Greg to keep the rallies going despite their frequent misses. After a morning of tennis, I did some individual build-up skills of the netball court whilst another assistant ran more advanced skills for the spinal-injured participants. Eventually I organised a game of netball, placing the two guys on opposite teams, but competing against one another in wing defence and wing attack. To ensure this worked, I played centre for one team, and another friend, an elite wheelchair basketballer who I had convinced to come away, played as centre for the other team. This allowed them to catch accurate passes and for them to be fully integrated into the game. Their parents watched and were thrilled; it was a great step forward for their children. This moment brought a tear to my eye, and showed the ability of all of us in the right environment, be it initially contrived or not. By the end of the weekend, they had not only had a wonderful time, but they had in fact won the hearts, the admiration and most importantly the friendship of the staff and all the other participants. Because all they were doing was their best.

At the hospital I saw the good, the bad and the indifferent from parents. One of the saddest times was when a mum came up to me and asked whether her son would ever be able to dress up, or whether he would have to wear tracksuit pants and moccasins for the rest of his life. If it hadn't been so sad it would have been amusing. But in the initial days of rehabilitation it is generally the clothing of choice for ease of dressing. Also, for swollen feet moccasins are perfect because they don't mark, and people at that early stage of rehabilitation are not used to the loss of sensation and caring for their feet. The answer was yes, he could dress up, but it would take some time, and he would probably have to have an additional fashion accessory made of metal.

Of course to run a department you need staff. Initially I was by myself but after one year a volunteer knocked on the door expecting to meet 'Sandie' the female Leisure Coordinator. Heather had been a primary-school teacher, and began volunteer work at the Austin at the start of 1989. By the end of the year she had become absolutely indispensable. Funds became available and she became a part-time staff member at the beginning of 1990, labelled with an appalling title of 'Half-Time Unqualified Leisure Assistant'. This was a little harsh, as her only disability was that she was a passionate Fitzroy supporter. We were a great team, and worked together without a senior–junior relationship.

One time Heather and I had a meeting at Moonee Valley Racecourse to discuss a proposed fundraising night. We arrived for the meeting and made our way to the offices where I introduced myself as the leisure coordinator and Heather as my assistant. We then toured the function rooms, and despite the introductions, throughout the entire tour every single question from the staff was directed to Heather. Choosing to not be assertive and correct this ridiculous situation, I let it continue, so after each question Heather would repeat the question to me, as an interpreter would. After I gave my answer she would then translate it back to the Moonee Valley staff member. It was unbelievable. In one hour I did not get one question asked directly to me. As we wandered back to my car after the meeting, Heather turned to me and said, 'Well, what was it like being Dickie Knee?' All they needed to do to really finish off their effort was to pat me on the head.

Treatment such as that at Moonee Valley highlighted the different way that some people see those of us in wheelchairs. Living it every day, you tend to forget, just seeing you as you. But it can lead to problems of its own, if you forget that you're on wheels. One day at dusk, not long after the Dickie Knee incident, I parked my car in the street outside the rented house that I had moved to after leaving the hospital flats. Being unsure of whether or not I was going to go out again, I had inadvertently left my car's automatic shift in neutral. I got out of the car and, having transferred into my wheelchair, I went to lock and shut the car door. It was as the door slammed that I noticed my wheelchair seemed strangely off balance. What in fact was happening was that the car was starting to roll down the gentle gradient in my street. With the car door now locked, I unthinkingly grabbed the car under the bonnet near the windscreen in an effort to stop it, as if I were on legs. I skidded down the road in my wheelchair, with one hand hanging onto the outside of the car and the other ineffectually locking one wheel of my chair. As the car slowly gained pace, and another car rounded the bottom of my street some fifty metres away, I surrendered to the unfolding nightmare and attempted to pull my hand from under the bonnet, only to find my fingers jammed. After several tugs, my hand came free. Mortified, I watched as the car rolled some twenty to thirty metres down the hill. It crossed the road, mounted the kerb and promptly ran its rear into a large tree, saving an unknown neighbour's fence. The car coming up the street had halted out of harm's way until my driverless car came to rest; the driver then pulled up alongside my chair to ask if I was all right. Embarrassed beyond words, I mumbled a response intimating that I was OK, and so they went on their way as I moved to rectify the situation. Quickly skulking to my truculent car's resting position, I hastily transferred into the driver's seat, praying that no-one else had seen my predicament. When I had safely parked my car in the driveway, I inspected the rear bumper bar and found no damage. I retired to the house, thankful that no-one had been hurt, far more appreciative of the trees in the street and anti-crush bumpers than before, and aware that the scene would have been fit for a Monty Python skit!

But back to the job. After being contacted by a group in Moorabbin who were promoting hand-control flying for spinal-injured people, Heather and I went and inspected their set-up. After a brief chat with our pilot, we wandered over to a very small aeroplane, and I began the process of getting in. In a slow and somewhat undignified manner, I bummed it up a wing and into the small cockpit. I strapped myself in with all available belts, and we taxied out. We were soon bumping down the runway and beginning our flight. As a person who hates flying at the best of times, I was a little taken aback when the pilot turned to me and said, 'Try this control out.' I had a little play, quickly handed control back to the pilot, and we eventually landed. I made a quick exit from the hangar with Heather, and as I got in to my car she said, 'Wasn't that fun!' She looked more closely when I didn't reply, and then added, 'Boy, are you green!' All I stammered was: 'Never, ever again am I going up in a light aeroplane.' The flying school offered a free flight or two to the patients, who obviously had similar stomachs to me; not a single in-patient took up the challenge.

Working at the hospital gave me a range of opportunities to understand my own and others' emotions, primarily because I was in the unusual situation of having been inside looking out (a patient) and outside looking in (a staff member). With this insight came the truest understanding of the random emotional waves sweeping over the in-patients, and of the importance that passion and perseverance have to attitude and outcome, no matter the task at hand. The greatest challenge for everyone in the specific setting of rehabilitation was to search for, find, and nurture an internal flame, and to carefully direct it to positive outcomes. Without it the journey back to normality, with or without residual functional loss due to the actual spinal injury, was more than difficult.

One time the medical director of the Unit asked me to organise two patients to attend a production of *Phantom of the Opera*. A visiting American professor and his wife wished to see the production, but the only way to get seats on such short notice was for them to accompany two wheelchair users, and use the

Back to the Austin

companion seats adjacent to the wheelchair viewing bays. The wheelchair bays were available, perhaps due to their poor location. After doing a round of the ward I found that no-one was prepared to attend. So it was up to me. Obviously I was one person in a wheelchair, but where to find another? I went home to the long-suffering Lisa, commented how attractive she looked, and told her that I was going to take her to *Phantom of the Opera*. She was thrilled, and I waited for her excitement to settle before I announced that there was a little catch. I explained my bind, and told her that she would have to go in a wheelchair. After a little resistance, she acquiesced, and when the big night arrived, her instructions were explicit and clear. The plan was to park well away from the theatre, where she could mount her wheelchair in privacy. Should she fall out at any stage of the evening—with the particular risk area being the crossing of the road which had tram tracks—she was to lie and groan, and then stoically attempt to get back into her wheelchair with minimal use of her legs. She was not to swear and leap to her feet, which would have led to visions of her on the front page of a local daily: 'Miracle Girl Walks Again'. We picked up the professor and his wife, who were in on the scheme, and all went according to plan, more or less. Despite being exceedingly nervous and jamming a finger in the rush to assemble her wheelchair, Lisa safely negotiated the tram tracks, which are an ever present hazard for the ill skilled, and successfully entered the foyer. But her night of experiences was just beginning. As she made her way to her seating area she was grabbed, unrequested, by an overzealous usher and whisked at speed to her seating bay. At the interval, as all women do, Lisa decided she wanted to visit the ladies' room. The very same usher patted her on the head, and then volunteered to whisk her to the toilet for people with disabilities. Confronted by a queue of able-bodied people standing in line for the same toilet, the friendly usher loudly announced that the toilet was only for people with disabilities, then bellowed at the locked cubicle door for whoever was occupying it to get out, unless they had a disability. A lady rushed from within, still straightening her attire; a crimson Lisa manoeuvred into the cubicle, locked the door and stood up, saying aloud, 'I am such a fraud.' On completing her business, she came out to find her usher friend standing guard, and was whisked back to her seating bay. At the end of the evening Lisa commented that she was better than I was. When I asked in what way, she answered with a twinkle in her eyes: 'One night out in a wheelchair, and someone patted me on the head. How did you go?'

Being in a wheelchair didn't just give me entree to theatre seats when I wanted them. It also gave me a little personal insight into some of the pain and emotions experienced by grieving parents, having seen it first hand through Al and Rosie. The parents at the Austin varied from wonderful to unhelpfully overprotective. From being there and allowing their child to grow, to patting them on the head and saying, 'Don't worry, don't listen to anyone, you will walk again.' Messages like that used to be not only frustrating but also desperately sad. Often the patient wouldn't walk again, but because of their family's input wouldn't accept that that was how it was, and so they wouldn't rehabilitate. The parents often saw me as a potential role model for their 'stricken' child since I appeared to have my life together. Whilst this was fantastic for me when helping paraplegics, I often felt inadequate in that role for anyone who had suffered a more significant injury. With all this giving of myself in many and varied emotional settings, I found that my greatest challenge was that there was always a new patient.

Of course my situation in the chair put me in a unique position as a staff member. There was little doubt that it gave me some advantages, but there was also a downside. At times, some patients felt more comfortable discussing particular issues with me, and this not only made me question my ability to handle such interrogations, it also brought other ongoing problems. It would often lead to feelings of role erosion by staff whose area the patient was requesting information about, or perhaps even gilding the lily. Statements such as 'Sandy said I should have this type of cushion' were seen by some patients as a means of attempting to get particular equipment, regardless of whether I had said anything of the kind. Walking this fine line was not just my challenge. One day, during a crowded staff in-service on sexuality, there was a discussion about an injection in the penis which could assist some spinal-injured people to gain erections. Midway through the in-service, the registrar suddenly directed a question at me, saying, 'Sandy, you tell us about it. I'm sure you've had more experience than the rest of us.' Stunned, I answered that I was not in need of assistance, and after a moment's uncomfortable silence the discussion moved on. At the conclusion of the session the registrar approached me and apologised; I'm sure it was one of those times we've all had, when we wish we could stop the words just after they've left the mouth. Yet to me it was another effect of my unique situation on the Unit, and typical of the stresses of rehabilitation.

It was the same topic that created one of the most direct confrontations in my time of employment at the hospital. Before I joined the Spinal Unit, a sexuality handbook had been developed to help new patients and their partners to learn about any aspects of function that may have changed. When the time came for an update, I was asked to join the review committee. The committee was made up of a number of staff, including one strong lady who had been one of the initial key contributors. After two or three meetings little had been achieved, as there was a dispute as to whether a new handbook should be written or the old one revised. All committee members agreed that the old one should be revised, except for the woman who had been involved in the original edition. She would not budge, pressing for a new book to be written, and denying that her opposition had anything to do with us wanting to change her initial work. The meetings continued to go nowhere and the frustration rose and rose. Finally, midway through another meeting, in disbelief at her denials, I challenged her with a rather direct attack: 'Come on, big girl, it's ego, isn't it? That's the reason you don't want a revision.' Stunned and angered she blurted back, 'Yes, it is. It is ego.' We finally stopped dancing around the subject. All the cards were on the table, and the handbook was revised. Rarely was there such room to pander to staff's interests when it came to providing the best possible care for patients.

The question most often asked of people who work or have worked in rehabilitation is 'How do you cope?' My answer is: 'You do.' The hardest thing is to find the right balance, and by that I mean if you give too much or if you get too involved you are wonderful for a few patients but you burn out. Yet if you stay removed, aloof and uncaring, bridges are not built and so you don't impact on individuals' rehabilitation processes; all you do is skim the surface. It was quite common in my time to see new staff get very involved with one, two or three clients and then burn out. And be gone.

I'd been at the Unit for four-and-a-half years when I was interviewing an elderly Italian man who'd had a fall that had resulted in him becoming a quadriplegic. After chatting to him for about four or five minutes, I realised that I was about to cry. His situation for some reason touched me, more than the norm. I cut the interview short, went back to the office and spoke to Heather, saying, 'I'm cracking up.' I told her the story and we just sat there and laughed madly.

Trying every day to brighten the lives of people who had little reason to feel brightened had a cumulative effect. This particular meeting simply caused the tank to overflow. His situation was tragic, but no more tragic than every other in-patient. You had to care, but if you cared too much or for too long, you went under.

A year after this—a year which included many moments of hilarity, frustration and sadness, observing those with fight and those without—my giving time was up. In September 1993, after five-and-a-half years at the Austin Hospital, I resigned.

Austin postscript

I left the Austin because I felt that I couldn't give to the required levels, as I was drained. My position was filled by Janet Walsh, and then Phillip Pingree, whilst Heather continued her fantastic work for years, taking redundancy eighteen months or so ago. The Austin basketball team eventually folded, and the number of people trying the game has dropped.

In 1998, the provision of full-time and part-time leisure workers stopped, due to the collapse of funding sources. Austin patients now have very little organised leisure experiences. I hold out some hope that the Unit will gain external funding over the next couple of years, arrange a board of management, and employ a leisure worker.

THE BIG WIDE WORLD

For some time before resigning from the hospital, I had given a lot of thought to what I wanted to do. I was keen to combine my basketball career with my professional life. Inspired by the thought of working for myself, and with a feeling that there was an unexplored niche market in the area of disability, I set out to establish a disability management company. Having seen life from both sides of the coin, so to speak, I felt well qualified to give some balanced consultation on issues pertaining to access, staff training and alleged discrimination conflicts in the corporate sector. This, in addition to my personal desire to make the world a more level playing field, saw the company initially focusing on physical-access audits of property, development of staff-training manuals and mediation of discrimination complaints. And so with the proportion of people with disabilities in the community on the rise (currently 18 per cent), and a lack of well-versed professionals dealing with access requirements, I went into business. My prospects were significantly enhanced with the bringing into effect in 1993 of the Federal Disability Discrimination Act, which, in brief, made it unlawful to discriminate against a person due to their disability in any number of ways. I formed my own company, Disability Dynamics, a few weeks after leaving the hospital, consulting to Australian businesses which were looking for guidance on how to comply with the changing landscape of what was and wasn't acceptable business practice in relation to people with disabilities.

As with my experiences in leaving the Austin as a patient, and going back to Ballarat College, and my initial move to Perth, I was in a sense stepping into the unknown, and away from the security of familiar environs. In this instance, my sacrificing of financial stability was compensated for by the excitement of the challenge, and the quest to establish a ground-breaking consultancy. The end of my emotional input at the hospital was both a huge relief and yet a loss. However, the corporate world held its own innate demands and requirements. With businesspeople being the economic rationalists they are, justifying and proving the benefits of using a disability-management specialist was a new experience for virtually all our contacts. It was a new consideration for business development, and had never been seen as an issue, let alone good business practice. But I was not the only one who saw this area as a growth market with immense potential.

Around the same time, two guys who I played basketball with over a number of years, along with another chap, had established a business akin to Disability Dynamics, also in pursuit of the corporate animal. Quite quickly we found ourselves working in similar areas of physical-access audits and the development of access for events. So, with our common backgrounds and different skill sets, a decision was made to amalgamate the two businesses, and so Morris–Walker

Consultants came into being. The business grew quickly, and the sharing of contacts took us from a hotchpotch of small clients to major corporations.

A broad range of clients allows the company to make a real difference to the opportunities for people with disabilities, and to make a commercial dollar. The Australian Grand Prix Corporation, for instance, asked us to ensure that the Formula One Grand Prix in Victoria had appropriate transport, suitable seating and facilities, and staff trained to deal with patrons with disabilities. We have also expanded into pre-construction design review work, plus physical-access audits of existing buildings for clients such as Ansett Australia, McDonald's, Telstra and AMP, making premises more accessible to not only people with disabilities, but for parents with prams, and for the elderly as well.

Another real passion was to further develop my skills and opportunities on the public-speaking circuit, using my life and sports experiences to entertain and inspire others. Having progressed from the 'Hope' presentation, I actively sought this work for the first time, rather than it coming to me on an *ad hoc* basis. I have spoken on such challenging topics and themes as 'Humanising the Myth of Disability' at an access-manual launch; I have addressed an AFL football team as a motivator during their build-up to a final; and I have appeared at conferences as an after-dinner speaker with a focus on humour. I quickly developed my own style and flair. I still feel the buzz when holding an audience with the spoken word, whilst taking them through a range of emotions. From uncontrolled mirth, to moments of individual and team empowerment, every speech is a different challenge. Each time, I hope that through the peaks and troughs of my tales, each member of my audience takes something from my life and uses it in their own.

At the end of 1995 an opportunity arose which utilised many of my skills, not only those I had developed through presentation work, but also during drama studies at Ballarat College, and in playing basketball. The Victorian WorkCover Authority, in an effort to promote the 'return to work' message, initiated an advertising campaign involving a number of aspiring Paralympic athletes, including me. My advert basically involved me chatting about how accidents can happen to anybody, and then tossing a foam ball into a ring. This may sound a simple task for a basketballer, but the foam ball is absolutely nothing like the real McCoy. So, in short, I couldn't boast that it was filmed in one take. The campaign was the first time that positive role models with disabilities had been used extensively in the media, consequently challenging perceived stereotypes. The feedback was particularly strong, and in many ways the series was the forerunner of sponsorship for Paralympians, since WorkCover had grasped that we were a marketable commodity.

Soon after the airing of the commercials I began work within a major corporation on a consultancy basis in a leadership-assessment program. In these sessions, mock interviews were held with me playing a role, varying from an Indian salesperson to a customer waiting for an important delivery. The senior managers would need to settle the issues at hand whilst being videotaped and having their performance assessed, with the intention of identifying those with leadership qualities. With the WorkCover commercial running at this time, one manager kept referring to the television advert, no matter how hard I tried to get him back to the job at hand, possibly ending his future leadership ambitions. But not everyone had seen the advert; my favourite comment after one particular day role-playing was: 'the actor pretending to be in a wheelchair seems pretty good at it'.

Despite all of my other commitments, my real passion remained sport.

BACK TO BASKETBALL

When I had come back to Victoria to take up my position at the Spinal Unit, I had also gone from the worst state team in Australia to a contender for the national title: the Vics. I was selected in the Victorian team to compete in the National Championships, where after making the final as long shots, we won, defeating South Australia by two points. Rosie and Al were amongst the spectators in attendance, and during the victory celebrations they overheard the coach paying me the ultimate compliment: 'Sandy added the bit of mongrel that the team needed.' When Rosie relayed the story to me I was chuffed, but she felt somewhat differently. To top off a day of days, at the closing ceremony the team for the Seoul Paralympics was announced, and I was in it.

This was to be the beginning of more than ten years of

continuous selection in the national team. In wheelchair basketball the national team is selected from performances at the annual National Championships, and in the National Wheelchair Basketball League (NWBL). The NWBL has developed since 1988, and is based very much upon the able-bodied National Basketball League, with a home-and-away format, and teams from Queensland, New South Wales, Victoria, South Australia and Western Australia. Since 1988, I have been fortunate that my football skills and continued coaching input have given me the tools to excel; however, you cannot excel without passion, drive and ongoing commitment. This is the national team's journey from the bottom of the ladder, striving for the top.

The Seoul team, as I was to learn, was not particularly strong. After a preparation trip to Los Angeles, we arrived at the Games with limited ambitions, lacking in international experience and squad depth. And so over the days of the competition our limitations were exposed. There being twenty teams competing, we only managed to come an inglorious tenth, struggling to beat even teams from small countries like Morocco. We were definitely no power, and it seemed that some players thought that they had had their victory, simply by making the team. I, along with a few others, was not in that group.

But it was an introduction to the intricacies of the Paralympics, and there was so much more than basketball to see and learn from the Seoul experience. It is only at such major events as the Paralympics that the basketball team competes alongside all the other athletes and is faced with people with a wide range of disabilities. At any Paralympic event, one is initially struck by the diversity of impairments, but amazed at the abilities. On one of my first trips to the food hall in Seoul I had taken a seat after selecting a meal, only to look up to find an amputee athlete sitting directly opposite and eating with his feet, an initially unnerving sight. Soon after, I learnt that vision-impaired athletes are broken into three categories: athletes with less than one per cent vision; those with one to five per cent vision; and those with five to ten per cent vision. In an unfamiliar environment, blind athletes would often walk with their hand on the shoulder of a more sighted blind athlete in front, giving a whole new meaning to the term 'the blind leading the blind'! This humour may seem flippant, but I was soon to learn that Paralympic athletes are no different from Olympic athletes or footballers, with rivalries and nicknames quickly evolving. From the blinkies (vision impaired), seagulls (amputees) or the generic term 'crips', in-house slang was accepted, and this medium of humour encouraged.

Another incident at the Games also heightened my awareness of some of the hazards presented by other athletes. One evening I had made a cup of black tea at one of the hot-beverage areas of the food hall. As I carried it back to my table, I was bumped by an athlete who was engaged in an activity very loosely related to walking and who probably shouldn't have been. With his stumbling gait, he inadvertently fell into me, knocking the scalding tea into my groin. Panicked as to the obvious consequences, I grabbed two glasses of nearby cooling orange juice and promptly tipped them into my lap in an attempt to save the burning flesh. Despite how ludicrous it looked, the results were effective and a later private inspection revealed only a minor burn. From then on I have wended my way around athletes with some caution.

But all these learning experiences couldn't sweeten the taste of tenth. With frustrations bubbling, the trip home always had potential! And so it proved to be. The flight home to Australia had a stopover in Bangkok, meant to be a day of R and R. As I lay on my bed late at night in the Bangkok Airport Hotel, my room mate asked me what I was doing. He, the socialiser from hell, said we were going out, and that was that. I quickly found myself in the back of a taxi, heading for the seamy side of the city. We visited a couple of bars before settling in one called the Butterfly Bar, which had a dark dingy interior but seemed quite hospitable. At first we were stunned at the youth of the near-nude women, and the brazen male customers, but we quickly relaxed, and whilst not drinking enjoyed the scenery. Many of the scantily clad bar girls were dancing on small podiums, and with nowhere else to dance, temptation—and the exhibitionism in me—took over. Transferring onto a podium and getting my mate to throw my chair up, I remounted and began to dance with one of the girls. I felt overdressed beside her, so began, of all things, a poor man's striptease! Watch, shoes, socks, shirt all departed, and the place went off, since all the girls rushed close to my podium. The manageress encouraged this impromptu show, however the moment of truth quickly arrived, since all I had left on were my jeans. I stopped the show (mind you, with my skinny legs and other god-given gifts I'm sure I saved all from disappointment) and got off the podium. At the end of the evening we were asked back to two of the girls' homes. We refused, and instead risked life and limb by hurtling for forty minutes in a 'tuk tuk' back to our hotel. A night to remember, and one never repeated.

The following year, 1989, saw me selected in the FESPIC Games team bound for Japan. We had just been runners-up in the National Basketball Championships held in Adelaide, where South Australia had triumphed, turning the tables on Victoria in the final. The Japanese hosts put on a sensational Games in Kobe, which was later to be decimated by an earthquake. All athletes were accommodated in a huge five-star hotel with first-class sporting facilities. What was similar to the FESPIC Games in Indonesia in 1986, however, was that the quality of the opposition varied greatly. We eventually secured second place after being defeated by Japan in the final. The only moment of real mirth or angst came in a match against India who, for the sake of entering a team, had track and field athletes playing. Outclassed and confused, they literally threw themselves at our players in an effort to stop our scoring. It was the first time I had been winded on a sports arena since my football days.

The Australian team's next international appearance was at

the World Championships in 1990, to be held in Brugge, Belgium. We had an eventful trip on our way to pre-training in Germany, when on approach to Dubai for a scheduled refuelling stop, part of one of the plane's wing flaps fell off. This necessitated an unscheduled stopover in the oil-rich city. With the airport staff totally lacking any idea of how to deal with a team of elite athletes who however couldn't walk, we sat on the plane for two-and-a-half hours after landing, the plane's air conditioner having been turned off shortly after touchdown.

Finally, we were unloaded and transferred to 1920s wheelchairs that airport staff had scrounged from somewhere, rather than our own chairs, and then taken through the airport medical centre, by staff wearing plastic surgical gloves!

Some fifty-five hours after departing from Melbourne, the team arrived in Munich, Germany, and since it was morning, promptly had a training run, the sole aim being to keep players out of bed. And then our hosts insisted on taking us out to a beer garden for lunch and Steinlagers. It was the longest day!

After three days' training with various German teams, we were taken to Dillingen, a regional town where a pre-tournament was to be held. Only for the amusement really to begin!

Generally you would think that anywhere hosting a wheelchair basketball tournament would be well organised, and that access to buildings would be straightforward. We arrived in a bus outside an old multi-level, dormitory-style building, and the team manager got off the bus to inspect the accommodation, only to return with a very furrowed brow. I guessed what the problem was and asked, 'Bob, are there no lifts in there?' He replied that there weren't. 'And we're not on the ground floor, are we?' I asked, to which he again said no.

Our means of vertical transport to and from the first level of the building was to be the German Army, whose job it was to stand by the stairs for the entire competition and carry athletes up and down, as required. After serious consideration, and an investigation of alternative accommodation which was found to be even more limited, we grudgingly acquiesced to our host's accommodation plans. So for every trip up and down the two flights of narrow wooden stairs over the week, four army privates would lift each of us in our chairs, holding onto whatever was available, and transport us. Each time we had the constant fear of being dropped. It certainly did not encourage a quick trip upstairs for little things such as cleaning teeth after meals. Any trip, anywhere, had to have real worth, since once you were downstairs you stayed down, and once you were upstairs you stayed up. Any pretence at independence had to be shelved for the duration of the stay. But the final indignity came on the last night at the completion of the tournament. The team had gone out for a few drinks and returned in dribs and drabs to our barracks at a late-ish hour, only to find that the human lifts had knocked off and gone home. Each team member was reduced to crawling up the stairs, with wheelchair in tow. After the week's experience, a sense of mad farce had long pervaded the situation; this just topped it off. And that was only the pre-tournament.

After bussing it the six hours from Dillingen to Brugge, we arrived to find that the doors to our rooms at the hotel were too narrow for wheelchairs, so we moved again. In the three days remaining before the Gold Cup, we trained, however I nearly didn't make it to the first game. For some reason, despite years of training with few previous problems, my hands blistered badly, to the extent that two days before the tournament I had a total of sixteen blisters, even in my palms. And it only hurt when I pushed my chair or caught the ball! Luckily, after a couple of days' rest I was ready to go for the first match.

The tournament was a success, and a great step forward for the Australian team. We finished fifth, beating reasonable teams such as Italy and Japan, and were on the verge of the top echelon of teams—Germany, America and France. But to get this far, I had had to fear for my life in a match against the USA.

Before the game, the coach had asked me to guard and

annoy one of their players, Tree Waller. Tree is approximately 210 centimetres tall, black, and has the huge disability of missing a few toes. He has been known to leap out of his chair after a game, and slam dunk the ball to celebrate. Considering that I was a 2.0 pointer and Tree was a 4.5 pointer, I was less than enamoured with the task. When I fell out of my chair I would have to get back up, whereas Tree would simply chase after his on his feet. Yet the coach had realised he had an ex-footballer in his midst, and was not going to miss an opportunity to maximise his team's unique talents.

Sure enough, five minutes into the game things were developing nicely. Tree had scored a number of points, and grabbed rebound after rebound, but yes, I was annoying him. I had knocked him out of his wheelchair a few times and watched him run after it and remount. I had at one stage, despite locking my wheels, been bulldozed backwards into the US key (a designated area close to the basket which offensive players are only allowed into for a three-second period). All this while being screamed at by the coach to 'Keep him out of the key'. With two minutes remaining in the first half, I elbowed him in the ribs, causing him again to 'fall' out of his chair. He had walked over to it, and wheeled it like a shopping trolley, back towards me. With sweat dripping off his harried brow he bent over and when his face was just above mine he said: 'Brother, you got a problem?' As this incident occurred directly in front of the Australian bench, the seven substitutes had all taken one roll back, but they all wanted to play, so I could not back down. I simply told Tree to go forth and multiply, or words to that effect. The rest of the US team who caught the conversation laughed, whilst I'm sure the Australian bench thought me a brave but stupid man. What I would like to have said was more conciliatory, however at the end of the match I found out that I had actually earned Tree's respect. At the final siren Tree got out of his wheelchair, walked over to me and wrapped me in the biggest bear hug I have ever been unfortunate enough to experience. It was like a rainforest—very hot and wet with lots of undergrowth. Yet the hug was the reward for standing up (so to speak) for myself.

Aside from this near-death experience the tournament had one other momentous occurrence, after the completion of all the matches. Immediately after our loss to the German team in the play-off for fifth and sixth, I was notified that, due to my function on court, I had been reclassified. To a 2.5 pointer! This meant that I had played with an apparent balance and function beyond that of my initial classification. The implications were clear: with the higher rating, I took up more of the team's total points; in short, it meant I had to be a better player to justify my court time. I was not happy, but I had already grasped through my brief time at international level that I was encroaching more and more on the territory of this higher classification as the understanding of my balance improved along with my wheelchair skills. Unfortunately many players have felt over the years that the harder they work the more likelihood there is of being penalised. Regardless of this sentiment, I had to improve.

I must have done enough, as I was selected in the Australian team for the Barcelona Paralympics. Due to the lack of international competition and also the lack of funding, the Australian team had not travelled at all in 1991. So in preparation for the 1992 Paralympics we went to a tournament in Lexington, Kentucky early in the year. The most memorable aspect of this tour came prior to departure. I arrived at Tullamarine Airport, with Lisa and a couple of mates to see me off, and went to check in. The middle-aged lady at the check-in counter methodically tagged my bags and wheelchairs, issued a boarding pass, and checked my passport. Then she walked around to me at the front of her counter, handed me my ticket and passport with one hand, and with the other hand patted me on the head, saying, 'There you go.' I didn't react; you never do in such situations, because the shock does tend somewhat to disarm you. However, my friends did, virtually falling to the floor in fits of laughter. After recovering my composure I chose to laugh it off too; if I took such things too seriously, it would no doubt have adverse effects on my blood pressure. I could only assume it was normal customer protocol, or that their staff training needed a review.

The Blue Grass Championships in Lexington brought with it a unique challenge to the Australian team, since the tournament featured the US classification system of 17.5 points rather than the international system's 14 points. Our opposition were the best US National Wheelchair Basketball League teams competing at the tournament, along with Australia and France as two invitational teams. With the team using the tournament as a lead in to Barcelona, our coaching staff chose to play to international points, despite conceding 3.5 points to all our opposition, bar the French team. But this had obvious consequences: it was a little like playing one player short, because the physical capability of the 17.5-point teams was significantly superior. In one match, however, in an effort to get a win the coach had resorted to putting the five players with the least disability on court; the combination of players was within the 17.5 ceiling. If nothing else it was good in the other games for 1.0 pointers to practise playing like 2.0 pointers, and 2.0 pointers to play like 3.0 pointers, and so on.

But with the tournament over, the major consequence of the points discrepancy was a lack of clarity as to how much we had improved from Brugge, if in fact we had at all. Regardless, we felt as if we were on an upward spiral and we prepared for the Paralympics with much optimism. All would be revealed in Barcelona.

As I waited in the departure lounge at Tullamarine Airport with other members of the team, the captain of the British Airways jumbo walked through and spontaneously invited me and another player to sit up the front with him on the Melbourne to Sydney leg of the trip. Neither of us hesitated, despite the flight of stairs up to the cockpit and upper deck.

Bumming it up the stairs, we entered the cabin and sat immediately behind the captain and co-pilot during their preparation and flight to Sydney. On final approach to Sydney, as the captain banked the plane above the water, he was to say, 'Ready for bombing run on Sydney.' It was a once in a lifetime experience. However, if I had known the outcome of the Barcelona Paralympics, I may have asked him to turn the bus round and take me back to Melbourne!

Barcelona was to be a great Paralympics because of the quality of the village and its accompanying amusements, all adjacent to a beachfront. Ten-pin bowling alleys, movie theatres, an art gallery, a music area, and an electronic games area were a few of the activities provided for the athletes. But it did not help our performance. The team played appallingly, and the coach did not exactly have a career tournament, to say the least. We lost again to the Germans in the first pool match, beat Egypt, and then basically fell apart, losing match after match, some close and some not, to France, Spain and the Netherlands to name but three. We eventually finished eighth after losing a close match to the USA in a quarter final; we had done everything in that game but won it, and were eventually beaten by the depth and quality of their bench players.

The positive to come from the smoking debris was that the team was starting to find young talent with a hard edge. Foremost amongst this new blood was the sixteen-year-old Troy Sachs. Troy, a 4.5-point player who had been born without a foot, had played extensive able-bodied sport (with a prosthesis) and brought a rare vitality and litheness to the game. Dubbed by the team with the nickname 'Puppy', he was seen to have the size and potential to grow into a 'Dog' in four years' time, developing a hardness that was to be crucial in Atlanta.

As for me, my tournament had been solid especially later in the week, with one particular incident standing out. In Brugge at the Gold Cup (the World Championships) in 1990, France had won the tournament thanks largely to their star, Michel

Gradelle, an emotional and fiery guard whose skills included a sweet shot and great speed. After their victory I had told our coach of his volatility, and how I thought he could be upset. Obviously I had not been alone in my observation: in the pre-tournament in Kentucky the USA, in a rematch of the Gold Cup final in Brugge, had wound Michel up until he fouled out of the game. In our game against France, his weakness was still on my mind. The game unfolded with France streaking to a seventeen-point lead at half time, in front of a capacity Spanish crowd, along with a pocket of five hundred flag-waving loud French supporters. Australia began a long comeback in the second half, which culminated with us being four points down with four minutes to go. An Australian player, Stewie, was called for an intentional foul; in response he threw the ball into the face of an adjacent French player, and the referees in turn threw him out of the game. At this moment, Michel was sitting immediately next to me, and looked as if he was about to explode. With the referees still busy ejecting Stewie, I spontaneously turned and grabbed Michel's lip, giving it a quick squeeze and then letting go. Then he did explode, swinging a round-arm punch at me, as I ducked. At the moment the punch was thrown, the referees turned back, and promptly ejected Michel as well. All the French players had seen what had happened and were ropeable.

We eventually lost by a few points. Immediately after the match, Al and Rosie, who had been in the stands and knew me rather well, asked a couple of questions. 'What dirty disgusting thing did you do to that poor French boy?' said Rosie. Al joined in with: 'I saw your hand go out, I just want to know what you grabbed.' As for poor Michel, he was suspended for one match, along with Stewie. At elite sport, only the hard and smart survive.

A month or two after the conclusion of the Paralympics, it became known that the captain of the USA team, David Kiley, had tested positive to a banned substance. Kiley had taken a tablet during the tournament due to phantom pain from his spinal injury, unaware that the drug was on the list of banned medications. After many appeals, the USA was stripped of their medal, and Australia was promoted to seventh. This appeared to be an innocent error, but it certainly enhanced athletes' precautions when taking prescriptions. To me, however, Barcelona had finished the day I left the village. The USA's disqualification in no way altered our lack of performance.

With the end of my commitments to the team in Barcelona, I left the village early one morning with Justine, my friend from the Austin, who at the time was travelling around Europe, and watched some of the Games. After catching a train from Barcelona to Toulouse in France, we hired a car, at which time Justine was less than thrilled to learn that I had not been able to fit my hand controls in my luggage. So she drove and I navigated, albeit badly. At one point, she asked me if the street we were in was one way. I had a look and informed her that it was, and that we were only going one way—the wrong way! We survived, and made it to Paris, where a visit to Euro Disney helped me to discover my true worth.

At Euro Disney a person in a wheelchair enters the rides through the exit paths. This means that, rather than standing in the queues for an hour or more, the wheelchair user and companions go straight to the front of the line! Then, after the ride, they are often asked whether or not they would like another go, while everyone else stands in the infinite line. At the first exit that we began to enter, an attendant asked me whether or not I could walk. Being a little surprised, I simply said no, upon which he said that I couldn't go on the ride, in case it broke down. I then intimated I could walk a little bit, and so with passage granted, on I went, along with Justine who had had three knee reconstructions, and certainly was not going to be able to carry me out of any predicament that we found ourselves in. As the day progressed, each time I was asked if I could walk by the exit attendants, my tendency to magnify my true mobility increased; by the end of the day, my disability only played up when I walked long distances! We in fact went on every ride imaginable in just one day. On leaving I remarked to a well-pleased Justine that I could rent myself out for a fee to frazzled families as the best guide to see all of Euro Disney!

But Paris did pose one novel problem for the wheelchair-using traveller. Paris is the home of the poodle, and of the poodle's many many brothers and sisters. The vast majority live in apartments, and when taken for walkies the poodles do what dogs do when walking. With dogs not allowed in the city's parks, the footpaths are like minefields to the wheelchair user. Walkers (infantry) can step over and around deposits, but wheelies (tanks) sometimes made tragic errors of judgement and simply plough through. When this did occur I would suddenly find myself friendless.

Due to our poor finish at Barcelona, the Australian team had to qualify for the World Championships, which were to be held in Edmonton in Canada. At a training camp in preparation for Edmonton it was mooted that the qualifier was to be held in Egypt, which was less than enthusiastically received. However, the venue was changed, from Egypt to Iran!

Iran was an experience not to forget. After arriving in Tehran, we were taken to our hotel under police guard. In the hotel foyer the words 'Down with USA' were emblazoned in permanent lettering across the entire length of one wall. Any T-shirts and the like with American logos or symbols quickly went to the bottom of one's suitcase. As hotels go, our accommodation was reasonable, but I didn't really feel at home—despite some of the television having an Australian theme. *Skippy the Bush Kangaroo* just isn't the same with everyone suddenly speaking in Iranian. No wonder Skippy looked so confused whenever he went 'Tch, tch, tch'!

Since independent touring around the city was not possible, we were limited to the occasional supervised shopping visit, and two visits to the Australian Consul. Shopping was an interesting experience; one particular moment when my taste must have abandoned me, I bought a suit and shirt. Later I was to realise there was a good reason for the items being so cheap. The visit to the Consul provided us with our haven of normality; despite the country's sanctions against alcohol and the like, the Consul's grounds were like a spring in a desert. At the end of one evening the entire consular staff were in wheelchairs, with a number of the team being even less able to walk than normal.

For me, though, the basketball part of the trip nearly finished before it began. The coach had organised us to push a number of times around a large hilly circuit near the hotel. With everyone in their day chairs, since our basketball chairs were yet to arrive, we set off in a tight pack, monoing quickly down a hill. Midway down the steep hill, when we were still tightly bunched and we had a bluestone wall on our right, one of my axle housings snapped, jerking my chair suddenly to the right. The pack of swiftly moving wheelchairs scattered, avoiding a massive pile-up, with me just managing to stay upright in my damaged vehicle. I was fortunate enough to complete my laps in a borrowed chair.

The tournament was made up of the home nation, Japan, several other weaker teams, and us. After losing to Japan, and defeating all the other teams, we arrived at the last match against Iran, essentially in a play-off for the second qualifying position for the World Championships. In front of a hugely noisy, trumpet-blowing home crowd jammed into an outdated stadium, we played. After a little while we had gained the upper hand, however our march to victory was slowed by full bags of peanuts being thrown onto the court—or, more specifically, at us. Never in my entire career have I seen a team as keen to sit on an aeroplane for a day or more as we were at the end of that tournament. At the Tehran airport our team manager was heard to say that he would come back again if we had to qualify for another tournament. Only to be met with a chorus of 'With another team'!

After Iran, Edmonton was like heaven. The team arrived confident of resuming their climb up the world rankings after the aberration of Barcelona.

Despite suffering a heavy loss to the USA early in the tournament, we confidently disposed of a number of teams in the pool round, including Germany, Brazil and Spain, and so found ourselves in a quarter-final match against Great Britain. The team led for thirty-seven of the forty minutes, yet these were all at the wrong end of the game. I had taken a shot when the scores were level with just two minutes to go, and the ball seemed to stick onto the end of my fingers, dragging the shot significantly short. I was not alone; the tension got to all of us and the buzzer sounded with the team four points in arrears. Shattered, we limped off the court. In our rooms after the game, players cried or simply sat in silence for an hour or more, or so it seemed.

The Great Britain team would play sixty or seventy international matches a year, whilst Australia would play ten to fifteen. It was our lack of international experience which let us down. The team most used to the heat, so to speak, would stay in the oven the longest. And that wasn't Australia. The positive side was that Great Britain had gone on to win their semi final, only to lose to the USA in the final, thus winning silver. This was a confirmation of how close our team was getting to the top rungs of the ladder. And young, up and coming individual players were reaching a genuine international standard. Troy Sachs (4.5) had taken great steps in the development of his game in the international arena, and the tournament also saw the impressive debut of new boy Nick Morris (1.0). Nick brought to the team not only the athletic traits remaining from his days as a promising footballer and cricketer, but also a gregarious nature and real determination after narrowly missing out on selection for the Barcelona Games. Ingrained from his youth as a winner, he showed scope to play beyond his 1.0-point classification, making him potentially invaluable.

Yet despite this growth, the negatives could not be ignored. We were sixth, and though we had given a far better performance, we did not reap any benefits from this in the world rankings. You can only have potential for so long; for it to mean anything, sooner or later the potential must turn into reality.

THE GOLD MEDAL JOURNEY

Following the devastation of Edmonton, a new coach was appointed. It was felt by many, although not all, that the previous coach had taken the team as far as he could, having been at the helm since 1989. He had led us to fifth, seventh and sixth, and there was a sense that we were marking time, and not progressing as we could. The position of coach had been readvertised and after a confused and drawn-out appointment process, Mark Walker was given the job.

Walker had coached the Victorian state team from 1993 to 1996. He was a career basketball coach, with broad experience gained in many settings. Intense to the extreme, and not generally a player's coach, Walker soon showed great abilities to read the game and make astute decisions under pressure. And like any new coach, he came to the team with his own agenda.

At our first training camp after his appointment, on the Queen's Birthday weekend of 1995, Coach Walker addressed the squad of thirty assembled basketballers about his vision: we could win gold medals, by gaining an edge in all facets of our game. Within that he included clear definition of roles within the team, individual fitness, and high performance in simple skill areas such as foul shooting (free throws) and lay-ups (easy shots from within the key), because it was these areas that had let us down in the past.

Having set the tone, he got down to business, and over the next eighteen months he put the team through the most rigorous preparation it had ever seen. At training camp after training camp—which now appeared on the calendar every month or so, slotted in between National League commitments—there was an intense focus on lay-ups, practised in a diverse range of drills, and continuous pressure foul-shooting drills. And whenever simple lay-ups were missed, or insufficient scores were returned from foul-shooting competitions, the entire team paid through numerous penalty sprints the length of the court. Coach Walker often appeared arrogant and aloof to many of the players, being unwilling or unable to build individual bridges with some. He didn't care; he saw winning as the only thing that mattered, and chose not to worry about small irrelevancies such as whether he was liked or not. He never lost sight of the big picture.

The time came for the team to go to Yamagata, Japan, for the qualifying tournament for the Paralympic Games. At the camp preceding the tournament, Coach Walker appointed David Gould (4.5) and myself as co-captains of the team. Gouldy and I had been great mates off court and best of enemies on, for many years. David had represented South Australia in junior able-bodied basketball prior to a shooting accident in his teens, and so he had a great base to launch what had become a superb wheelchair basketball career for South Australia and Australia. With my competitive streak mirroring his, we had had many explosive battles over the years, with perhaps the highlight being during a National League game in Adelaide. Having fallen out of his chair whilst still holding the ball, David was lying on his back on the court with the ball firmly in his grasp above his head. I attempted to take the ball from him, to pass it to the referee and restart the game. David refused to relinquish the ball, so I grasped a fair amount of his underarm hair and pulled—hard—unbeknown to the referee. Yelping, he released the ball, and so with a handful of hair I presented the ball to the referee and the game recommenced. As I headed down court, I sprinkled the hair onto the seething Adelaide bench. But with him having had his victories over me, most importantly we liked and respected one another.

However, in the weeks leading up to the tournament I had been close to withdrawing from the team due to severe tennis elbow. In the last week, I reasoned that although I was not fully fit, the team was missing a number of senior players, so I had better just grin and bear it. So with new tennis-elbow straps, I packed my bags.

Troy Sachs was unavailable since he was studying in the USA, Troy Andrews missed selection and Stuart Ewin had yet to be coaxed out of retirement. So three players who ultimately missed selection or were to be unavailable for Atlanta were in the Yamagata team. Brook Quinn (3.5), a small up and coming forward from Victoria, Daryl Taylor (1.5), a shooting guard from South Australia, and Michael Callahan (3.0), a veteran and a player's player, were all off to Japan.

Yamagata is a regional city, some six hours out in the country. On arrival in Japan, the team learned that we were to make the remainder of the trip by bus, as a sightseeing opportunity organised for us by the hosts. After seeing the sights through the inside of my eyelids, we arrived at the hotel in Yamagata, and quickly gained an understanding of the space restraints that Japan is reputed for.

Whilst the hotel itself was of an excellent standard, the

accessibility of the rooms was not. Despite having an easily reached single bed, each room had a bathroom up a 20-centimetre step, with a door far too narrow for a wheelchair and non-existent circulation space inside. With no alternative, each player used the sanitary facilities by bumming it up the step and around the bathroom itself.

The day after our arrival, a welcoming function for the visiting teams was held in a nearby hotel, which housed some of the other teams. Having lost a toss of the coin with David, I went onto the stage to introduce the members of our delegation, accompanied by an interpreter. Having used interpreters during my time working at the Austin, I understood the protocol. However, when I stopped speaking, he didn't start. In fact the interpreter spoke very good Japanese but very little English. This limited the effectiveness of our duo. I did manage to mention how much the team had enjoyed the six-hour sightseeing tour, because I felt sure that my interpreter would make his own translation of whatever I said anyway!

The tournament unfolded somewhat similarly to the qualifying tournament in Iran, in that the five teams present had diverse skill levels, with Korea being the only team that approached the standard of Japan and Australia. After a number of easy wins we came up against Korea, whose game was run through the skills of a small but clever left-handed point guard. Coach Walker instructed me to: 'Ruin his life'. I was told to guard him everywhere he went. And I think that meant even if he went to the toilet. I spent the match harassing the guard, who eventually lost interest in the game and started having friendly staring matches with me. Meanwhile we ran away to a comfortable victory.

Due to the order of the draw we played Japan in the last match of the tournament, and despite never having beaten Japan in Japan, we went into the match with quite some confidence. In front of a patriotic Japanese crowd, with our only support being a small group of young female students who had befriended the team, we eked out a narrow three-point victory. Without Troy, Richard Oliver and Michael Callaghan, the two 3-point veterans of the team, played key roles, whilst David Gould (4.5) had a superb game, taking control of the match in the second half.

This victory meant we were off to Atlanta and the team as a whole was on a high. That evening, a team mate who had been abstaining from alcohol in the long lead-up to the tournament was given a bottle of Japanese scotch at the closing dinner. He was last seen in his room, in a bath, mumbling something akin to 'Don't let me die'. And that, I suppose, is why athletes don't drink.

But all was not well in Australia. Al had been diagnosed with prostate cancer and, while undergoing further scans for the cancer, had had another unwanted discovery. The additional tests had disclosed a potentially dangerous aortic aneurism. With this new prognosis, the priority of the prostate cancer was downgraded, and the urgent need for surgical intervention with regard to the aneurism took precedence. I learnt of not one, but both health issues whilst a long way away. I flew home as soon as the tournament concluded, before the remainder of the team. I managed to secure a regional flight from Yamagata to the international terminal and so missed out on my second opportunity to sightsee on the six-hour bus trip. Pity that.

As 1995 drew to a close, during the National Basketball Championships held in Melbourne in late November, Al had a successful aneurism operation, and Victoria capped off a great week by winning the national title. With my week filled with regular trips to Geelong Hospital to keep an eye on Al and to support Rosie, in between games it was a more than busy time. Six weeks later, to the disbelief of hospital staff, the tough old bugger backed up and put himself back on the operating table for an operation relating to his cancer. After an extended recovery, he was back to his old self by the close of 1996.

In 1996, my first major international commitment was a trip

to Europe to play a number of Paralympic contenders and get some quality match practice. Having triumphed in Yamagata, we went with high spirits, despite the long trip ahead, first to Spain and then on to Great Britain.

The day after arriving in Madrid, we were due to play the Spanish national team. With weary minds and bodies we stepped up to the line. For the first half of the match, things proceeded reasonably. However, we fell away in the latter stages of the game and we were soundly beaten. When this scenario was repeated the next day, tails dropped and rumblings began. We packed up our bags and ball and departed for Great Britain the next day, hoping for a change in fortune.

It didn't happen. On arrival in Great Britain things got worse. Transported from Heathrow Airport to Stoke Mandeville, we were accommodated in one large dormitory within the grounds of the old rehabilitation hospital. With this building having been constructed in the forties and fifties, it was not what you would call salubrious. The crowded living quarters, the hospital-style food, and the standard grey English sky, on top of the removal from any type of normal community was significantly depressing and destructive. In a way it was like going back to hospital.

In an effort to create some privacy, four members of the team instigated a breakaway from the first dormitory, setting up camp in an adjoining one. With the dormitories having separating walls which did not reach the ceiling, war quickly broke out over the dividing barrier. Initially apples and light ammunition were used. As days passed, and frustration rose, eventually whole mattresses were sent over the wall to the enemy. With the main dormitory having numbered lockers next to the beds, I snuck into the enemy's dormitory and rearranged their lockers. Anyone who was not paying attention, and in particular Evan Bennett, the elder statesman assistant coach, had significant problems opening what he thought was his locker with his allocated key. This did not help to establish a ceasefire.

Over the next few days we played Sweden, only to lose by

a couple of points, and the Netherlands twice. Despite being within touch and in fact leading at half time, we were humiliated come the end of the games. The host nation didn't do us any favours. Despite being eight points down at half time, they ran over the top of us to record a sound victory. The final humbling experience occurred in a game against a club side where a British national player took us to task. Joey Jayaratne could not miss, and it was only in the final minutes that we secured a hollow victory.

The team was not having a good time. When the chips are down, simmering tensions are exposed. Bickering between players rose as the week went on. For me, as co-captain, I found that I spent much of my time trying to broker peace and glue things together. On court, whilst playing reasonably but not at my peak, the final humiliation was to be when I was shirt-fronted. With my head down, chasing a speedy player flat out down court, an opponent who I can only imagine was a tough Welsh miner in a previous life, set an illegal screen and landed me in the score bench. A legal sceen in wheelchair basketball is a stationary block using the wheelchair (or the body in upright basketball) to free up team mates from opposition players. This was something else. Coming from my blind side, he hit me whilst anything but stationary, and the resultant impact was akin to being run over by an English double-decker bus. At least in this match we were in control at the time of the incident. However, I was hit so hard I couldn't even find the perpetrator.

Come the completion of the week the successes of Yamagata were long gone, and it was as a chastened group that we boarded the flight home. The road back seemed oh so long. Only five days after arriving in Australia after a thirty-hour flight, Coach Walker called a training camp in Adelaide, much to the players' chagrin. And so still weary from the flight home, players fronted up in Adelaide to address our weaknesses, particularly half-court offence and zone defence. In regard to offence, the team was very good when in quick transition out of defence; however, when the opposition managed to slow the game down and set their defence, making us play a structured offence and create a quality shot, we struggled. In contrast the European teams had very good structured half-court offences that exposed weaknesses in our zone defence. And it was on these aspects that we focused. During the camp it also became clear that we were not the only ones unimpressed with the tour. Over the weekend, Coach Walker met with a member of the Australian Paralympic Federation (APF) who expressed his concerns at the team's performance in Europe, intimating that he had doubts about the coach's future. Yet the team in the main continued to train in ignorance of the behind-the-scenes rumblings. Come Sunday evening, our spirits had lifted. The wheels were back on, albeit loosely.

Two training camps followed where further steps were taken. The final camp was held at the Australian Institute of Sport, with the feature being the attendance of Patrick Farrell, a sport psychologist from the Victorian Institute of Sport. One afternoon Patrick called a meeting to set team goals and to create a forum for airing grievances, or areas of concern. All team members attended, apart from Troy Sachs, who was still studying in the USA. Through much discussion, initially individually and eventually as a team, a goal structure was set for the Atlanta Paralympic Games. These goals were set out in a phased, or stepped, format which basically featured winning our first game and then making the top four in our pool, and so on. It was less daunting to look at it in stages rather than looking at the whole task.

With team unity back at its normal level, we left Canberra and waited impatiently for the pre-tournament in Canada, and for the first games of the Paralympics. We felt we could do no more.

At departure time, every trip overseas is seen as 'the one'. The flight bound for Canada, from where we'd go on to the

1996 Paralympics, was no different. On arriving at the airport I was confronted by the usual assortment of players, spouses and friends. But what was unusual was that I was in the wrong uniform. There had been two uniforms issued, one with stars and one without, and everyone had gone with being a star. I hadn't. Nothing like leading by example. After a quick search of my baggage I decided that either it was on my bed in Deepdene or was right at the bottom of my bag, under much other gear. No time for any changes now.

The Melbourne team members, me included, passed through passport control and on to wait in the departure lounge—which I have always found to be a place of thoughtful boredom. My thoughts then were: 'Is it all worth it?' and 'How sore will my backside be on arrival?' This thinking time is always interrupted just prior to our boarding as I make my last visit to an accessible toilet, since toilets on planes are not. I am still amazed when people talk of their love of flying. I envy them. Sitting in the same crowded spot with strangers and repetitious food is not my idea of a good time. How do they do it?

The LAX flight was called, and since we board first and get off last, we get to enjoy extra plane time. The flight was relatively uneventful apart from Nick slowing up a little. I was seated in the middle row with Stewie and Nick and Coach Mark when, after four or five hours, Nick became aware that I was the proud owner of what he was to dub 'the dispensary'. Sleeping pills. After much pleading, Nick conned me into assisting his sleep pattern with three pills. It was like tranquillising a large bull. There was significant slowing of language, movement and attention, until finally he virtually passed out during dinner. Suffice it to say there were no more problems from Nick for a few hours. Coach Walker also visited the dispensary, while Stewie refrained. His abstinence, however, was not to last for long.

Arrival at Los Angeles was greeted with much relief. Canada was getting closer, and slowly the team was aisle-chaired off the plane in dribs and drabs. We made our way through the airport to collect our luggage and move it to the right area since we were changing airlines. All seemed well, and I was pleased to see my basketball wheelchair amongst all the other chairs on my way to the Air Canada departure lounge. Loaded onto the smaller plane with no great fuss, the onward flight passed with no hitches. On arrival in Toronto, some thirty hours after leaving Melbourne, accommodation of any description looked very appealing; but first the baggage and equipment had to be accounted for. Quickly, all bags and chairs were collected; except for my basketball chair, which was nowhere to be seen! I reported the loss to baggage claims, but no-one at the airport seemed particularly interested. So we left the airport, hopeful that my chair would turn up tomorrow.

The following evening, I headed back to the airport accompanied by one of the team's staff. Graeme had been with the team since the early eighties and was the expert in such matters. He filled the role of wheelchair mechanic, acted as an occasional masseur and general assistant, and was part of the heartbeat of the team. We felt sure that my chair would be with the Australian women's wheelchair team, who were also arriving for a training camp. After much time spent at the lost baggage counter, we were both disappointed. The following three days saw Graeme repeating his fruitless visits to the airport, and eventually pulling out what was left of his hair. I did the same.

The team's frustration level was rising, and I remained very, very fresh, as I could not participate in training. Finally we received a call from the Australian wheelchair rugby team in camp at Birmingham, Alabama who had somehow ended up with my chair. It had been misdirected by a whole country and, despite the efforts of the Australians in Birmingham to get it on a flight for a reunion with me, had sat at the wrong airport for two days, enjoying a sojourn down south. When it did arrive, Graeme came up to me carrying the wheels, saying that now only the frame was missing! Good joke, mate.

The Gold Medal Journey

Travelling with a wheelchair basketball team brings with it a whole range of inherent challenges, and makes different demands of everyone involved, including the coach. During our stay in Toronto we hired three vehicles, one of which was driven by Mark and was used to transport all of the day chairs. The other two vehicles we used for player transport. One day, after we finished a training session, the two vehicles had gone directly back to the hotel, loaded with sweaty, weary players, only to find that Mark was not there with the chairs. This meant everyone sat and waited in the vans. Meanwhile, Mark had simply forgotten the importance of his cargo and had stopped off to do some personal banking on the way back to the hotel. This caused significant angst amongst some members of the team.

By the time my basketball wheelchair arrived, the team had a remaining three days of training, with two sessions per day, before the commencement of a preliminary tournament involving two Canadian teams, Mexico and us. As the days progressed, training varied from very good to poor, as did Coach Walker's humour. He, as much as anybody, was feeling the pressure of the build-up, and was challenged by the need to nurse the veterans in the team so as to bring them to their peak for Atlanta, and not to burn them out. As co-captains, David and I discussed the situation with Mark on the way to training one day, and everything came to a head. The training session was coordinated by Gerry, Richard and myself, as Mark chose to simply sit and observe energy levels. I felt Mark needed a visit from me to clarify pertinent issues. So, borrowing a lipstick from one of the members of the women's team, I knocked on Mark's door. I went in and told him that things were not that bad. And as such he should smile, and build bridges with individual players rather than withdrawing. I used the lipstick to draw on the mirror in his room, and I said how a smiley face was better than a grumpy face. Meanwhile the team waited for Mark before going out for a couple of hours' sightseeing to

Niagra Falls. Little did they know why they were waiting. He saw the humour, accepted my direct thoughts and moved on, invigorated for the pre-tournament, which started the following day.

A few days before the tournament a players' meeting had also been held to run Troy through the goal-setting process which had been run by Patrick Farrell at our last camp in Australia. Richard and I coordinated the forum, and Troy, with significant input of his own, joined the mission. At a further team meeting days later, something happened which at the time passed with little fanfare, but in a way was to grow to inspire a base and culture of belief within the team. Gerry Hewson (1.5), one of the veterans and a key motivator, had been urging for a focusing game call to be adopted. After the failure of a number of his previous suggestions, he coined the phrase: 'What time is it? Our time!' This was unanimously adopted. It was nearly time.

After the debacle that was the practice tour of Spain and England, the importance of our success at the pre-tournament in Toronto could not be underestimated. It was to be our last chance to rebuild confidence and team spirit before Atlanta. With the Canadian national team having been split, we were a little unclear as to each team's strength, however we beat each Canadian team, and a combination of both, and Mexico, all convincingly. Since the Canadian matches had all been comfortably won, it was difficult to tell how we were actually playing, what sort of form we were really in and what our strengths and weaknesses were. Mexico was a little different, as they were an improving team.

When Australia play Mexico, I have always found that the best way to prepare is to watch the cartoon *Speedy Gonzales*. The Mexican team, like the animated mouse, go very, very fast, but often not on the shortest route, nor can I understand a lot of what's being said. They are, however, a team on the improve. Coach Walker matched me up with Raoul Ortega, an unbelievably quick guard, who like Speedy, takes the long route from basket to basket. Eventually I chased Raul down, only to come out of my chair. I landed heavily on the metal upright of his chair's back support, jamming it up under my ribcage, and collecting a foul from the referee in the process. The coach took me off, but, most importantly, as I left the game we were well and truly in control of the proceedings.

We won the tournament, which in itself meant little. But the victories sent positive vibes throughout the team, and these were to be so important in our next competitive venue. Atlanta.

Another flight, another sore backside, and so it was that we arrived at Atlanta Airport and were welcomed by members of the Paralympic Games Organising Committee. After baggage collection, and ensuring that my basketball wheelchair had not gone astray, we were all shepherded to the accreditation area. With the majority of countries descending on the one day, the process, as is the norm, was slow. Eventually every player had their photo taken, and then collected their personal accreditation card, which allowed them to enter and move within the village. Along with showbags full of questionable memorabilia, we were loaded onto a bus bound for the village.

As the team drove through the streets enroute from the airport to the Games village, the looks throughout the bus varied from the keen anticipation of the rookies such as Orf, Nick and Selbs, through to the apparently calm exterior of Gould, Oliver and Hewson. The bus arrived at the village with little fanfare; after the tensions of Seoul, security has never appeared to reach equivalent levels. We were waved in to the college campus that made up much of the village, and the anticipation rose. This was to be home for two and a bit weeks, and it's not meant to get any better than this. This is the Paralympics.

Disappointment awaited. Unloaded in the middle of the village and directed up a hill, the team straggled in search of the Australian quarters, finally finding them right at the top of the campus. Going anywhere was great, coming back would not be so easy. The team was stunned on arrival to learn that we were housed as one. Not only did we have to play together as a team, but also sleep together. All twelve players were ensconced in a single unit, comprising six tiny bedrooms, which were so small that many of the players made the beds into bunks to maximise their floor space, with the higher point players (being able to stand or walk) of course on top. I roomed with Stewie (3.0) and whenever he wanted to come in or out of the room I invariably had to move my wheelchair out of the way since I was closer to the door. Immediately after our arrival the two toilets in the unit blocked. It was far from the Ritz. After the toilets exploded, the unit became known as 'Animal House'.

In an attempt to quell the steamy Atlanta weather the House had been fitted with a state-of-the-art air conditioner, which kept its confines cool; in fact, downright freezing. The organisers had not provided any blankets for the beds, so on the first two nights in Animal House, the team froze. It took so long to get any blankets allocated, and when they arrived they were only blankets under a loose definition, thin, green and scratchy army surplus. During this Antarctic time, one member of the team had a unique 'advantage' over his mates. Orfeo Cecconato (4.0), the big Italian, above-knee double amputee was considered lucky, and the team had pleasure in telling him that at least only half of him was cold!

The food hall at any Paralympic Games Village is often an area where people congregate. In the Atlanta village this occurred for the wrong reason. In the first few days the time queuing to eat often amounted to more than an hour. Feeding enormous numbers of hungry athletes needs to be well planned, and it wasn't. It did thankfully improve after a time, but the food itself stayed at a stable and mundane level.

The major problem that the team encountered on a basketball front was the transport system. With long waits being the norm for buses to training venues, in the early days it was not uncommon for some teams to actually miss their allocated training times altogether.

But perhaps the greatest disappointment of the village was the lack of entertainment. After the wonderful experiences of Barcelona, the veterans in the team had expected at least something. There was nothing and worse, as we passed Centennial Park, which had hosted enormous entertainment and was the site of the bombing during the Olympics, we were to see that it had been all but packed up after the Olympics, and before the Paralympics.

Later we were to learn that there had not been great co-ordination between the American Committee for the Olympic Games (ACOG) and the American Paralympic Organising Committee (APOC). Consequently the funding, sponsorship linkage and Games organisation had been particularly poor.

But in reality, as management reminded the entire Australian team prior to competition and soon after arrival, all accommodation issues and the like were extraneous to the real reason for being in Atlanta, and that was to be the best we could be. With this in mind, our humour and morale was good and upbeat. I said to the rookies in a raspy voice, 'It doesn't get any better than this,' with a twinkle in my eye, and a story or two about Barcelona, just to make them drool.

With Animal House developing its own personality as the days passed, the team had grown closer; with the living confines as they were, if it hadn't, war would have broken out. One player did so much to make the House a home that he became as valuable off the court as on. Tim Maloney, with his laid-back personality, quickly became the House's chief scrounger, stocking the fridge to overflowing capacity with drinks and the like procured from vending machines with his accreditation card. He bested this performance by somehow managing to get every sort of food and implement out of the dining room, so there was always in-house nourishment available.

The House quickly developed a floor covering of deep litter

and its own particular aroma, whilst its incumbents played cards in the lounge. David Selby, the rookie 1.0 pointer, was the leading card shark, displaying his on-court trait of steely focus, hour upon hour around the table. Meanwhile others slept and bantered caustically with one another, all while waiting impatiently for the first match against Spain to arrive. When not in the House, the days after arrival were spent training and exploring the village (there was little to discover), and of course thinking; all the training, costs, injury, frustration, goal setting and sacrifice were about to come to fruition.

And fruition meant winning early matches to give us a chance of entering the medal rounds. At the Paralympics, twelve teams are divided into two pools of six, Pool A and Pool B. Each team then plays all the other teams in their pool, thus establishing a ranking system. The first four teams in each pool then cross over, playing one another, with victors of these matches moving through to semi-final matches. The quarter-final match-ups are decided with the first-ranked team in Pool A playing the fourth team in Pool B, the second team in Pool A playing the third team in Pool B, and so on. In short, what this meant was that to maximise your chances you had to perform consistently and get early wins on the board.

Before any victories could be sought, there was the small matter of the opening ceremony at the Olympic Stadium. At the previous Paralympics in Barcelona, I had chosen not to attend, due to the length of the ceremony and the heat, with an eye on being extra prepared for the tournament. My absence had done little to prevent our failure in Barcelona, so I went. Opening ceremonies, whilst often being a wonderful spectacle, are a logistical nightmare for the organisers. The number of athletes needing to be transported from the village to the ceremony venue invariably puts the already questionable transport system under pressure. With Australia being at the front of the alphabet, we always seem to have to depart the village particularly early, and wait at the site. This time was no different, with the wait being in the vicinity of three hours before we entered the stadium. Boring. So much so, that Stewie went to sleep leaning against a wall whilst still in his chair. But when the time came to enter the stadium, the wait proved to be worth it. With the roar of the 100,000 spectators, we marched down the straight and the hair on the back of my neck stood up. And I'm sure I was not alone in this feeling, because that's what it's all about, representing our country. We were grouped in lines for the spectacular show, which seemed to go on for ever. One moment though stood out. Due to his recent spinal injury, Christopher Reeve was one of the guest speakers. During his address he spoke of his dream to walk again. Upon his uttering these words, he received a chorus from the thousands of athletes before him: 'Get in line!' A very, very funny moment! Soon after, to avoid the rush and crush to get home, I and a number of team mates left early. The Games were now officially underway.

Australia versus Spain

Despite losing to Spain in both matches on our European tour, we felt confident of a win in Atlanta. We were fresh and had had a positive build-up. Everything had been directed to this game. It was our pre-determined goal.

In the rooms beforehand, Coach Walker had organised key match-ups of David Gould (4.5) to guard Diego De Paz (4.0) and myself (2.5) to be the stopper on the super-shooting veteran Antonio Henares (4.0), with Sachs (4.5), Hewson (1.5), and Morris (1.0) rounding off our starting five.

David and I had decided that he would lead the team out, and continue to do so, so long as we won. If we lost we would swap, and if we lost again we would swap back, and so on.

'What time is it? Our time!'

The match starts with both teams tentative. Spain is especially keen to do well since one of their national icons, Antonio Samaranch, the Spanish International Olympic Committee Chief, is in attendance. Scoring the first field goal for Australia I feel positive, but as the half progresses we struggle to get any offensive flow. Half time shows Australia trailing 29–33 with the team shooting poorly, and things continue to go awry until finally we are 13 down, five minutes into the second half. Then suddenly the elusive offensive rhythm is found, along with defensive intensity, and we go on a run for four minutes and level the scores. And then disaster as I pick up a cheap and stupid fourth foul, quickly followed by an unlucky fifth, fouling out of the game with eleven minutes to go. To say that I am livid with myself is an understatement. With me being the only 2.5 player Coach Walker must change his combinations, makes an error and puts too many points on court and is subsequently called for a technical foul. David and Troy then foul out over the closing minutes, with all this resulting in a 13-point blow out at the end 56–69.

The rooms are silent. Foul problems cost us again. De Paz was unstoppable for Spain, scoring 31 points, despite David having done all that was possible defensively as well as scoring 20 points at 50 per cent. No-one else had shot that well. The focus must now be to regroup; we must look to the next game against Argentina, and move on.

As we clear the changing rooms the call goes out that the photographer taking the team photo is ready. Sometimes people's timing is off, and the photographer's certainly is today. Smiles are plastered on, but the normal frivolity of team photos is lacking. He uses the age-old trick of getting the team to say 'Sex!' to raise some smiles. By all considerations, he didn't do a bad job.

The bus drive back to the village with the women's team is not cheery. It feels all too like the beginning in Barcelona.

Australia versus Argentina

Before the game I feel confident of one thing, and that is that the contest will be an absolute rough-house. It seems in all sports that a team lacking in skill often aims to compensate by bringing the level of the game down through physicality; wheelchair basketball is no exception. Coach Walker reminded us in the dressing room before the match that if we don't control our individual foul count, we take the game out of his control as far as keeping a consistent line-up on the court is concerned. We needed to have intensity in defence with hustle and intelligence. I lead the team out for what is meant to be an easy win.

And from the huddle: 'What time is it? Our time!'

The game opens with the regular starters for Australia aiming to move the ball quickly down court for easy shots. Argentina responds by fouling, fouling and belting. I'm in my element since its like being back in the old football days; obviously no-one has told the Argentines that basketball is supposed to be a non-contact sport. There seems to be a general lack of flow again, but it is hard to play against such a team. Eventually we win 70–37, having accumulated a few bruises in a game which goes for over two hours due to the huge foul count.

Prior to the game all the veterans noted that the huge, vicious-looking Juan Horez (4.5), fondly known as 'Magilla the Gorilla', was still playing for Argentina. He had been in their team the last time the two teams met, in Seoul. In that match he had grabbed Stuart Ewin's chair and thrown it backwards, laughing as Stewie, 'The Bear', was launched into orbit. He was one mean man.

In an effort to get a laugh and to raise morale in the changing room, I had tried to persuade someone to pay me something if I belted him. I had found no takers, either because they were cheap or because they feared for my safety. Nevertheless, at one stage of the game, with Magilla trapping me in a corner of the court, I wave a large elbow just past his nose, missing by millimetres. Moments later he lays flesh on flesh, removing just a little skin from my head. In the closing minutes of the match Stewie exacts revenge, coming up behind Magilla and belting him behind the ear as he is focused on rebounding. Stewie follows his particularly brave effort by turning to the bench and in his falsetto voice screaming: 'I've waited eight years for this, eight years!' upon which the whole team dissolves in laughter. The game continues with Stewie quite keen to be subbed out because he's got a very angry Magilla chasing him.

The other memorable incident occurs when a small Argentine double amputee falls out of his wheelchair in front of me with the ball the other side of him. The referee fails to blow his whistle, so I'm left with a choice: either let the ball go on to another opponent, or run the amputee over. So I run him over and get the ball—not a great moment in sport!

The true test would be in the next game against Great Britain, ranked number two in the world. This game would make or break the whole tournament.

Australia versus Great Britain

And just before the huddle broke came 'What time is it? Our time.'

We get away to a very slow start, again struggling to score in the first half. Come half time we have scratched our way to a 26–24 lead.

In the second half Great Britain open up a 10-point lead. Then things turn around. Veterans Stuart Ewin and Richard Oliver come off the bench for 7.5 minutes, and play an instrumental role in steadying and lifting the team to a stronger offensive half, in which we score 37 points. I manage to draw a lot of fouls whilst carrying the ball, getting to the foul line 16 times and shooting a reasonable 62 per cent. I finish with a total of 12 points, while Troy scores 13 and David 20.

Our nemesis on the tour to England, Joey Jayaratne, is again destructive, scoring 16 points at 66 per cent. However, the old enemy folds in the final minutes, allowing us to eke out a victory, with a final score of 63–55.

Finally, we are on a roll. If we hadn't won this match, who

knows what would have happened to the fabric of the team. Bring on the 'Canucks'.

Australia versus Canada

The dressing rooms, although tense, now have some genuine belief. With the previous day's victory against Great Britain under our belts, and the feeling that we have a reasonable understanding of the Canadian team following our time in Toronto, we go into the match confident.

With morale on the up, from within the huddle Orf screams: 'What time is it?' He is greeted with a chorus of 'Our time!' and our self-belief can be heard in our voices. Our chant is getting louder.

The match opens and continues as a defensive battle. Offensively, David and Troy struggle to get going, but are compensated for by a great point spread throughout the team. Orf and myself each score 9, Troy and Gerry 8, and Stuart 7.

In the closing 3.5 minutes, with David and Troy both fouling out, Tim Malony plays particularly solidly, making three out of four foul shots and grabbing two rebounds. The buzzer sounds and Australia wins again, with a score of 52–42. The input from the bench is invaluable: of the twelve players in the squad, ten make it onto the court in this game.

After this victory, we are guaranteed to make the quarter-final crossovers in a reasonable position, drawing a supposedly weaker opponent from the other pool.

Australia versus Mexico

Before taking on Mexico, we watch Canada play Great Britain. If Canada win we will avoid the USA in the semi-final—assuming, of course, that we get past whomever we play in the quarter-finals. Canada lose, so Great Britain, despite not having won more matches, get a preferred draw.

With that on our minds, the team starts the warm-up looking very glum and flat, as though we are going to a funeral.

Everyone knows there is nothing to be done about it, but it is still hard. Bridges, though, can only be crossed when you get to them, and Mexico could be a danger team, having run Canada, Great Britain and Spain to within a few points.

The game opens with us shooting to a 20–4 lead. Again I'm put on Raoul (4.0), and I find that he hasn't got any slower. Transition is superb, but Troy (4.5) is nursing an elbow injury, playing only ten minutes. The range of substitutions loses us momentum. However, we regroup, winning 65–47. I get on the end of a few lay-ups and finish with 22 points proving that I can score big numbers. It's funny in these games, as the opposition become so concerned about the big guys that they just let me go. I spoil what would have been a perfect 9 for 9 by missing the easiest lay-up. Orf (4.0) plays well for 20 points while Troy Andrews (1.5) seems to be running into some form. Nick (1.0) plays only 17 minutes, which is good, considering what his workload has been and will continue to be. He still thinks he is a 4.0 pointer and that's why he is so good.

Two teams, Spain and Australia, have now had only one loss. We finish second in our pool, and the Netherlands are third in theirs. So it is a case of bring on the Dutch.

Australia versus the Netherlands
This is the team that humiliated us twice at Stoke Mandeville. Despite us having stayed close for a half, they found a way to blow us out of the water in the second half of both these matches.

A quarter-final makes or breaks a team's campaign. The outcome of the game determines whether or not you are playing off for positions one to four if you win, five to eight if you lose. We had made the quarter-final crossovers in Barcelona, despite our poor performance, and at the World Championships in 1994, only to lose on both occasions. From exhilaration to devastation in forty minutes.

In the rooms before the game, we focus on Gert Van Der

Linden (4.5) (also known as 'Stumpy' since he is a double amputee) the Dutch guard, and Koen Jansens, their big free-scoring forward. They are not a two-man team, but the two are unquestionably the team's superstars, and have to be stopped if we are to win. Coach Walker's address stresses the need to transition the ball quickly into offence and to stay out of foul trouble. I lead the team out to battle.

With nervous anticipation, Orf screams: 'What time is it?' to be greeted with a chorus of 'Our time.' This time hope can be heard in each man's voice.

As the game begins, nerves and tension dominate and the scores fluctuate throughout a defensive slog for the first half. On the half-time buzzer, Stumpy throws a last-second fluky hook shot from the corner of the court immediately in front of the Dutch bench. It's all net as it goes through the hoop, eliminating the two-point lead that we had held so grimly and putting the Dutch in front by one point, 25–26. This shot had the effect of lifting the battling Dutch team and deflating us as we headed for the changing rooms.

After half time the Dutch get straight into an offensive flow, jumping to a 10-point lead. Koen Jansens has scored 14 points, but with 10.5 minutes remaining on the game clock he is on four fouls. I get the ball and drive at him in an effort to draw his final foul. He refuses to touch me as I shoot, but as the ball rebounds towards me and I catch it, I jump my chair into his. The Japanese referee, Mitsuya Satou, then makes the call of his life, blowing his whistle, awarding a pushing foul and effectively finishing Koen's game. It's a questionable call, but it is just what the team and I need. Though having a very average game, I have found a way to make my impact. With our defence giving up only 4 points in the next 11 minutes, our offence takes over. With 30 seconds remaining, the scores are level. Bringing the ball down the floor, we run a long offence which culminates in David making a great pass inside to Troy for a lay-up. Eight seconds remain on the clock. Again Stumpy grabs the ball and, in an effort to repeat his hook-shot prayer of the first half, he launches it from half court. It misses and the buzzer sounds, leaving us with the narrowest of victories, 46–44. And with that, pandemonium breaks out.

Players hug and fall from their chairs. Coach Walker dances: we are now top four, a position that we have never been in before. And tomorrow we face the might of America. Bring 'em on!

Australia versus USA

Massaged, taped, stretched and pumped. It was time. Coach Walker's address tells us not to be intimidated by the 'Dream Team' tag. US coach Brad Hendricks had identified Spain, Canada, Holland, Sweden, Great Britain and France as his team's threats for the gold medal. What about us?

As we file out of the changing rooms and pass the opposition's rooms, I hear one thing, and that is the USA team saying it was their gold medal! It is like being told that we are not even a consideration, that we're not respected. This is like a red rag to a bull. As we sit just off court and wait for the Spain–Great Britain semi final to finish, we stew. The USA have given us one last lift by insulting Australia again.

The time comes to enter the court, with Great Britain having vanquished a now devastated Spain. The crowd is large and loud, and of course local. We are in the lion's den, playing the 'Dream Team on Wheels' at their national game at their home Paralympics. I lead the team out, still at the front, and David quips that he hopes I'm at the front next time we play. Me too, because that would mean that Australia was playing for gold.

Introductions and anthems pass in a blur, as the moment approaches for the underdogs from downunder.

The game starting fives are announced. The USA go with twin towers, Reggie Colton (3.0) and the infamous Tree (4.5), along with supreme shooter Trooper Johnson (2.5), Mark Shepherd (2.0) and Mike Schlappi (1.5). Walker goes with his regular starters, Sachs (4.5), Gould (4.5), Blythe (2.5), Hewson (1.5) and Morris (1.0). Key match-ups have Troy on Tree, and although outreached he has the better chair skills; David has Reggie, the biggest double amputee in the world; and I have Trooper, and have to stop him shooting the lights out, yet score myself.

In our final huddle Coach Walker talks of defence and belief. With the crowd in our face, their favourites at the ready, and our backs to the wall, Orf screams: 'What time is it?' There follows a defiant heartfelt chorus: 'Our time!'

The referee holds the ball aloft, with Sachs and Tree lining up for the tap. Tree wins it and so the US head into offence, but miss their first shot. Troy does the same, only for me to get the rebound and hand it off to David who also misses. Everyone is as tight as a drum.

Eventually, after a minute-and-a-half, Colton opens the US account, from a hook-pass assist from Schlappi. This is quickly followed by a basket from Tree from the foul line. 4–0. Troy fakes Colton, and with a great spin move puts us on the scoreboard through a driving lay-up; only for Schlappi to get free on an open lay-up. Gerry chases him down, fouling him heavily to the floor and preventing the basket. He goes to the line and hits one from two. He is earning his keep, and the next time he heads down the floor, Nick puts him on it again! Troy rebounds a US miss, and goes coast to coast, helped by a great block from Nick. Moments later, I throw a full-court pass to David for a lay-up and we are in front, but it is only early days. Gerry has picked up early fouls, so Doggy the ultimate team man and defensive specialist comes into the game. A couple of baskets by Troy, one from my assist, and with 14 minutes to go it's 8–6 to us. It continues, basket for basket, until Randy Snow substitutes into the game for Shepherd. Snow (2.0) explodes, scoring 8 points on 100 per cent in 5 minutes; his deadly accuracy is difficult to counter due to his clever use of screens. He takes the US to a 10-point lead. I score, but Trooper scores twice. Then I score again. 26–18.

Troy has a purple patch, being fouled on a lay-up which goes in, and then hitting two consecutive three-pointers tying the scores at 27-all. In desperation, being outreached for a loose ball, Troy is called for a technical foul for lifting out of his chair. It's his third foul of the game, so Coach Walker sits him on the bench and sends on Orf. A long miss from David becomes good when a tap back by Doggy is slammed in off the backboard by Orf. Half time sees us one point down 30–29, after a lay-up and a foul shot from the US in the dying seconds of the half.

Troy, with a huge 17 points and 10 rebounds, seems to be causing the US problems with his size, quickness and aggression. David has been a little quiet, but knowing him, he will find something. Gerry is in foul trouble, whilst Doggy has been solid, Nick hard at it, and Orf giving a solid few minutes. Defensively, I have controlled Trooper, but I need to find some more points. I only have 4, as does he.

We head to the rooms where Coach Walker exhorts us to lift our defence. He believes we can score against the US. The key defensive adjustment is not to slide in under screens, but to fight over the top, stopping outside shooters like Snow. Everyone is pumped as the starters assemble on court for the second half.

The US go for the same starters, apart from Snow, whose shooting streak means he is in for Shepherd. The half begins with Tree again winning the tap for the US, this time receiving it back in a post-up move for an easy two points. David replies with a basket for us, only for his man Colton to outreach him for an immediate answer. Again each team trades baskets until Troy and big Colton have a coming together over a loose ball at the 16-minute mark. With animal aggression, Troy rips the ball free as the referee blows his whistle, upsetting a couple of US players. The US goes cold, missing a string of shots. With a succession of baskets—including one from myself, three from the lifting David, and culminating in a behind-the-head pass by David to Troy, waiting under the basket—we see the score advance in our favour to 49–42 at the 6.11 minute mark. In desperation, Coach Hendrick calls a time-out to talk it over with his players, and to change his line-up. The heat in the kitchen is going up. Australia basically holds a 3 to 6 point lead, but the US refuses to go away until they make their last run. My man Trooper, scoreless so far in the second half, hits a three-pointer from what seems like the car park, and is fouled in the act of shooting. He sinks the bonus foul shot, bringing the scoreline to an uncomfortably close 55–53 in our favour, with 3.15 minutes left. With the US over the foul limit, Troy is soon fouled again and sent to the foul line, scoring one from two. In another visit moments later he hits both baskets. The scoreline is 58–53 with 2.45 minutes on the game clock when Chuck Gill (3.5), a US substitute, scores. This is followed by an Australian turnover instigated by a mix-up between Troy and myself, and an overthrown pass from David. It gets hotter! A defensive breakdown sees Gill score again. With 1.25 minutes on the clock and Australia with a one-point lead, I find myself on the foul line. With ball in hand, weight on my shoulders, exhausted and feeling ill with fear due to the moment of my life being before me, I know that I will score. Or so I tell myself. The first foul shot is all net. The second rims out, only for it to fall free, allowing me to grab it from a scrimmage of players and bank it off the backboard for two points. A three-point play, putting us four points up. After a succession of desperate three-point attempts by Trooper and others, the ball comes free from a long defensive rebound and as I drive towards the basket, a desperate Tim Kazee of the US intentionally fouls me. With 20 seconds remaining I sink both foul shots, closing the game at 63–57. We play the game out and as the buzzer sounds, the place is stunned.

Chuck Gill lies on his back distraught, still strapped in his chair. Nick lies on his back too, but in disbelief. Wheelchairs again go everywhere as players embrace whilst the mainly US crowd sit in shocked silence. Troy embraces Peter Corr, the

Australian Women's Coach, with emotion pouring from within. We have just shot Bambi! Or so it feels.

Finally, back in the rooms, is our moment of private elation. All the planning and timing has come together. Troy has had a sensational game of 28 points and 22 rebounds; David has had 18 points at 50 per cent, having been superb in his execution; I have 11, complemented by 9 rebounds and 7 assists. Nick and Gerry have performed heroics, with Doggy not alone in giving a stunning display from off the bench. Yet the job is not over. I, along with many others, quickly look to the next game, our gold-medal chance!

As we slowly file out of the rooms to the bus to take us back to the Games village, the Omni Stadium has emptied to a fair degree. It has the feel of a place where something extraordinary has occurred, and it doesn't know how to react. The bus ride to our temporary home passes in a blur, only for the scenes at the end of the game to be relived at the village drop-off point. Enormous numbers of Australian officials and athletes, plus other countries' athletes, have surged down the hill from our accommodation to welcome us off the bus with cheers, hugs and looks of awe, all under the balmy American night. Our victory has sent shockwaves through the entire village.

The team wanders back to Animal House, attracting effusive comment as we go. Despite it being well past 11 p.m. no-one can sleep. But we do have a day to recover, since the final is not until the day after tomorrow. Over takeaway food, the team ponders the immediate past and the immediate future in a manner of ways. Predominantly I worry; we must grasp our chance, as such chances are not often on offer.

Australia versus Great Britain—the Gold Medal Game

It's a pretty quiet bus ride to the Omni Stadium. I think everyone knows that you don't often get moments like this, or, more precisely, opportunities like this. But we have. The day has dragged slowly, but our 7.30 p.m. appointment with the Brits has finally arrived.

The changing rooms are their normal hotch-potch affair. Each player does his own thing as I get my usual pre-game rub from Alan and tape up my ever loose thumbs. The elbow straps go on for the last time, protecting the tennis elbow, which will get a rest after it's over, come what may. Troy looks composed and hard. What will he offer today? As I leave the massage room, one of the American coaches compliments me on my game against the States and then asks me which Troy Sachs is showing up tonight. I answer, 'The real one,' and hope like hell. David is toey; he's waited a long time for this. This is his fourth Paralympics, and all his excellence has yet to be rewarded with team success. It might be today. Richard probably reviews the twenty-one years he has put into this team. It's his time. Gerry, the hard man from New South Wales, has a steely intent. He once headbutted a referee in the stomach; his aggression in the right direction is paramount today. Nick, the tumbleweed whose warmth is infectious, is in his first Paralympics and now has his chance; he really wants it. Coach Walker brings everyone together for the pre-match, yet it seems some of the players can't believe we are even here. Nick is distracted, asking if anyone has got any champagne, while Orf says he is going to frame his uniform. You have got to be kidding; before the game expect nothing. Coach Walker asks me to say a few words. I can't believe players are making celebration plans and assuming the best outcome, so my words are strong: 'You have not achieved all of it. Don't let yourselves down. Don't be so bloody arrogant. We may never get this fucking chance again.'

Walker outlines key match-ups. I've got Joey Jayaratne (3.0), one of the sweetest shooters in the competition, and he has hurt us before. Troy has Simon Munn (4.0), the key big man for Great Britain. And Nick has Mark Cheaney (1.0), a clever shooting guard. David has David Bramley (4.0), an underrated all-rounder. Gerry has Steve Caine (2.0) the controlled point guard with goggles.

Leading the team out, goose bumps run up and down my neck. I suck this moment in and it seems to last no time and yet for ever. How do you describe this: 10,500 people at the gold-medal game at the Paralympics all paying to watch us? The stands are missing two people, Al and Rosie, who due to Al's slow recovery have not been able to make the trip. However, there is a good contingent of Australian spectators in sight to cheer us on. And of course a lot of Americans who have pre-bought tickets expecting that either or both the men's and women's teams would be in the gold-medal play-off. They're not. So bad, so sad.

As I run the team through our last warm-up, I hope that the players have enough gas in the tank. Against the US, the team had used a limited rotation of players, with four of the starters playing 37 minutes or more. I don't hope, I pray!

As we come together for the pre-game huddle, one last time the big Italian asks the question: 'What time is it?' and is greeted with a believing chorus of 'Our time!'

The controlling referee comes to centre court and tosses the ball to start the game. Munn and Sachs compete for the tap, but it falls free, and after clipping David's fingers goes direct to Jayaratne who is on the move. Collecting the ball, he drives straight to the basket and at the last minute passes the ball to Bramley on the opposite side of the key for the lay-up. GB have scored within the first five seconds! And over the next thirteen minutes it seems that they cannot miss. Cheaney (1.0), of all people, is doing the damage, shooting six from six from down low outside the key. And again it seems that we refuse to chase over the top of screens; rather we play the 'hide inside and hope they miss' game. They don't, and so with 7 minutes remaining, again we find ourselves staring at a deficit, this time of 28–15. Coach Walker makes a desperate move and puts me on Cheaney. It's the first time I've ever guarded a 1.0 pointer. In the meantime, nothing is going right until Troy nails a three-point shot, which is quickly followed by Nick forcing a turnover, only for us to miss another shot and Dan Johnson to reply with a basket for the Brits. Having got to the foul line a number of times, Troy then cans another three-pointer, bringing us closer, and then follows up with a dynamic move through four defensive players for two more. It's starting to happen. Moments later I drive the ball at the GB captain, Colin Price (2.5) and draw his fourth foul from him. Since they are in the bonus, I go to the foul line and hit one from two. With 1.24 on the clock, I get the ball from Gerry, drive it down court and with a hook pass to David, see him score, levelling it up at 32–32. We have scored 19–4 in the last 7.5 minutes. In the closing minutes of the half, Nick sets up one of the GB high pointers for a charging foul. Two foul shots are awarded to him. However, high pointers usually shoot foul shots better than low pointers; with that in mind, I manage to get onto the foul line instead of Nick. The GB team are unaware of the swap, but I miss the first with an appalling shot; with pressure building I hit the second. With little more ado, apart from a couple of late foul shots from GB, we are back in it as the buzzer sounds. The score is 33–34 to GB.

In the rooms the whiteboard comes out and everyone is instructed to hustle in defence and jump out and pressure the GB shooters. Roughly drawn sketches are constructed, reinforcing our defensive commitments. Sweaty players have direct conversations and pleas are made for everyone to stay focused by Coach Walker. Focus is the key, because everything else is now running smoothly. After a few moments of quiet contemplation, drinks and towelling down, the team re-enters the court to a mass of entertainment and noise. We just want to get on with it; since we feel we were now on a roll. After a few minutes, the time comes to find out if fairytales can come true.

Again GB control the tap only to miss their first shot of the half; but alas, so do we. I then foul Munn and, according to the referee, he was in the act of shooting. The big man hits one from two. David then replies with a long shot from the top of the key, bouncing it in over the front of the ring, only for Jayaratne to reply by hitting his first open hoop. We need timing, and we have it, because after this shot we play our best basketball ever. Troy hits his third three-pointer of the match. On the next play I steal the ball, push hard down the court, and pass it to David for a lay-up, on which he is fouled; he gets to shoot a bonus and makes it count. Troy, in the zone of zones, responds to another GB miss with the move of his life. Spinning his man, he loops a finger roll with his left hand off the backboard for two, screaming in the face of his opponent as it goes down. With that the GB coach, frantic with panic, calls a time-out to try and regroup. Our time-out is dominated by Nick's impassioned plea: 'One fucking stop, one fucking basket.' Immediately on resumption of play, Troy does another spin move for two, and David matches him with a finger roll for two. After this offensive burst, we now hold a 47–37 lead. Each time a British player becomes an offensive threat, Coach Walker switches me onto them. At one stage, so wrapped up in the game, he shouts for me to guard two different players. 'I'm a stopper, but I can't guard two at one time,' my inner voice yells. With 4.5 minutes still remaining, we hold a 67–58 lead when David fouls out, having contributed a terrific 18 points. He is replaced by Orf, who straight off the bench, throws a full-court baseball pass to me which I catch one handed above my head, only to be heavily fouled as I attempt the lay-up. I hit both foul shots. This is followed by a prayer three-pointer from Troy. Amidst a copious number of desperate three-point attempts by GB, the game draws to a close. In the closing minute, Troy leaves the game with a world-record score of 42 points to a huge ovation from the crowd, along with all the remaining starters. Bench players, who have given so much, play out the final seconds, as celebrations begin amongst those just substituted.

The Gold Medal Journey

The buzzer goes, freezing our victory scoreline at 78–63. Let the real celebration begin!

Exhausted beyond belief, both physically and emotionally, I just sit there amongst the euphoria and I ask myself, 'What time is it?' And from deep within, I hear my inner voice say quietly, 'Our time.' And it was.

GOLD AND HOME

At the conclusion of the medal ceremony, the team had been inadvertently scattered. Troy and Nick were dragged off to be drug tested, whilst various players, me included, did interviews with awestruck media from Australia. Later I was to learn that we had made the first section of one of the national news bulletins back home—a first for wheelchair basketball.

After finishing our individual commitments within the stadium, the team floated in dribs and drabs, enveloped in a disbelieving mix of euphoria and emotional exhaustion, to an adjacent English-style bar for well-deserved drinks. Over a few minutes, the bar filled with members of both teams, most accompanied by family, friends and supporters. Though the feeling in the bar was of elation, there was also an aura of disbelief. Australian players, the majority proudly wearing their medals around their necks, sat and drank, some slowly, some more quickly. Some players talked and whooped, others sat in relatively mute contemplation. As for me, after three beers I felt both so full and, in a way, empty. Full of emotion and elation, yet utterly spent. Much to our disappointment, after only an hour or so, time was called by the prudish barkeepers, who had failed to grasp the enormity of the moment. With that, the team broke into smaller groups, intent on taking Atlanta by storm. And we did!

During a night on the tiles in many and varied settings, the team celebrated the win in their own individual way. Come dawn, as one can imagine, Animal House—which, despite its name and reputation, had been filled with routine and regimentation over the preceding two weeks—was not looking its pristine best. Some inmates of the house had returned somewhat carefree, but the House was also minus a few who had not managed to find their way back from the frolics of the post-game festivities.

I saw only a little of the morning, surfacing just before lunch, thankfully to find that the win was not a dream; or, if it was, everyone I saw had had the same dream. I still had the feeling that I should pinch myself, to ensure that I was living in reality; this sense dissipated slowly over the day as the true significance of the tournament sank comfortably into my being. And whenever I wanted reassurance, I peeked in the bottom of my bag to stare at the circular medal, gold in colour, that through its presence created clarity of the moment. It was truly mine. Over the day I did this more times than I can count, and suspect I was not alone.

The day floated by, wonderfully pressure- and deadline-free, with no more teams to conquer. All that was left of the Games was the formality of attending the closing ceremony, with the entire Australian Paralympic entourage.

Australia was to depart for the stadium last, due to our country having been named host of the next Games, so the usual wait was much shorter. With Yothu Yindi, Australia's best-known indigenous band, performing in some ways it felt like home. The Paralympic flag was presented to Sydney as host city for the Paralymic Games in 2000. This moment brought to my heart a proud feeling of our achievement. With the ceremony bringing the Games to a close, part of me was so excited to soon be going home to share our triumph with family and friends, and yet there was also a tinge of sadness. The longest journey with my team mates was now truly over. We would be going back to our individual lives, leaving the magic of the past weeks for ever, and consigning it to our memories for the remainder of our lives.

Over the following couple of days, the team did just that and went their own ways. Some went on pre-arranged holidays with partners and family, and others went home.

And so, with the dream having come true, we spent a day sightseeing in Atlanta, then prepared to board the Qantas flight bound for Oz. After the closing ceremony I was one of the last to leave the quiet shell that had been the once boisterous Animal House. I had organised to catch an earlier flight to Los Angeles so as to spend a day at Disneyland with a few other athletes. However, we were stranded in a plane sitting on a tarmac in Salt Lake City because of an electrical storm, and were forced to abort our plan. The delays were so extensive that there was a mad scramble in LAX airport to catch the flight home.

Breathless after a sprint through the terminal to the departure gate, I arrived at the door of the plane via the aerobridge. I was waiting for an aisle chair to transport me onto the plane, and who should appear having heard my voice? Unbelievably, as fate would have it, it was Cathy, who since the days of the Austin had gone on to become a senior flight attendant with Qantas. Despite going our separate ways so long ago, she and I had maintained regular but occasional contact over the fourteen years that had passed since my discharge from the hospital.

She had followed the progress of the team and was as stunned as I was. She knew more than anyone from where and how far I had come. Only slightly interrupted by our boarding, we spent a deal of time catching up on all and sundry, and one can imagine the treatment I received during the thirteen-hour forty-minute flight to Sydney. Come our arrival in Sydney, and a couple of hours waiting for my connecting flight to Melbourne, I was home, thirty-eight hours after leaving Animal House. The dream was over, but the welcome-home celebrations were about to begin!

Yet not for me. Two days after my arrival home, during a routine skin check of my backside (for the fourteen years since my discharge I had had to use a mirror to do regular checks of my tail to ensure that I had not developed any pressure areas) I was shocked to find a large red area reflected back at me. I had never had a pressure problem before. Whilst for the general public a red mark the size of three twenty-cent pieces on their backside is of little concern, for me it was the end of the world. The only way to cure such an ill was to remain off the bright red area until it faded. This meant no sitting (no wheelchair) at all. I spent a full month lying face down in a beanbag. Al and Rosie came to Melbourne to feed and water the animal, and the only time throughout each day that I would sit would be on one or two quick trips to the toilet. Showering meant crawling to the bathroom and hanging over the edge of the bath, precariously balanced on my knees, every few days. And of course, apart from during the Games themselves, it could not have happened at a worse time because so much was going on.

Upon the team's return home, a large welcome-home ticker tape parade had been organised for all the athletes in Sydney. I missed that. Melbourne had organised its own parade for the Victorian athletes, where I had been asked to accept the key to the city on behalf of the athletes. I missed that. The Victorian athletes had been invited to do a lap of honour in open top cars at half time during the AFL final. I missed that. I was even asked to appear on *The Footy Show*. And you guessed it. I missed that.

What I didn't miss was the camaraderie of various members of the Paralympic team. On the night of the Victorian parade, Nick Morris, Louise Sauvage (Australia's premier Paralympic track racer) and Shona Casey (a staff member of the Paralympic team), dropped around to visit at various times of the evening, all trying to paint a picture of the day's events.

By the time my tail had recovered—a painstakingly slow process—Atlanta was long gone. And with the fanfare over, like it or not, it was time to look towards new horizons.

NEW HORIZONS

With basketball on the back burner for a little while, it was time to get back to Morris–Walker, since the company had been bereft of my input for what seemed an inordinate amount of time. And over the next months it became a focus for my life.

The major development in the business was the consistency and level of public speaking that I was invited to do, often motivational, but always with a humorous delivery. It seemed everyone—and Australians more than most—loves a winner, and with an awareness of the team's achievements as portrayed through the media, corporations wanted to listen to me talk about the key factors involved in our victory, or in my own personal journey.

This diverse range of speaking engagements, in conjunction with a constant stream of audit work, meant I was more than busy. In what seemed like no time at all, I found myself preparing for the 1997 National League season, and 2000 was sneaking ever closer. Both on court and off.

I decided to seek professional representation in the sports management field, making negotiations easier for any sports-related endorsements, and widening my scope of opportunities. After having informal chats with a couple of managers, I met with Rob Woodhouse from Elite Sports Properties (ESP), who agreed to represent me. This was at the time a great fillip for me, as I was aware that very few Paralympians are represented by leading sports management companies in Australia; to an extent, corporate Australia is yet to grasp the potential of Paralympic athletes.

With Sydney hosting the Paralympic Games soon after the Olympic Games in 2000, another opportunity arose. The Sydney Paralympic Organising Committee (SPOC) decided to appoint ten media ambassadors throughout Australia to spread the word of the coming Games, and I was honoured to be one of them. As an ambassador, I speak to a variety of groups including key sponsors of the Games, ranging from functions with the Melbourne City Council, to events held to raise the awareness of the Paralympics. Unlike our parallel games, the Olympics, there are significant myths and a lack of knowledge and understanding of what the Paralympic Games are about and what is on show. My role as an ambassador is to spread the word that the Games are for real; highlight ticketing opportunities; and assist the media in portraying the elite image that the Games deserve. Personally, it is exciting to be one of the faces of the Games, aiming to make the Sydney Games the best so far, and therefore setting the bar at a higher level for the Games of tomorrow.

The memories of Atlanta were rekindled at the ceremony awarding the Order of Australia Medal (OAM) to all gold-medal winners at both the Paralympic and Olympic Games as a recognition of their achievements. Our medals were presented to us at Government House in Melbourne by the Governor of

Victoria, Richard McGarvie, AC on a fine autumn afternoon in April. I was joined by the Victorian members of the team, and Al and Rosie, who were fitted out in their best attire and revelled in the occasion. It was a special day for me, however I couldn't but feel humbled when various bravery-award citations were read. As we drove home, I remarked to Al and Rosie that there were many colleagues from the Austin as deserving of recognition for their work as any of us gold medallists. Nevertheless I was more than chuffed to have an OAM. Some people told me it suited me, since I was in fact an Old Angry Man!

Upon returning from Atlanta, and over the following twelve months, Coach Walker had been at odds with the Australian Paralympic Federation (now the Australian Paralympic Committee) on the issue of payment. His argument was that he lost significant job opportunities because of his commitments to the Australian team. And as he was not being reimbursed for these losses, Coach Walker felt disadvantaged, since many of the coaching and support staff sent to Atlanta were on leave with pay or in positions which saw them receiving their normal wage. With an enhanced sense of his value, having taken the team to gold, Coach Walker felt further justified in his stance. And so after to-ing and fro-ing as to his tenure, despite some efforts being made to raise funds, Walker resigned in late 1997, since the Australian Paralympic Committee was not in a position to meet his demands. The financial reality of Paralympic sport meant that there was no money, and consequently no choice, and Coach Walker did know his terms of appointment throughout. In a way, staff as well as athletes in the Paralympic movement are following the financial trends of Olympic sport. However, we are some thirty years in arrears at this time, and so in most instances our commitment depends on the most natural ideology—our love of the game. The news of Coach Walker's resignation was met by the players with varied emotions due to his often standoffish and at times abrasive nature. Essentially, with his departure came time for a new beginning.

And this new beginning was an exciting one. After the advertisement of the position of coach for the 1998 World Championships and 2000 Paralympic Games, the new appointment, following an initial approach by one of the Australian players, was Bob Turner, a name synonymous with the development and promotion of basketball in Australia for more than twenty years.

Having first come to Australia from America to play, Bob had eventually moved into the coaching of National Basketball League teams, and had accumulated vast experience, initially with the Newcastle Falcons, then with the Canberra Cannons, leading them to successive titles in the 80s. He then headed up the renowned Sydney Kings franchise in the 90s. Bob's passion is the marketing of the game of basketball; his teams have always received the most publicity. His appointment to lead our campaign, following years of an uphill battle to open the media door, created a new opportunity to take our game to the public in the march towards 2000.

Bob had only ten months to meet and select a squad, and prepare a team for the 1998 World Championships to be held in Sydney in October. The first training camp was held in Melbourne, and despite all the team members having played one another over the previous year or more since the victory in Atlanta, no group debriefing had ever been held. Bob introduced himself to the players, then asked the remaining veterans from the gold-medal team to share some of their experiences with one another and with new squad members. And, of course, to try and capture and share the essence of what it had taken to win. Then training commenced, just as it was to continue, at a frenetic pace up until October.

Helped by Bob's marketing ability, the team now dubbed 'the Rollers', began to attract media attention, with articles appearing in Olympic sponsor Ansett's in-flight magazine, *Panorama*; *Ralph*, a blokie magazine; and *Aussie Post*. We also got significant interest from the electronic media. All this was important, but it doesn't win games, something which Bob repeatedly highlighted by reminding the team that no-one is interested in anyone who doesn't win. He had arranged us some international competition as a benchmarking exercise, and also as a chance for him to learn who could do what on court, along with coming to grips with the nuances of wheelchair basketball.

The first team we played were the silver medallists from Atlanta, Great Britain, who came to Australia and played in five test matches throughout New South Wales. Our team having lost four players from Atlanta, many new faces were given an opportunity throughout this series, which we convincingly won five–nil. This, however, was not as easy as the scoreline may suggest as a number of the games were particularly close. The real highlight was the crowds that filled the stadiums to watch the Rollers play. This was new.

What was also different was that during the 1998 lead-in to the Gold Cup and National Wheelchair Basketball season, I had begun seeing a member of the Australian women's wheelchair basketball team with whom I had been friends for years. Paula, a below-knee amputee (seagull), had the advantage of being eligible for wheelchair basketball, and yet in her non-playing guise had no need for a wheelchair as a mobility aid. Having each had varied relationships, both short-term and long-term over the years, we found ourselves single at the same time, and due to our existing friendship, knew one another's pedigree. Putting aside the common advice that ducks shouldn't play in their own pond, we decided to explore the step beyond friendship. And we have found that having a relationship with someone chasing similar goals, and sharing constant strict training regimes, creates a unique understanding. At times though it can be testing, as both of us are experiencing the emotional and physical rollercoaster ride associated with sport at an elite level.

The commitments to a relationship are many and varied and,

in the following case, a little frightening. On an interstate National League trip with the Dandenong Rangers, handicapped by a lack of support staff able to drive manual vehicles, Paula found herself in charge of the truck hired to carry all of the baggage and wheelchairs for the team. After being bombarded with her bragging of her abilities to drive manual vehicles, and given no choice in the matter, I was summonsed to accompany her in the high cab of the truck. Unconvinced of her ability with (or without) a prosthesis to fully engage the clutch, I seconded another team member, Campbell, to share my experience. The three of us set off in convoy, following the two hired Tarago vans transporting the remainder of the team. On reaching the first set of lights leaving Sydney Airport, Campbell all but abandoned the cab (without his wheelchair) when Paula attempted to proceed with the green light and put the truck into reverse. She began to move backwards, only to brake on hearing the gasps from her travelling companions. Following with a second attempt with an identical outcome, her bragging soon quietened and an executive decision was made that I would become the co-pilot. With me changing the gears and Paula concentrating on using the prosthesis on her left leg to engage the clutch, almost requiring her to stand on the pedal, we battled on. Meanwhile, with Campbell holding a stable heart rate of 180 or more, we proceeded for forty minutes or more through Sydney, an amputee grinding her way through the gears (with a paraplegic changing them) and steering a vehicle far bigger than anything she'd ever driven before. As the driving relationship developed, a sense of absolute hilarity, mixed with a false sense of normality descended on the cabin, finally seeing us arrive at our Parramatta accommodation with all and sundry smelling the assault perpetrated on the gearbox. Campbell's colour slowly returned to normal and, despite his protestations, he became our regular companion, slowly coming to terms with the anomalies of our dual-pilot driving arrangement. Paula finally mastered the intricacies of manual driving twenty minutes from the airport on our return journey. At the time of writing she has never been given the opportunity to show her newly acquired skills.

After the GB tour, Canada came to our shores in early July for a series around Australia. Each game was followed by the Australian Boomers, the men's national basketball team, taking on their Canadian counterparts. This linkage of the two types of basketball was a first. It came about from our closer association with Basketball Australia through Bob, and was a huge step forward for the credibility of our game. Spectators on the tour were introduced to an entirely new game, and they loved it. During our last match the entire Boomers team sat in the stands and watched us fight out a close finish.

In the four tests against Canada, played in Hobart, Adelaide, Newcastle and Sydney, we split the series with two wins each. After winning comfortably in Hobart and taking our unbeaten run including Atlanta to thirteen, we received our wake-up call. Being flogged in Adelaide and Newcastle, the team regrouped to score a gritty and nailbiting victory in the final match in Sydney.

Our last international preparation for the Gold Cup was to be at the Roosevelt Cup in Warm Springs, Atlanta, where a four-team tournament was held. The teams were Canada, USA, the Netherlands and Australia. Similar to our tour of Europe pre-Atlanta, the team flew in and began playing within a couple of days of arrival, only to lose four out of five. This tournament, although it was not known at the time, was to include the top four teams from the next World Championships. And where did we finish?

Following a number of further training camps, the team entered the Games village in Sydney with, for the first time in our lives, the pressure of being number one. The Rollers were becoming known.

After a practice match in which we comfortably defeated a battling Japanese team, we were ready to step up to the line again. Me, only just, since in the second half of the game against Japan, I had snapped an axle for the first time in my entire career, and was assisted ingloriously from the court, minus a functioning rear wheel. The axle could not be quickly removed despite the urgent attentions of Graeme, so repairs were not completed until after the game. I felt I was ready anyway.

With Bob coming to the team with no preconceived ideas, he had trialled a number of captains throughout the preliminary games. I was quietly thrilled to be announced as captain for the World Championships. Captaincy to me is all about directing the traffic on occasions, and always providing an available ear. However, with the maturity and experience of a number of the Rollers, I often find that I simply lead the team out, conduct formalities with the referees, and get on and play. But as a players' player, someone who has had to work far harder at their basketball than their football, it is probably best to lead by example, which is what I always try to do. Because I believe it's the little things and the hard things that bring teams together and get them over the line. It is this quality that made the difference in Atlanta, and kept our performance solid since.

The biggest challenge of leadership for me is that, at times, I have to forgo the luxury of expressing how I really feel on and off the court, instead taking a path that will be conducive to positive outcomes and increased chances of success. After the World Championships at the Australian Paralympic Committee annual awards dinner, a number of people came to me and said that they were happy to see me smiling. I replied that I do, but not often on a basketball court, because there is always some job to be done. It's all about next.

And our next next was the Gold Cup, which had been retitled the 'Energy Australia Gold Cup' having attracted a major naming-rights sponsor. This was an exciting time for the Rollers, since we were now playing in front of a home crowd. In the weeks preceding the Gold Cup, a large advertising campaign had been run. With Energy Australia's backing, the team appeared on the side of Sydney buses and on various billboards, with one of the slogans being 'Nobody pushes these guys around'. And we hoped they wouldn't.

The first match, in front of the biggest crowd I'd ever seen at a wheelchair basketball match in Australia, was against Finland, who we knew virtually nothing about, since they had only recently had a vast rise in performance in the European Championships. The game opened with me shooting well and, along with Troy and David, scoring the majority of points. We won the game narrowly after a late Finnish comeback. Yet the turning moment in the game came not from a scorer, but from Nick, who took on a 4-pointer, and managed to steal the ball in the closing minutes, halting their charge. One down.

Mexico was next. They had developed little since Atlanta, and we inflicted the same result upon them. Later in the week the other weaker team in the pool, Egypt, was to suffer the same fate after putting up early resistance.

The rematch with Spain saw the Rollers seeking revenge for their one and only defeat in Atlanta. And following a dynamic 41 points from Troy, 24 from myself, and great minutes off the bench by Orf, we got home by 4 points. A spectacular match for the crowds. And the Rollers were on a winning streak.

The last match to confirm our ranking in the pool was against Canada, who were also unbeaten. Following the test series, it was obvious that there was little between the two teams, and so it was to prove. We were defeated 54–58. David contributed a game-high total of 20 points along with 7 rebounds. Troy finished with 15 and I finished with 8. This meant we were to play Great Britain in the quarter final, a game which was to be similar to the Netherlands match in Atlanta.

After trailing by 4 points at half time, the team had rallied and with 35 seconds left, GB was leading by one point. Bringing the ball down the court, I passed to Troy, and then in a heavenly moment, a clear path to the basket opened for me. Troy, with great vision, then threw a crisp hook pass, hitting me with the ball as I flashed to the basket, and scored with a simple lay-up. With the Brits scrambling back and throwing a half-court prayer, the buzzer sounded, leaving us the victors, 61–60. We were back in top-four territory. I was massively relieved; as I quipped in an interview later, if I'd missed the shot, I would have kept going off the court and out of the door, since I could not have faced the wrath and disappointment of my fellow Rollers.

As in Atlanta, we were drawn to play the USA in the semi final. However, this time there was to be no fairytale. With the US team having gone through significant development and a youth program in the two years since Atlanta, they were too good. They went from a 25–35 lead at half time to a blow-out of 46–64, despite the Rollers closing to within 5 points at one stage in the second half. The final score, whilst exaggerating the difference between the teams, was in some ways irrelevant. We had lost. This was the end of our gold quest.

In the other semi final, Canada had also suffered defeat at the hands of the Netherlands, and so the bronze play-off was to be against our now regular foes. Signifying the closeness of the teams, the scores were locked at 29–all at half time. With a lift from the young Canadian star Patrick Anderson, Canada claimed victory 63–56. And there are no prizes for fourth.

On conclusion of the final between the US and the Netherlands, which had gone to the USA by a two-point margin, medal presentations and individual awards were made. When the dynamic Australian women's team member, Liesel Tesch, was honoured with selection in the All Star Five Team, I was thrilled for her. And when the men's All Star Team was announced, I was surprised and honoured to be selected, but also embarrassed; whilst individual recognition in a team sport is nice, it's not what you play for and it certainly is no replacement for a team victory. It's not the same celebrating on your own. In football parlance, it was a little bit like winning the Brownlow Medal with your team finishing out of the finals. Hollow.

New Horizons

The team and I went and had a consoling drink or two, with our eyes soon turning towards defending the Paralympic gold medal on home soil.

TOWARDS 2000

In the wash-up over the months after the Gold Cup, the changes in the nature of wheelchair basketball were clear, and there was much to consider in the planning and preparation for the ultimate challenge that is Sydney.

With the USA team being young and dynamic and in many ways similar to the Canadian team, a focus on finding new blood to supplement the veterans of Atlanta was required, since whilst experience is irreplaceable, so is the enthusiasm and vibrancy of youth. The squad which will ultimately make up the Rollers team in 2000 is a very changed one from the gold-medal winning team of Atlanta. It's likely that there will be only about six remaining members. But in their place comes a number of new faces intent upon emulating their predecessors.

Adrian King, a 200-centimetre tall 2.0 pointer, aspires to be the first Queenslander in the team for many a year, bringing an enormous wing span and the work ethic befitting a player with true basketball potential.

Shaun Groenewagon, a tall, willowy, left-handed 4.0 pointer who was brought up through an elite junior able-bodied basketball program, has come to the squad in a rush. With his background, he has superb technical shooting skills and his touch is special. Though he is still raw, he recently highlighted his potential by shooting four three-pointers in a row during a National League final. He is one seventeen-year-old not to get into shooting competitions with at the end of training, if you want to keep the shirt on your back.

Brad Ness is a big 4.5 pointer, an ex-footballer from the west whose boisterous personality has led him to be termed 'Australia's cultural attache'. He brings true physicality and aggression to the court. Hungry to mirror his football successes, Brad has moved to the USA on a basketball scholarship, intent on refining his skills for the Sydney stage.

Shane Porter, a 1.0 pointer and another Queenslander, aims to take the step from untapped potential to realised ability. Again tall, his unusually good rebounding and shooting bring a new dimension to the team, as does the constantly changing colour of his hair.

Having grown together through years of junior wheelchair basketball in Victoria, Campbell Message, a 2.5 pointer, and Brook Quinn, a 3.5 pointer, reached the pinnacle of their basketball careers playing in the Gold Cup for the Rollers. Fighting to maintain their positions, their electrifying speed and intensity will hopefully see them in the team in Sydney.

And amongst all this new-found youth is a veteran aiming to bring his wealth of experience and infectious enthusiasm to the team. Mick McFawn, having represented Australia in the late eighties and early nineties, is a driven man, seeking to reclaim his position of years gone by and be the best he can be for the Rollers come 2000.

There are other remaining veterans on the cusp of the team,

trying to resecure their positions, and other new hopefuls trying to get the chance to show their wares. Selection in mid-2000 will be a dogfight, and one that will ensure the Rollers go to the Sydney Dome with the best that Australia has to offer.

With probably seven different teams having the ability to win the basketball gold medal in Sydney, it is not only about selecting the best team and having a great preparation and a little luck; it is also about peaking at the right time. Exactly as in other sports, with the ebbs and flows of individual and team performance, to triumph in Sydney is all about being the best that we can be in late October 2000, not before or after. The Gold Cup not only highlighted the changing faces of the game, but what a small but gaping chasm of difference there is between first and fourth. Although fourth didn't match any of the team's goals or aspirations, it has certainly fired the group as a whole and individuals within to bridge the gap, reclimb the mountain and defend the Paralympic gold medal.

And as for preparation, it will be a long trek. Over the final year the Rollers will have two overseas trips to various international competitions, a test series in Australia, plus individual National League commitments squeezed between. There are also monthly training camps, culminating in an extended stay at the Australian Institute of Sport (AIS) in early October.

Sometimes though, preparation for Sydney veers well away from the basketball court in a lateral approach to the team training schedule and fitness regime, as with one recent experience at the AIS. When I received the required-item list for the camp at the AIS, I was somewhat surprised to see bathers on the list. I'd been a less than average swimmer prior to my accident, and things had certainly not improved since. After arriving at the camp, the team was instructed to meet at the pool rather than the basketball courts, so it was with a mixture of mirth and apprehension that the team grouped poolside, sporting a range of swimming attire, most of it unique. On being instructed to get into the pool, the higher-point players gracefully jumped in and promptly started swimming up and down, heads ensconced in bathing caps captioned 'I Swam At The AIS'. For the lower- and middle-point players, me included, getting into the pool was far from graceful, and featured a variety of entries. And over the swimming session, purportedly only an hour, the team was instructed to do a range of exercises aimed to introduce new ways of individual fitness training. With the higher-point players enjoying the lower-point players' 'survival' techniques, it was a session shrouded in humour, with me being told that I was competing for the award of worst swimmer. My hat was false advertising, since it should have been captioned 'I Nearly Drowned At the AIS'. Whilst proving that there is no risk of me swimming at the Paralympics, such breadth of preparation can only help.

The Rollers' team commitments provide the cream on the cake in regard to preparation for Sydney, but it is the preparation away from the team that lays the true base. At the time of writing, more than two-thirds of the squad are virtually full-time basketballers, training without the constraints of full-time employment. Any available time will be spent sprinting up hills, picking up weights, developing individual skills and deepening their fitness reserves for a climactic coming together of individual talents in October 2000.

For me, the next year will be more than busy. Having chased sport at an elite level from the days of kicking the dew off the ground at Derrinallum as an aspiring junior footballer, to preparing for my fourth Paralympics, I would be lying if I didn't say that at times it seems like a long road. But without question, as has been said so many times by so many athletes, nothing will surpass the feeling of entering the stadium come the opening ceremony of the 2000 Games. Regardless of tennis elbow in both elbows, perennially sloppy thumb joints, and shoulders that at times scream 'enough', I am in the midst of another heavy weights program, trying to become bigger and stronger than ever before; because somewhere right now an opponent will be doing the same.

But at the same time, it should be said that life, while revolving around my training and match commitments, does go on in other facets. There is a constant challenge to all athletes to maintain some sort of balance. In the lead-up to the Games long-suffering friends will again be lost for a time, whilst Morris–Walker will see less and less of me as the year rolls on. And then of course there are various speaking commitments, and the search for fun and laughter in any shape or form.

Through any training routine there are highs and lows, with a constant quest to find some humour, to keep one's spirits and enthusiasm up. And sometimes people unknowingly volunteer their services to help out in this regard. Recently, during an individual on-court shooting session, I was approached by two chaps, one of whom asked whether or not I had a footbrake on my wheelchair. Trying to answer his serious question in a like manner I said no, to which he replied how useful it would be when coming in to shoot a lay-up. Undeterred by the strained look on my face, he then said to his mate that the provision of such would be a good idea to make some money! I continued to try and shoot whilst shaking my head in bewilderment.

But then again, it could be said that with the second biggest sporting event in the world coming to our shores, it is not just a few members of the general public who are a little naïve about the nuances of paralympic sport.

The media face the challenge of giving Paralympic athletes genuine coverage, not exposure that is superficial, patronising, condescending or, perhaps worse, non-existent. Two recent instances highlighted a sensationalist approach, and one based on naïvety.

A Sydney newspaper recently published a colour wraparound purportedly promoting the Paralympics, only to devalue it by heading each page with 'The Brave Games'. And recently, with my buddy Louise Sauvage winning the overall Female Sportsperson of the Year Award, a furore erupted as to her worthiness in many ranks, media included. Despite being shouted at, and down, by the vast majority of an enraged general public, the question of her athletic ability was seemingly forgotten, souring her deserved moment in the sun. Whilst it may appear to be impossible to compare the likes of Cathy Freeman, Carrie Webb and Louise, to name but three of the contenders for the award, what should have been noted was the excellence of each. Hopefully in the lead-in and at the Games, the media will learn this. Because that's what the Games are about: excellence. Somewhere amongst the waves of emotion, and the guff that is washed over Paralympic athletes, one important thing is often missed. Olympic athletes and Paralympic athletes are exactly the same: people striving to be the best they can be. Paralympic athletes have simply had one additional obstacle to overcome on the obstacle-strewn path to the podium.

Corporate Australia has not been assisted by the media in identifying and grasping true marketing opportunities as they apply to Paralympic athletes. Personally, whilst having been relatively fortunate to attract true sponsorship—which is significantly different to charity—I hope this situation will change, before Australia's Games, creating a winning combination for athletes, sponsors and the Games themselves.

Regardless, do yourself a favour and come and watch a game. Because wheelchair basketball is a spectator sport. I guarantee you won't be disappointed. The Rollers will put up a hell of a fight, because it's been so hard to get there one way or another. And after the setback of the World Championships, I can assure you that there are a lot of hungry, motivated Australian wheelchair basketballers out there.

EPILOGUE

As I sit and write the final pages of this book, it is a time of reflection, of contemplating the journey that my life has been, and where it is at the moment, and where it will be tomorrow.

Throughout the time of writing, many people have asked whether putting the words on paper has been something of a cathartic personal experience. Whilst I do not believe it has been, some of the topics have stirred mental images long since stored in a cupboard at the back of my mind.

We all tend to forget aspects of our life as we move on, and past images fade over time. On looking back, I'm probably a little surprised at the speed with which I forced things immediately after my accident, particularly resuming and completing my degree. As for where the accident sits in my psyche, it is something which is lived with, rarely thought of, but not entirely forgotten. Only a short time ago I was conducting an access audit on a school that happened to be holding their annual school athletics carnival on the same day. I reminisced with Paula as to my own running days at school and my long ago successes. Thinking a little more of this, it was only later when hearing the foreign yet distantly familiar sound of an athlete's running spikes on concrete that the real sense of loss came to the fore. This is a rare occurrence, and probably a healthy one due to the positive memories, but it still catches me by surprise when it surfaces.

Al and Rosie, who are now happily in retirement and free of the trials and tribulations of the antique shop, now focus on lowering their golf handicaps, and on developing a garden to rival the Royal Botanical. With an annual trip to Queensland to avoid Victoria's more severe winters, and the odd trip back to Derrinallum to see lifelong friends and scenery such as Mount Elephant, life for them is more than busy. I have had many discussions with them in writing this, aimed at enhancing some cloudy hospital memories. These brought many unwanted feelings flooding back to them. For Al, it reminded him of the dream which he has had repeatedly over the years but had never told me about, of me walking using callipers but seemingly having an unimpaired gait. And for Rosie, it brought back memories of her battles with the physiotherapists, and her determination at the time to do her best for her boy.

Recently I went back to Derrinallum as guest speaker at my old football club, which has now merged with the adjoining town of Lismore, forming the Lismore Derrinallum Lions. I was accompanied by Al, Rosie and Paula, and it really was a trip down memory lane. For the first time since 1981, I saw photos of the premiership teams of my youth hanging on the new function-room walls and faces from my upbringing, prompting an absolute recognition of how long ago those days were. And with this, a pin-pricked awareness of the effort that had been spent in what turned out to be a quest left unfulfilled.

Epilogue

After speaking at the evening function on some of the humorous aspects of my basketball travels, and staying the night in the town's only hotel, the following morning I was invited to give a pre-match address to the club's junior team, made up of keen fresh-faced country youngsters, who could all have been mirrors of me twenty years ago. After my talk about passion and desire, they gave me a buzz by going on to grasp a hard-fought one-point victory over the top team on the ladder. We watched a little of the following reserves game, then drove away. Although it was wonderful to go back, it also highlighted that, no matter who you are, fate sometimes means that you can't go back to your yesterdays and truly belong.

From the early days of Austin desperation to the reality of today, my accident has had many consequences, one of which—to borrow a phrase from Rosie—is the understanding that 'you can't be a shrinking violet in a wheelchair'. And there is no doubt she has a point, since the chair's appearance in my world has forced me to become more than assertive in many instances, and refine my non-physical fighting skills. From the battles of Ballarat, to the confrontations when representing the defenceless patients of the Austin, to the education of the occasionally recalcitrant corporate client, there are fewer chances to choose to be passive and peaceful than there would be if I were on two legs, not four wheels. And I would be lying if I said that such drive has no cost, or is not wearisome and outside my nature.

Yet there have been enormous unplanned positive aspects. The real benefit of my accident was that it gave me two lives. It threw me, without warning, out of my subconscious comfort zone. It drew a line in my life at the age of nineteen. Having lost virtually everything that I had taken for granted, I was forced to look at myself more than I ever would have otherwise. This in turn has given me the advantage of getting to know myself well, and an outlook on life to live it moment by moment, to maximise it; because it's not just a training run.

And of the tomorrows? In life one should never say never, and it is with this in mind that I contemplate basketball beyond Sydney. But with the game quickening, and other horizons beckoning, I admire more and more any athlete from any arena that chooses to get out before the inevitable slide.

Work-wise, over the last year or so I have had the chance to do some radio work on Melbourne's 3AW Sunday Sports show, which I have enjoyed and has been well received. The sports media is something that I would like to explore in the future, if given the opportunity. However, I am somewhat handicapped by the limited profile that wheelchair basketball receives, and there is no question had I become a mediocre half-back flanker for St Kilda, more doors would have opened than will for a gold medallist Paralympian. Nonetheless, with a broad and diverse knowledge of sport, and the reputation of not being short of a word, such work is far more appealing to me than the disability-management field, which although valuable and profitable is often somewhat less than stimulating for me. One can only measure up so many buildings and retain one's sanity, regardless of the gains both to the community and oneself.

And finally, as to my current relationship with Paula, the truck driver from hell, I am proud of my clean skin when it comes to marriage and children, but I am told constantly by others that I'm not getting any younger. And in a way the pitter patter of little feet, followed by the thud of a junior football smashing a house window, does have its own eccentric appeal. And as I and a lot of other people know, you never know what tomorrow brings.

And with this in mind, live life to the fullest. Dream your dreams, love like you have never been hurt, and work like you don't need to be paid. Step up to the line, and hopefully I'll see you there!